The Handbook of
Risk

Founded in 1807, John Wiley & Sons is the oldest independent publishing company in the United States. With offices in North America, Europe, Australia and Asia, Wiley is globally committed to developing and marketing print and electronic products and services for our customers' professional and personal knowledge and understanding.

The Wiley Finance series contains books written specifically for finance and investment professionals as well as sophisticated individual investors and their financial advisors. Book topics range from portfolio management to e-commerce, risk management, financial engineering, valuation and financial instrument analysis, as well as much more.

For a list of available titles, please visit our Web site at www.WileyFinance.com.

The **INVESTMENT MANAGEMENT CONSULTANTS ASSOCIATION** (**IMCA**) is a nonprofit organization with members in the United States, Canada, Britain, Asia, and Australia that promotes education, ethics, and standards for the investment consulting profession. The association's 5,000 members benefit from peer networking opportunities, information sharing, and cutting-edge forums on risk management, portfolio construction, and practice management. IMCA's Certified Investment Management Analyst designation assures clients of a consultant's expertise and commitment to professional ethics. IMCA Practice Standards, Performance Reporting Standards, and Questionnaires for Investment Managers offer practical guidelines to members seeking to enhance their client relationships. The semiannual *Journal of Investment Consulting* publishes original research and in-depth articles on investment theory and practice, and *The Monitor*, a bimonthly membership publication, informs members of the latest news on industry trends and investment strategies. IMCA also publishes regular updates on important legislation and regulatory developments in Washington, D.C., and the fifty states through the association's Legislative Network.

The Handbook of
Risk

Edited by
Ben Warwick

John Wiley & Sons, Inc.

Published by John Wiley & Sons, Inc., Hoboken, New Jersey.
Published simultaneously in Canada.

For general information on our other products and services, or technical support, please contact our Customer Care Department within the United States at 800-762-2974, outside the United States at 317-572-3993 or fax 317-572-4002.

Wiley also publishes its books in a variety of electronic formats. Some content that appears in print may not be available in electronic books.

Library of Congress Cataloging-in-Publication Data:

ISBN 0-471-06412-2

Printed in the United States of America.

10 9 8 7 6 5 4 3 2 1

contents

PREFACE   VII

PART ONE
The Nature of Risk   1

CHAPTER 1
The Failure of Invariance by Peter L. Bernstein   3

CHAPTER 2
Inverted Reasoning and Its Consequences: Confusing the Present
with the Future-Discounting by George C. Selden   17

CHAPTER 3
A New Paradigm for Portfolio Risk by Robert H. Jeffrey   27

CHAPTER 4
The Likelihood of Loss by Mark Kritzman   35

PART TWO
Measuring Risk   43

CHAPTER 5
Measuring and Managing Investment Risk by Roger G. Clarke   45

CHAPTER 6
An Assessment of Alternative Models of Financial Market
Volatility by John F. O. Bilson   57

CHAPTER 7
The Case for the Relevancy of Downside Risk Measures
by David Nawrocki   79

CHAPTER 8
Measuring Risk for Asset Allocation, Performance Evaluation,
and Risk Control: Different Problems, Same Solution
by Christopher L. Culp, Ph.D., and Ron Mensink   97

CHAPTER 9
Model Risk by Emanuel Derman   129

CHAPTER 10
Technology and the Capital Markets by Ben Warwick   143

CHAPTER 11
Horizon Problems and Extreme Events in Financial Risk
Management by Peter F. Christoffersen, Francis X. Diebold,
and Til Schuermann   155

PART THREE

The Investment Manager's Viewpoint   **171**

CHAPTER 12
A Behavioral Framework for Time Diversification
by Kenneth Fisher and Meir Statman   173

CHAPTER 13
Converging Correlations and Market Shocks:
Implications for Managing Risk by Louis Llanes   189

CHAPTER 14
Investing on the Edge of Chaos by Mike Howell   207

CHAPTER 15
Hedge Fund Risk by Brian Cornell   219

CHAPTER 16
The Risk of Informationless Investing: Hedge Fund Performance
Measurement Bias by Andrew B. Weisman   247

INDEX   265

I believe that the most important contribution that Modern Portfolio Theory has made to the practice of investing is the integration of risk as a fundamental element. Probably the most important principle of modern investment thought is the idea that one cannot earn a return over the risk free rate without taking on incremental risk. This is the essence of the principle of no risk free arbitrage in our capital markets. I contend that this single, simple principle is the most important insight stemming from the financial academic community in the 20th century. It's as a result of this principle that markets behave properly with asset prices coherently reflecting the constant flux of market conditions.

This principle must be kept in mind with every investment decision we make: if we seek to earn incremental return we are by necessity going to take on risk. However, like any fundamental principle, it provides little practical guidance. It provides no guidance, for instance, as to the character or structure of an investment's associated risks. The associated practical problem then lies in understanding, measuring and managing these risks.

In a portfolio context we have many opportunities to control risk. We seek diversification against individual security risk, we use multiple asset classes to reduce exposure to individual market risks and we use statistical methods to try to quantify the magnitude of these risks.

Managing an investment portfolio is essentially about selecting a set of risks and assembling them into a coherent whole. Every investment professional is by necessity a risk manager; and to be successful must be able to translate investment goals, individual financial circumstances and personal comfort with risk into recommended portfolios. Obviously in order to do this one needs to be armed with tools and insights that can be used to lend structure to the problem.

This book has assembled under one cover some of the seminal work on the topic of investment risk. An investment professional who is master of this topic will be better positioned to avoid the failures and anguish that arise from investment disappointments. In more basic terms, every investor wants to make money but has a limited appetite for losses. Mastery of the contents in this book will help you position portfolios to achieve investment goals while keeping losses within expected tolerances.

Edward D. Baker
Editor-in-Chief
The Journal of Investment Consulting

The Handbook of
Risk

.

The Nature of Risk

The Failure of Invariance

Peter L. Bernstein

Can everyone be "above average"? According to the author, there are significant differences between how people should make decisions and the way decisions are actually made. From ignoring nature's tendency to regress toward the mean to placing too much emphasis on current events in shaping our view of the world, Bernstein presents a lively and interesting view of behavioral finance and risk aversion.

All of us think of ourselves as rational beings even in times of crisis, applying the laws of probability in cool and calculated fashion to the choices that confront us. We like to believe we are above average in skills, intelligence, farsightedness, experience, refinement, and leadership. Who admits to being an incompetent driver, a feckless debater, a stupid investor, or a person with an inferior taste in clothes? Yet how realistic are such images? Not everyone can be above average. Furthermore, the most important decisions we make usually occur under complex, confusing, indistinct, or frightening conditions. Not much time is available to consult the laws of probability. Life is not a game of balla. It often comes trailing Kenneth Arrow's clouds of vagueness.

And yet most humans are not utterly irrational beings who take risks without forethought or who hide in a closet when anxiety strikes. As we shall see, the evidence suggests that we reach decisions in accord with an underlying structure that enables us to function predictably and, in most instances, systematically. The issue, rather, is the degree to which the reality in which we make our decisions deviates from the rational decision models of the

Reprinted from *Against the Gods: The Remarkable Story of Risk* (John Wiley & Sons, 1996, pp. 269–283).

Bernoullis, Jevons, and von Neumann. Psychologists have spawned a cottage industry to explore the nature and causes of these deviations.

The classical models of rationality—the model on which game theory and most of Markowitz's concepts are based—specifies how people should make decisions in the face of risk and what the world would be like if people did in fact behave as specified. Extensive research and experimentation, however, reveal that departures from that model occur more frequently than most of us admit. You will discover yourself in many of the examples that follow.

The most influential research into how people manage risk and uncertainty has been conducted by two Israeli psychologists, Daniel Kahneman and Amos Tversky. Although they now live in the United States, one at Princeton and the other at Stanford, both served in the Israeli armed forces during the 1950s. Kahneman developed a psychological screening system for evaluating Israeli army recruits that is still in use. Tversky served as a paratroop captain and earned a citation for bravery. The two have been collaborating for nearly thirty years and now command an enthusiastic following among both scholars and practitioners in the field of finance and investing, where uncertainty influences every decision.[1]

Kahneman and Tversky call their concept *Prospect Theory*. After reading about Prospect Theory and discussing it in person with both Kahneman and Tversky, I began to wonder why its name bore no resemblance to its subject matter. I asked Kahneman where the name had come from. "We just wanted a name that people would notice and remember," he said. Their association began in the mid-1960s when both were junior professors at Hebrew University in Jerusalem. At one of their first meetings, Kahneman told Tversky about an experience he had had while instructing flight instructors on the psychology of training. Referring to studies of pigeon behavior, he was trying to make the point that reward is a more effective teaching tool than punishment. Suddenly one of his students shouted, "With respect, Sir, what you're saying is literally for the birds . . . My experience contradicts it."[2] The student explained that the trainees he praised for excellent performance almost always did worse on their next flight, while the ones he criticized for poor performance almost always improved.

Kahneman realized that this pattern was exactly what Francis Galton would have predicted. Just as large sweet peas give birth to smaller sweet peas, and vice versa, performance in any area is unlikely to go on improving or growing worse indefinitely. We swing back and forth in everything we do, continuously regressing toward what will turn out to be our average performance. The chances are that the quality of a student's next landing will have nothing to do with whether or not someone has told him that his last landing was good or bad.

"Once you become sensitized to it, you see regression everywhere," Kahneman pointed out to Tversky.[3] Whether your children do what they are told to do, whether a basketball player has a hot hand in tonight's game, or whether an investment manager's performance slips during this calendar quarter, their future performance is most likely to reflect regression to the mean regardless of whether they will be punished or rewarded for past performance.

Soon the two men were speculating on the possibility that ignoring regression to the mean was not the only way that people err in forecasting future performance from the facts of the past. A fruitful collaboration developed between them as they proceeded to conduct a series of clever experiments designed to reveal how people make choices when faced with uncertain outcomes.

Prospect Theory discovered behavior patterns that had never been recognized by proponents of rational decision making. Kahneman and Tversky ascribe these patterns to two human shortcomings. First, emotion often destroys the self-control that is essential to rational decision making. Second, people are often unable to understand fully what they are dealing with. They experience what psychologists call *cognitive difficulties*. The heart of our difficulty is in sampling. As Leibniz reminded Jacob Bernoulli, nature is so varied and so complex that we have a hard time drawing valid generalizations from what we observe. We use shortcuts that lead us to erroneous perceptions, or we interpret small samples as representative of what larger samples would show.

Consequently, we tend to resort to more subjective kinds of measurement: Keynes's *degrees of belief* figure more often in our decision making than Pascal's Triangle, and gut rules even when we think we are using measurement. Seven million people and one elephant!

We display risk aversion when we are offered a choice in one setting and then turn into risk seekers when we are offered the same choice in a different setting. We tend to ignore the common components of a problem and concentrate on each part in isolation—one reason why Markowitz's prescription for portfolio building was so slow to find acceptance. We have trouble recognizing how much information is enough and how much is too much. We pay excessive attention to low probability events accompanied by high drama and overlook events that happen in routine fashion. We treat costs and uncompensated losses differently, even though their impact on wealth is identical. We start out with a purely rational decision about how to manage our risks and then extrapolate from what may be only a run of good luck. As a result, we forget about regression to the mean, overstay our positions, and end up in trouble.

Here is a question that Kahneman and Tversky use to show how intuitive perceptions mislead us. Ask yourself whether the letter *K* appears more often as the first or as the third letter of English words. You will probably answer that it appears more often as the first letter. Actually, *K* appears as the third letter twice as often. Why the error? We find it easier to recall words with a certain letter at the beginning than words with that same letter somewhere else.

The asymmetry between the way we make decisions involving gains and decisions involving losses is one of the most striking findings of Prospect Theory. It is also one of the most useful where significant sums are involved, most people will reject a fair gamble in favor of a certain gain—$100,000 certain is preferable to a 50–50 possibility of $200,000 or nothing. We are risk averse, in other words.

But what about losses? Kahneman and Tversky's first paper on Prospect Theory, which appeared in 1979, describes an experiment showing that our choices between negative outcomes are mirror images of our choices between positive outcomes.[4] In one of their experiments they first asked the subjects to choose between an 80% chance of winning $4,000 and a 20% chance of winning nothing versus a 100% chance of receiving $3,000. Even though the risky choice has a higher mathematical expectation—$3,200—80% of the subjects chose the $3,000 certain. These people were risk averse, just as Bernoulli would have predicted.

Then Kahneman and Tversky offered a choice between taking the risk of an 80% chance of losing $4,000 and a 20% chance of breaking even versus a 100% chance of losing $3,000. Now 92% of the respondents chose the gamble, even though its mathematical expectation of a loss of $3,200 was once again larger than the certain loss of $3,000. When the choice involves losses, we are risk seekers and not risk averse.

Kahneman and Tversky and many of their colleagues have found that this asymmetrical pattern appears consistently in a wide variety of experiments. On a later occasion, for example, Kahneman and Tversky proposed the following problem.[5] Imagine that a rare disease is breaking out in some community and is expected to kill 600 people. Two different programs are available to deal with the threat. If Program A is adopted, 200 people will be saved; if Program B is adopted, there is a 33% probability that everyone will be saved and a 67% probability that no one will be saved.

Which program would you choose? If most of us are risk averse, rational people will prefer Program A's certainty of saving 200 lives over Program B's gamble, which has the same mathematical expectancy but involves taking the risk of a 67% chance that everyone will die. In the experiment, 72% of the subjects chose the risk averse response represented by Program A.

Now consider the identical problem posed differently. If Program C is adopted, 400 of the 600 people will die, while Program D entails a 33%

probability that nobody will die and a 67% probability that 600 people will die. Note that the first of the two choices is now expressed in terms of 400 deaths rather than 200 survivors, while the second program offers a 33% chance that no one will die. Kahneman and Tversky report that 78% of their subjects were risk seekers and opted for the gamble: they could not tolerate the prospect of the sure loss of 400 lives.

This behavior, although understandable, is inconsistent with the assumptions of rational behavior. The answer to a question should be the same regardless of the setting in which it is posed. Kahneman and Tversky interpret the evidence produced by these experiments as a demonstration that people are not risk averse: they are perfectly willing to choose a gamble when they consider it appropriate. But if they are not risk averse, what are they? "The major driving force is *loss aversion*," writes Tversky (italics added). "It is not so much that people hate uncertainty but rather, they hate losing."[6] Losses will always loom larger than gains. Indeed, losses that go unresolved —such as the loss of a child or a large insurance claim that never gets settled—are likely to provoke intense, irrational, and abiding risk-aversion.[7]

Tversky offers an interesting speculation on this curious behavior: "Probably the most significant and pervasive characteristic of the human pleasure machine is that people are much more sensitive to negative than to positive stimuli . . . [T]hink about how well you feel today, and then try to imagine how much better you could feel . . . [T]here are a few things that would make you feel better, but the number of things that would make you feel worse is unbounded."[8]

One of the insights to emerge from this research is that Bernoulli had it wrong when he declared, "[The] utility resulting from any small increase in wealth will be inversely proportionate to the quantity of goods previously possessed." Bernoulli believed that it is the pre-existing level of wealth that determines the value of a risky opportunity to become richer. Kahneman and Tversky found that the valuation of a risky opportunity appears to depend far more on the reference point from which the possible gain or loss will occur than on the final value of the assets that would result. It is not how rich you are that motivates your decision, but whether that decision will make you richer or poorer. As a consequence, Tversky warns, "our preferences . . . can be manipulated by changes in the reference points."[9]

He cites a survey in which respondents were asked to choose between a policy of high employment and high inflation and a policy of lower employment and lower inflation. When the issue was framed in terms of an unemployment rate of 10% or 5%, the vote was heavily in favor of accepting more inflation to get the unemployment rate down. When the respondents were asked to choose between a labor force that was 90% employed and a labor force that was 95% employed, low inflation appeared to be more important than raising the percentage employed by five points.

Richard Thaler has described an experiment that uses starting wealth to illustrate Tversky's warning.[10] Thaler proposed to a class of students that they had just won $30 and were now offered the following choice: a coin flip where the individual wins $9 on heads and loses $9 on tails versus no coin flip. Seventy percent of the subjects selected the coin flip. Thaler offered his next class the following options: starting wealth of zero and then a coin flip where the individual wins $39 on heads and wins $21 on tails versus $30 for certain. Only 43 percent on heads and wins $21 selected the coin flip.

Thaler describes this result as the *house money effect*. Although the choice of payoffs offered to both classes is identical—regardless of the amount of the starting wealth, the individual will end up with either $39 or $21 versus $30 for sure—people who start out with money in their pockets will chose the gamble, while people who start with empty pockets will reject the gramble. Bernoulli would have predicted that the decision would be determined by the amounts $39, $30, or $21 whereas the students based their decisions on the reference point, which was $30 in the first case and zero in the in the second.

Edward Miller, an economics professor with an interest in behavioral matters, reports a variation on these themes. Although Bernoulli uses the expression "any small increase in wealth," he implies that what he has to say is independent of the size of the increase.[11] Miller cites various psychological studies that show significant differences in response, depending on whether the gain is a big one or a small one. Occasional large gains seem to sustain the interest of investors and gamblers for longer periods of time than consistent small winnings. That response is typical of investors who look on investing as a game and who fail to diversify; diversification is boring. Well-informed investors diversify because they do not believe that investing is a form of entertainment.

Kahneman and Tversky use the expression *failure of invariance* to describe inconsistent (not necessarily incorrect) choices when the same problem appears in different frames. Invariance means that if A is preferred to B and B is preferred to C, then rational people will prefer A to C; this feature is the core of von Neumann and Morgenstern's approach to utility. Or, in the case above, if 200 lives saved for certain is the rational decision in the first set, saving 200 lives for certain should be the rational decision in the second set as well.

But research suggests otherwise: "The failure of invariance is both pervasive and robust. It is as common among sophisticated respondents as among naive ones . . . Respondents confronted with their conflicting answers are typically puzzled. Even after rereading the problems, they still wish to be risk averse in the 'lives saved' version; they will be risk seeking in the 'lives lost' version; and they also wish to obey invariance and give consistent answers to the two versions . . . . The moral of these results is disturbing. Invariance is normatively essential [what we should do], intuitively compelling, and psychologically unfeasible."[12]

The failure of invariance is far more prevalent than most of us realize. The manner in which questions are framed in advertising may persuade people to buy something despite negative consequences that, in a different frame, might persuade them to refrain from buying . Public opinion polls often produce contradictory results when the same question is given different twists.

Kahneman and Tversky describe a situation in which doctors were concerned that they might be influencing patients who had to choose between the life-or-death risks in different forms of treatment.[13] The choice was between radiation and surgery in the treatment of lung cancer. Medical data at this hospital showed that no patients die during radiation but have a shorter life expectancy than patients who survive the risk of surgery; the overall difference in life expectancy was not great enough to provide a clear choice between the two forms of treatment. When the question was put in terms of risk of death during treatment, more than 40% of the choices favored radiation. When the question was put in terms of life expectancy, only about 20% favored radiation.

One of the most familiar manifestations of the failure of invariance is in the old Wall Street saw, "You never get poor by taking a profit." It would follow that cutting your losses is also a good idea, but investors hate to take losses, because, tax considerations aside, a loss taken is an acknowledgment of error. Loss aversion combined with ego leads investors to gamble by clinging to their mistakes in the fond hope that some day the market will vindicate their judgment and make them whole. Von Neumann would not approve.

The failure of invariance frequently takes the form of what is known as *mental accounting*, a process in which we separate the components of the total picture. In so doing we fail to recognize that a decision affecting each component will have an effect on the shape of the whole. Mental accounting is like focusing on the hole instead of the doughnut. It leads to conflicting answers to the same question. Kahneman and Tversky ask you to imagine that you are on your way to see a Broadway play for which you have bought a ticket that cost $40.[14] When you arrive at the theater, you discover you have lost your ticket. Would you lay out $40 for another one? Now suppose instead that you plan to buy the ticket when you arrive at the theater. As you step up to the box office, you find that you have $40 less in your pocket than you thought you had when you left home. Would you still buy the ticket?

In both cases, whether you lost the ticket or lost the $40, you would be out a total of $80 if you decided to see the show. You would be out only $40 if you abandoned the show and went home. Kahneman and Tversky found that most people would be reluctant to spend $40 to replace the lost ticket, while about the same number would be perfectly willing to lay out a second $40 to buy the ticket even though they had lost the original $40.

This is a clear case of the failure of invariance. If $80 is more than you want to spend on the theater, you should neither replace the ticket in the first instance nor buy the ticket in the second. If, on the other hand, you are willing to spend $80 on going to the theater, you should be just as willing to replace the lost ticket as you are to spend $40 on the ticket despite the disappearance of the original $40. There is no difference other than in accounting conventions between a cost and a loss.

Prospect Theory suggests that the inconsistent responses to these choices result from two separate mental accounts, one for going to the theater and one for putting the $40 to other uses—next month's lunch money, for example. The theater account was charged $40 when the ticket was purchased, depleting that account. The lost $40 was charged to next month's lunch money, which has nothing to do with the theater account and is off in the future anyway. Consequently, the theater account is still awaiting its $40 charge.

Thaler recounts an amusing real life example of mental accounting.[15] A professor of finance he knows has a clever strategy to help him deal with minor misfortunes. At the beginning of the year, the professor plans for a generous donation to his favorite charity. Anything untoward that happens in the course of the year—a speeding ticket, replacing a lost possession, an unwanted touch by an impecunious relative—is then charged to the charity account. The system makes the losses pain less, because the charity does the paying. The charity receives whatever is left over in the account. Thaler has nominated his friend as the world's first Certified Mental Accountant.

In an interview with a magazine reporter, Kahneman himself confessed that he had succumbed to mental accounting. In his research with Tversky he had found that a loss is less painful when it is just an addition to a larger loss than when it is a freestanding loss: losing a second $100 after having already lost $100 is less painful than losing $100 on totally separate occasions. Keeping this concept in mind when moving into a new home, Kahneman and his wife bought all their furniture within a week after buying the house. If they had looked at the furniture as a separate account, they might have balked at the cost and ended up buying fewer pieces than they needed.[16]

We tend to believe that information is a necessary ingredient to rational decision making and that the more information we have, the better we can manage the risks we face. Yet psychologists report circumstances in which additional information gets in the way and distorts decisions, leading to failures of invariance and offering opportunities for people in authority to manipulate the kinds of risk that people are wining to take.

Two medical researchers, David Redelmeier and Eldar Shafir, reported in the *Journal of the American Medical Association* on a study designed to reveal how doctors respond as the number of possible options for treatment is increased.[17] Any medical decision is risky—no one can know for certain what the consequences will be. In each of Redelmeier and Shafir's experiments, the introduction of additional options raised the probability that the physicians would choose either the original option or decide to do nothing.

In one experiment, several hundred physicians were asked to prescribe treatment for a 67-year-old man with chronic pain in his right hip. The doctors were given two choices: to prescribe a named medication or to "refer to orthopedics and do not start any new medication;" just about half voted against any medication. When the number of choices was raised from two to three by adding a second medication with "refer to orthopedics," three quarters of the doctors voted against medication and for "refer to orthopedics."

Tversky believes that "probability judgments are attached not to events but to descriptions of events . . . the judged probability of an event depends the explicitness of its description."[18] As a case in point, he describes an experiment in which 120 Stanford graduates were asked to assess the likelihood of various possible causes of death. Each student evaluated one of two different lists of causes; the first listed specific causes of death and a generic heading like "natural causes."

Table 1.1 shows some of the estimated probabilities of death developed in this experiment:

TABLE 1.1 Probabilities of Death

	Group I	Group II	Actual
Heart disease	22	34	
Cancer	18	23	
Other natural causes	33	35	
Total natural causes	73	58	92
Accident	32	5	
Homicide	10	1	
Other unnatural causes	11	2	
Total unnatural causes	53	32	8

These students vastly overestimated the probabilities of violent deaths and underestimated deaths from natural causes. But the striking revelation in the table is that the estimated probability of dying under either set of circumstances was higher when the circumstances were explicit as compared with the cases where the students were asked to estimate only the total from natural or unnatural causes.

In another medical study described by Redelmeier and Tversky, two groups of physicians at Stanford University were surveyed for their diagnosis of a woman experiencing severe abdominal pain.[19] After receiving a detailed description of the symptoms, the first group was asked to decide on the probability that this woman was suffering from ectopic pregnancy, a gastroenteritis problem, or "none of the above." The second group was offered three additional possible diagnoses along with the choices of pregnancy, gastroenteritis, and "none of the above" that had been offered to the first group.

The interesting feature of this experiment was the handling of the "none of the above" option by the second group of doctors. Assuming that the average competence of the doctors in each group was essentially equal, one would expect that that option as presented to the first group would have included the three additional diagnoses with which the second group was presented. In that case, the second group would be expected to assign a probability to the three additional diagnoses plus "none of the above" that was approximately equal to the 50% probability assigned to "none of the above" by the first group.

That is not what happened. The second group of doctors assigned a 69% probability to "none of the above" plus the three additional diagnoses and only 31% to the possibility of pregnancy or gastroenteritis—to which the first group had assigned a 50% probability. Apparently, the greater the number of possibilities, the higher the probabilities assigned to them.

Daniel Ellsberg (the same Ellsberg as the Ellsberg of the Pentagon Papers) published a paper back in 1961 in which he defined a phenomenon he called *ambiguity aversion*.[20] Ambiguity aversion means that people prefer to take risks on the basis of known rather than unknown probabilities. Information matters, in other words. For example, Ellsberg offered several groups of people a chance to bet on drawing either a red ball or a black ball from two different urns, each holding 100 balls. Urn 1 held 50 balls of each color; the breakdown in Urn 2 was unknown. Probability theory would suggest that Urn 2 was also split 50–50, for there was no basis for any other distribution. Yet the overwhelming preponderance of the respondents chose to bet on the draw from Urn 1.

Tversky and another colleague, Craig Fox, explored ambiguity aversion more deeply and discovered that matters are more complicated than Ellsberg suggested.[21] They designed a series of experiments to discover whether people's preference for clear over vague probabilities appears in all instances or only in games of chance.

The answer came back loud and clear: people will bet on vague beliefs in situations where they feel especially competent or knowledgeable, but they prefer to bet on chance when they do not. Tversky and Fox concluded that ambiguity aversion "is driven by the feeling of incompetence . . . [and] will be present when subjects evaluate clear and vague prospects jointly, but it will greatly diminish or disappear when they evaluate each prospect in isolation."[22]

People who play dart games, for example, would rather play darts than games of chance, although the probability of success at darts is vague while the probability of success at games of chance is mathematically predetermined. People knowledgeable about politics and ignorant about football prefer betting on political events to betting on games of chance set at the same odds, but they will choose games of chance over sports events under the same conditions.

In a 1992 paper that summarized advances in Prospect Theory, Kahneman and Tversky made the following observation: "Theories of choice are at best approximate and incomplete . . . Choice is a constructive and contingent process. When faced with a complex problem, people . . . use computational shortcuts and editing operations."[23] The evidence in this chapter, which summarizes only a tiny sample of a huge body of literature, reveals repeated patterns of irrationality, inconsistency, and incompetence in the ways human beings arrive at decisions and choices when faced with uncertainty.

Must we then abandon the theories of Bernoulli, Bentham, Jevons, and von Neumann? No. There is no reason to conclude that the frequent absence of rationality, as originally defined, must yield the point to Macbeth that life is a story told by an idiot.

The judgment of humanity implicit in Prospect Theory is not necessarily a pessimistic one. Kahneman and Tversky take issue with the assumption that "only rational behavior can survive in a competitive environment, and the fear that any treatment that abandons rationality will be chaotic and intractable." Instead, they report that most people can survive in a competitive environment even while succumbing to the quirks that make their behavior less than rational by Bernoulli's standards. "[P]erhaps more important," Tversky and Kahneman suggest, "the evidence indicates that human choices are orderly, although not always rational in the traditional sense of the word."[24] Thaler adds: "Quasi-rationality is neither fatal nor immediately self-defeating."[25] Since orderly decisions are predictable, there is no basis for the argument that behavior is going to be random and erratic merely because it fails to provide a perfect match with rigid theoretical assumptions.

Thaler makes the same point in another context. If we were always rational in making decisions, we would not need the elaborate mechanisms we employ to bolster our self-control, ranging all the way from dieting resorts, to having our income taxes withheld, to betting a few bucks on the horses but not to the point where we need to take out a second mortgage. We accept the certain loss we incur when buying insurance, which is an explicit recognition of uncertainty. We employ those mechanisms, and they work. Few people end up in either the poorhouse or the nuthouse as a result of their own decision making.

Still, the true believers in rational behavior raise another question. With so much of this damaging evidence generated in psychology laboratories, in experiments with young students, in hypothetical situations where the penalties for error are minimal, how can we have any confidence that the findings are realistic, reliable, or relevant to the way people behave when they have to make decisions?

The question is an important one. There is a sharp contrast between generalizations based on theory and generalizations based on experiments. De Moivre first conceived of the bell curve by writing equations on a piece of paper, not, like Quetelet, by measuring the dimensions of soldiers. But Galton conceived of regression to the mean—a powerful concept that makes the bell curve operational in many instances—by studying sweet peas and generational change in human beings; he came up with the theory after looking at the facts.

Alvin Roth, an expert on experimental economics, has observed that Nicholas Bernoulli conducted the first known psychological experiment more than 250 years ago: he proposed the coin-tossing game between Peter and Paul that guided his uncle Daniel to the discovery of utility.[26] Experiments conducted by von Neumann and Morgenstern led them to conclude that the results "are not so good as might be hoped, but their general direction is correct."[27] The progression from experiment to theory has a distinguished and respectable history.

It is not easy to design experiments that overcome the artificiality of the classroom and the tendency of respondents to lie or to harbor disruptive biases—especially when they have little at stake. But we must be impressed by the remarkable consistency evident in the wide variety of experiments that tested the hypothesis of rational choice. Experimental research has developed into a high art.*

---

*Kahneman described being introduced to experimentation when one of his professors told the story of a child being offered the choice between a small lollipop today or a larger lollipop tomorrow. The child's response to this simple question correlated with critical aspects of the child's life, such as family income, the presence of one or two parents, and the degree of trust.

Studies of investor behavior in the capital markets reveal that most of what Kahneman and Tversky and their associates hypothesized in the laboratory is played out by the behavior of investors who produce the avalanche of numbers that fill the financial pages of the daily paper. Far away from laboratory of the classroom, this empirical research confirms a great deal of what experimental methods have suggested about decision making, not just among investors, but among human beings in general.

NOTES

[1]A large literature is available on the theories and backgrounds of Kahneman and Tversky, but McKean, 1985, is the most illuminating for lay readers.

[2]McKean, Kevin, 1985. "Decisions." *Discover*, June, p. 24.

[3]*Ibid.*, p. 25.

[4]Kahneman, Daniel and Amos Tversky, 1979. "Prospect Theory: An Analysis of Decision under Risk." *Econometrica*, Vol. 47, No. 2, p. 268.

[5]McKean, 1985, p. 22; see also Kahneman, Daniel and Amos Tversky, 1984. "Choices, Values, and Frames." *American Psychologist*, Vol. 39, No. 4 (April), pp. 342–347.

[6]Tversky, Amos, 1990. "The Psychology of Risk." In Sharpe, 1990, p. 75. For more information on this subject, see Kahneman and Tversky, 1979.

[7]I am grateful to Dr. Richard Geist of Harvard Medical School for bringing this point to my attention.

[8]Tverksy, 1990, p. 75.

[9]*Ibid.*, p. 75.

[10]*Ibid.*, pp. 58–60.

[11]Miller, Edward M., 1995. "Do the Ignorant Accumulate the Money?" Working paper. University of New Orleans, April 5.

[12]Kahneman and Tversky, 1984.

[13]McKean, 1985, p. 30.

[14]*Ibid.*, p. 29.

[15]This anecdote appears in an unpublished Thaler paper titled "Mental Accounting Matters."

[16]McKean, 1985, p. 31.

[17]Redelmeier, Donald A., and Eldar Shafir, 1995. "Medical Decisions making in Situations that offer Multiple Alternatives." *Journal of the American Medical Association*, Vol. 273, No. 4, pp. 302–305.

[18]Tversky, Amos, and Derek J. Koehler, 1994. "Support Theory: A Non-extensional Representation of Subjective Probability." *Psychological Review*, Vol. 101, No. 4, pp. 547–567.

[19]Redelmeier, Donald A., Derek J. Koehler, V.Z. Lieberman, and Amos Tversky, 1995. "Probability Judgment in Medicine: Discounting Unspecified Alternatives," *Medical Decision-Making*, Vol. 15, No. 3, pp. 227–231.

[20]Ellsberg, Daniel, 1961. "Risk, Ambiguity, and the Savage Axioms." *Quarterly Journal of Economics*, Vol. LXXV, pp. 643–669.

[21]Fox, Craig R., and Amos Tversky, 1995. "Ambiguity Aversion and Comparative Ignorance." *Quarterly Journal of Economics*, Vol. CX, Issue 3, pp. 585–603.

[22]*Ibid.*, pp. 587–588.

[23]Tversky, Amos, and Daniel Kahneman, 1992. "Advances in Prospect Theory: Cumulative Representation of Uncertainty." *Journal of Risk and Uncertainty*, Vol. 5, No. 4, pp. 297–323.

[24]Kahneman and Tversky, 1979.

[25]Thaler, Richard H., 1995. "Behavioral Economics." *NBER Reporter*, National Bureau of Economic Research, Fall, pp. 9–13.

[26]Kagel, John H., and Alvin E. Roth, eds., 1995. *The Handbook of Experimental Economics*. Princeton, New Jersey: Princeton University Press, p. 4.

[27]Von Neumann, John, and Oskar Morgenstern, 1944. *Theory of Games and Economic Behavior*. Princeton, New Jersey: Princeton University Press, p. 5.

CHAPTER 2

Inverted Reasoning and Its Consequences: Confusing the Present with the Future-Discounting

George C. Selden

In Psychology of the Stock Market *(1912), George Selden presented some of the results of his early studies of human attitudes and behavior in the stock market. Many of his observations have a remarkably contemporary quality.*

INVERTED REASONING AND ITS CONSEQUENCES

It is hard for the average man to oppose what appears to be the general drift of public opinion. In the stock market, this is perhaps harder than elsewhere for we all realize that in the long run the prices of stocks must be controlled by public opinion. The point we fail to remember is that public opinion in a speculative market is measured in dollars, not in population. One man controlling $1 million has double the weight of 500 men with $1,000 each. Dollars are the horsepower of the markets—the mere number of men is insignificant.

This is why the great body of opinion appears to be bullish at the top and bearish at the bottom. The multitude of small traders must be, as a plain

From *Psychology of the Stock Market.* (Burlington, Vermont: Fraser Publishing Company, 1965, originally published in 1912), 21–29, 43–54. Printed with permission.

necessity, long when prices are at the top and short or out of the market at the bottom. The very fact that they are long at the top shows that they have been supplied with stocks from some source.

Again, the man with $1 million is a silent individual. The time when it was necessary for him to talk has passed—his money now does the talking. However, the 500 men who have $1,000 each are conversational, fluent, and verbose to the last degree.

It will be observed that the previous course of reasoning leads up to the conclusion that most of those who talk about the market are more likely to be wrong than right, at least so far as speculative fluctuations are concerned. This is not complimentary to the molders of public opinion, but most seasoned newspaper readers will agree that it is true. The daily press reflects, in a general way, the thoughts of the multitude. In the stock market, the multitude is necessarily, as a logical deduction from the facts of the case, likely to be bullish at high prices and bearish at low.

It has often been remarked that the average man is an optimist regarding his own enterprises and a pessimist regarding those of others. Certainly, this is true of the professional trader in stocks. As a result of the reasoning outlined previously, he comes habitually to expect that nearly everyone else will be wrong, but is, as a rule, confident that his own analysis of the situation will prove correct. He values the opinion of a few people whom he believes to be generally successful; however, aside from these few, the greater the number of bullish opinions he hears, the more doubtful he becomes about the wisdom of following the bull side.

This apparent contrariness of the market, although easily understood when its causes are analyzed, breeds in professional traders a peculiar sort of skepticism, leading them always to distrust the obvious and to apply a kind of inverted reasoning to almost all stock market problems. In the minds of traders who are not naturally logical, this inverted reasoning often assumes the most erratic and grotesque forms, and it accounts for many apparently absurd fluctuations in prices that are commonly charged to manipulation.

For example, a trader starts with these assumptions. The market has had a good advance, all the small traders are bullish, and somebody must have sold the trader stock that he was carrying. Therefore, the big capitalists are probably sold out or short and ready for a reaction or perhaps a bear market. Then if a strong item of bullish news comes out—one, for instance, that really makes an important change in the situation—he says, "Ah, so this is what they have been bulling the market on! It has been discounted by the previous rise." Or he may say, "They are putting out this bull news to sell stocks on." The trader proceeds to sell out any long stocks he may have or perhaps sells short.

His reasoning may be correct or it may not; at any rate, his selling and that of others who reason in a similar way is likely to produce at least a temporary decline on the announcement of the good news. This decline looks absurd to the outsider and he falls back on the old explanation: "All manipulation."

The same principal is often carried further. You will find professional traders reasoning that favorable figures on the steel industry, for example, have been concocted to enable insiders to sell their steel or that gloomy reports are put in circulation to facilitate accumulation. Hence, they may act in direct opposition to the news and carry the market with them, for the time at least.

The less the trader knows about the fundamentals of the financial situation, the more likely he is to be led astray in conclusions of this character. If he has confidence in the general strength of conditions, he may be ready to accept as genuine and natural a piece of news that he would otherwise receive with cynical skepticism and use as a basis for short sales. If he knows that fundamental conditions are unsound, he will not be so likely to interpret bad news as issued to assist in the accumulation of stocks.

The same reasoning is applied to large purchases through brokers known to be associated with capitalists. In fact, in this case, we often hear a double inversion. Such buying may impress the observer in three ways:

- The *rank outsider* takes it at face value as bullish.
- An experienced trader may say, "If they really wished to get the stocks, they would not buy through their own brokers, but would endeavor to ·conceal their buying by scattering it among other houses."
- A suspicious professional may turn another mental somersault and say, "They are buying through their own brokers so as to throw us off the scent and make us think someone else is using their brokers as a blind." By this double somersault, such a trader arrives at the same conclusion as the outsider.

The reasoning of traders becomes even more complicated when large buying or selling is done openly by a professional who is known to trade in and out for small profits. If he buys 50,000 shares, other traders are quite willing to sell to him and their opinion of the market is little influenced, simply because they know he may sell 50,000 the next day or even the next hour. For this reason, great capitalists sometimes buy or sell through such big professional traders in order to execute their orders easily and without arousing suspicion. Hence, the play of subtle intellects around big trading of this kind often becomes very elaborate.

It should be noted that this inverted reasoning is useful chiefly at the top or bottom of a movement when distribution or accumulation is taking place on a large scale. A market that repeatedly refuses to respond to good news after a considerable advance is likely to be *full of stock*. Likewise, a market that will not go down on bad news is usually *bare of stock*.

Long stretches in which capitalists have very little cause to conceal their position will be found between the extremes. Having accumulated their lines as low as possible, they are then willing to be known as the leaders of the upward movement and have every reason to be perfectly open in their buying. This condition continues until they are ready to sell. Likewise, having sold as much as they desire, they have no reason to conceal their position further, even though a subsequent decline may run for months or a year.

It is during a long upward movement that the lamb makes money because he accepts facts as facts, whereas the professional trader is often found fighting the advance and losing heavily because of the overdevelopment of cynicism and suspicion.

The successful trader eventually learns when to invert his natural mental processes and when to leave them in their usual position. Often he develops a sort of instinct that could scarcely be reduced to cold print. However, in the hands of the tyro, this form of reasoning is exceedingly dangerous because any event can have an alternate construction. Bull news is either significant of a rising trend of prices or indicates that people are trying to make a market to sell on. Bad news may indicate either a genuinely bearish situation or a desire to accumulate stocks at low prices.

The inexperienced operator is therefore left very much at sea. He is playing with the professional's edged tools and is likely to be cut. What use is it for him to try to apply his reason to the stock market conditions when every event may be interpreted in two ways?

Indeed, it is doubtful if the professional's distrust of the obvious is of much benefit in the long run. Most of us have met those deplorable mental wrecks, often found among the chairwarmers in brokers' offices, whose thinking machinery seems to have become permanently demoralized as a result of continued acrobatics. They are always seeking an ulterior motive in everything. They credit (or debit) Morgan and Rockefeller with the smallest and meanest trickery and ascribe to them the most awful duplicity in matters that those high financiers would not stoop to notice. The continual reversal of the mental engine sometimes deranges its mechanism.

Perhaps the best general rule to follow is to *stick to common sense*. Maintain a balanced, receptive mind and avoid abstruse deductions. However, a few further suggestions may be offered.

If you already have a position in the market, do not attempt to bolster up your failing faith by resorting to intellectual subtleties in the interpretation of obvious facts. If you are long or short of the market, you are not an unprejudiced judge and you will be greatly tempted to put an interpretation upon current events that will coincide with your preconceived opinion. It is hardly too much to say that this is the greatest obstacle to success. The least you can do is to avoid inverted reasoning in support of your own position.

After a prolonged advance, do not call inverted reasoning to your aid in order to prove that prices are going still higher; likewise, after a big break, do not let your bearish deductions become too complicated. Be suspicious of bull news at high prices and bear news at low prices.

Bear in mind that an item of news usually causes only one considerable movement of prices. If the movement takes place before the news comes out as a result of rumors and expectations, then it is not likely to be repeated after the announcement is made; however, if the movement of prices has not preceded, then the news contributes to the general strength or weakness of the situation and a movement of prices may follow.

CONFUSING THE PRESENT WITH THE FUTURE-DISCOUNTING

It is axiomatic that inexperienced traders and investors, and indeed a majority of the more experienced as well, are continually trying to speculate on past events. Suppose, for example, railroad earnings as published are showing constant large increases in net. The novice reasons, "Increased earnings mean increased amounts applicable to the payment of dividends. Prices should rise. I will buy."

Not at all. This trader should say, "Prices *have risen* to the extent represented by these increased earnings, unless this effect has been counterbalanced by other considerations. Now what is next?"

It is a sort of an automatic assumption in the human mind that the present conditions will continue, and our whole scheme of life is necessarily based to a great degree on this assumption. When the price of wheat is high, farmers increase their acreage because growing wheat pays better; when it is low, they plant less. I remember talking with a potato farmer who claimed that he had made a good deal of money by simply reversing the previous custom. When potatoes were low, he planted liberally; when they were high, he cut down his acreage. He did this because he reasoned that other farmers would do just the opposite.

The average man is not blessed—or cursed, depending on how you look at it—with an analytical mind. We see "as through a glass darkly." Our ideas are always enveloped in a haze and our reasoning powers work in a rut from which we find it painful, if not impossible, to escape. Many of our emotions and some of our acts are merely automatic responses to external stimuli. Despite the wonderful development of the human brain, it originated as an enlarged ganglion and its first response is still practically that of the ganglion.

A simple illustration of this is found in the enmity we all feel toward the alarm clock that arouses us in the morning. We have carefully set and wound that alarm and if it failed to go off, it would perhaps put us at serious inconvenience; however, we reward the faithful clock with an anathema.

When a subway train is delayed, nine-tenths of the people waiting on the platform are anxiously craning their necks to see if it is coming, whereas many people on it who are in danger of missing an engagement are holding themselves tense, apparently in the effort to help the train along. As a rule, we apply more well-intentioned but to a great extent ineffective physical and nervous energy to the accomplishment of an object rather than the analysis or calculation.

When it comes to the complicated matter of the price of stocks, our haziness increases in proportion to the difficulty of the subject and our ignorance of it. From reading, observation, and conversation, we imbibe a miscellaneous assortment of ideas from which we conclude that the situation is bullish or bearish. The very form of the expression "the situation is bullish"— not "the situation will soon become bullish"—shows the extent to which we allow the present to obscure the future in the formation of our judgment.

Catch any trader and pin him down to it and he will readily admit that the logical moment for the highest prices is when the news is most bullish, yet you will find him buying stocks on this news after it comes out, if not at the moment, at any rate on a reaction.

Most coming events cast their shadows before arriving and it is on this that intelligent speculation must be based. The movement of prices in anticipation of such an event is called *discounting*. The process of discounting is worthy of a little careful examination.

The first point to keep in mind is that some events cannot be discounted, even by the supposed omniscience of the great banking interests, which is usually more than half imaginary. The San Francisco earthquake is the standard example of an event that could not be foreseen and therefore could not be discounted; however, an event does not have to be purely an act of God to be undiscountable. There can be no question that our great bankers have been as much in the dark in regard to some recent Supreme Court decisions as the smallest piker in the customer's room of an odd-lot brokerage house.

If the effect of an event does not make itself felt before the event takes place, it must come after. In all discussions of discounting, we must bear this fact in mind so our subject does not run away with us.

At the same time, an event may sometimes be overdiscounted. If the dividend rate on a stock is to be raised from 4 to 5 percent, earnest bulls, with an eye to their own commitments, may spread rumors of 6 or 7 percent, so that the actual declaration of 5 percent may be received as disappointing and cause a decline.

Generally speaking, every event that is under the control of capitalists associated with the property or any financial condition that is subject to the management of combined banking interests is likely to be thoroughly discounted before it occurs. There is rarely any lack of capital to take advantage of a sure thing, even though it may be known in advance to only a few people.

However, the extent to which future business conditions are known to insiders is usually overestimated. So much depends (especially in the United States) upon the size of the crops, the temper of the people, and the policies adopted by leading politicians that the future of business becomes a complicated problem. No power can drive the American people. Any control over people's action has to be exercised by cajolery or by devious and circuitous methods.

Moreover, public opinion is becoming more volatile and changeable year by year, owing to the quicker spread of information and the rapid multiplication of the reading public. One can easily imagine that some of our older financiers must be saying to themselves, "If I only had my present capital in 1870, or else had the conditions of 1870 to work on today!"

A fair idea of when the discounting process will be completed may usually be formed by studying the conditions from every angle. The great question is when will the buying or selling become most general and urgent? In 1907, for example, the safest and best time to buy the sound dividend-paying stocks was on the Monday following the bank statement that showed the greatest decrease in reserves. The market opened down several points under the pressure of liquidation, and many standard issues never sold so low afterward. The simple explanation was that conditions had become so bad that they could not get any worse without utter ruin, which all parties must and did unite to prevent.

Likewise, in the presidential campaign of 1900, the lowest prices were made on Bryan's nomination. Investors said at once, "He can't be elected." Therefore, his nomination was the worst that could happen—the point of time where the political news became most intensely bearish. As the campaign developed, his defeat became more certain, and prices continued to rise in accordance with the general economic and financial conditions of the period.

It is not the discounting of an event thus known in advance to capitalists that presents the greatest difficulties, but cases where considerable uncertainty exists, so that even the clearest mind and the most accurate information can result only in a balancing of probabilities with the scale perhaps inclined to a greater or lesser degree in one direction or the other.

In some cases, the uncertainty that precedes such an event is more de-pressing than the worst that can happen afterward. One example is a Supreme Court decision upon a previously undetermined public policy that has kept businessmen so much in the dark that they feared to go ahead with any important plans. This was the case at the time of the Northern Securities decision in 1904. Big business could easily adjust itself to either result. It was the uncertainty that was bearish. Hence, the decision was practically dis-counted in advance, no matter what it might prove to be.

This was not true to the same extent of the Standard Oil and American Tobacco decisions of 1911 because those decisions were signs of more trou-ble to come. The decisions were greeted by a temporary spurt of activity based on the theory that the removal of uncertainty was the important thing; however, a sensational decline started soon after and was not checked until the announcement that the government would prosecute the U.S. Steel Corporation. This was deemed the worst that could happen for some time to come and was followed by a considerable advance.

More commonly, when an event is uncertain, the market estimates the chances with considerable nicety. Each trader backs his own opinion strongly if he feels confident or moderately if he still has a few doubts that he can-not down. The result of these opposing views may be stationary prices, a market fluctuating nervously within a narrow range, or a movement in either direction, greater or smaller in proportion to the more or less emphatic pre-ponderance of the buying or selling.

Of course, it must always be remembered that it is the dollars that count, not the number of buyers or sellers. A few great capitalists having advance information that they regard as accurate may more than counterbalance thousands of small traders who hold an opposite opinion. In fact, this con-dition is seen frequently.

Even the operations of an individual investor usually have an effect on prices accurately adjusted to his opinions. When he believes prices are low and everything favors an upward movement, he will strain his resources in order to accumulate the heaviest load of securities that he can carry. After a fair advance, if he sees the development of some factor that might cause a decline—though he doesn't really believe it will—he thinks it wise to lighten his load somewhat and make sure of some of his accumulated profits. When he feels that prices are high enough, he is a liberal seller. If some danger appears while the level of quoted values continues to be high, he "cleans house" to be ready for whatever may come. Then if what he considers an unwarranted speculation carries prices even higher, he is likely to sell a few hundred shares short by way of occupying his capital and mind.

It is, however, the variation of opinion among different men that has the largest influence in making the market responsive to changing conditions.

A development that causes one trader to lighten his line of stocks may be regarded as harmless or even beneficial by another so that he maintains his position or perhaps buys more. Out of a worldwide mixture of varying ideas, personalities, and information emerges the average level of prices—the true index number of investment conditions.

The necessary result of the previous line of reasoning is that not only probabilities, but even remote possibilities are reflected in the market. Hardly any event can happen of sufficient importance to attract general attention that some other process of reasoning cannot construe as bullish and some other process cannot interpret as bearish. No doubt even our old friend of the news columns to the effect that "the necessary activities of a nation of 100 million souls create and maintain a large volume of business" may influence some red-blooded optimist to buy 100 Union, but the grouchy pessimist who has eaten too many doughnuts for breakfast will accept the statement as an evidence of the scarcity of real bull news and will likely enough sell 100 Union short on the strength of it.

It is the overextended speculator who causes most of the fluctuations that look absurd to the sober observer. It does not take much to make a man buy when he is short of stocks up to his neck. A bit of news that he would regard as insignificant at any other time will then assume an exaggerated importance in his eyes. His fears increase in geometrical proportion to the size of his line of stocks. Likewise, the overloaded bull may begin to throw his stocks on some absurd story of a war between Honduras and Roumania [*sic*] without even stopping to look up the geographical location of the countries involved.

Fluctuations based on absurdities are always relatively small. They are due to an exaggerated fear of what the other fellow may do. Personally, you do not fear a war between Honduras and Roumania; but may not the rumor be seized upon by the bears as an excuse for a raid? You have too many stocks to be comfortable if such a break should occur. Moreover, even if the bears do not raid the market, will there not be a considerable number of persons who, like yourself, will fear such a raid, and will therefore lighten their load of stocks, thus causing some decline?

The professional trader, following this line of reasoning to the limit, eventually comes to base all his operations for short turns in the market not on the facts, but on what he believes the facts will cause others to do—or, more accurately perhaps, on what he *sees* that the news is causing others to do. Such a trader is likely to keep his fingers constantly on the pulse of buying and selling as it throbs on the floor of the U.S. Stock Exchange or as recorded on the tape.

The nonprofessional, however, will do well not to let his mind stray too far into the unknown territory of what others may do. Like the *They* theory of value, it is dangerous ground in that it leads toward the abdication of common sense; after all, others may not prove to be such fools as we think they are. Although the market is likely to discount even a possibility, the chances are very much against *our* being able to discount the possibility profitably.

In this matter of discounting, as in connection with most other stock market phenomena, the most useful hint that can be given is to avoid all efforts to reduce the movement of prices to rules, measures, or similarities and to analyze each case by itself. Historical parallels are likely to be misleading. Every situation is new, although it is usually composed of familiar elements. Each element must be weighed by itself and the probable result of the combination must be estimated. In most cases, the problem is by no means impossible, but the student must learn to look into the future and consider the present only as a guide to the future. Extreme prices will come at the time when the news is most emphatic and widely disseminated. When that point is passed, the question must always be, "What is next?"

CHAPTER 3

A New Paradigm for Portfolio Risk

Robert H. Jeffrey

Risk is not the same thing as riskiness. Whereas agents (portfolio managers) can experience riskiness, or price volatility, only owners can experience true investment risk—the risk of being unable to meet cash obligations—as Robert Jeffrey explains.

Thomas Kuhn, in his landmark book *The Structure of Scientific Revolutions,* describes the fall of a so-called rational model as a paradigm shift. "Scientists in any field and in any time," he writes, "possess a set of shared beliefs about the world, and for that time the set constitutes the dominant paradigm . . . Experiments are carried on strictly within the boundaries of these beliefs and small steps toward progress are made." Citing the example of the Ptolemaic view of the universe with the earth at its center, Kuhn observes, "Elaborate mathematical formulas and models were developed that would accurately predict astronomical events based on the Ptolemaic paradigm," but it was not until Copernicus and Kepler discovered "that the formulae worked more easily . . . " when the sun replaced the earth as the center of the universe model that a paradigm shift in astronomy began and laid the foundation for even greater steps toward progress.[1]

The thrust of this paper is to put forth a similar proposition. I will assert, on a more mundane level, that our portfolio management process should also work more easily and rewardingly if a paradigm shift were to occur in the *rational model* or shared belief that portfolio risk is strictly a function of the volatility of portfolio returns.

Reprinted from *The Journal of Portfolio Management* 11 (Fall 1984): 33–40. New York: Institutional Investor, Inc.

THE CASE IN BRIEF

This paper will suggest that the current paradigm is incomplete. More important, the paradigm is often misleading for a vast number of portfolio owners because it fails to recognize that risk is a function of the characteristics of a portfolio's *liabilities* as well as its *assets* and, in particular, of the cash-flow relationship between the two over time. Consequently, I will offer a modification in the rational model's proxy for risk that, by considering liabilities, which tend to be highly parochial, has the salutary effect of involving the portfolio owner more intimately in the risk-determination process.

Finally, the paper will demonstrate how the acceptance of this modification in the definition of portfolio risk can naturally lead, in many cases, to the development of an asset mix policy tailored specifically to the particular, and often peculiar, needs of each portfolio owner. Such an asset mix is, after all, what sophisticated investors presumably seek but largely fail to achieve. The result is that most institutions have look-alike portfolios, even when the institutions themselves are markedly different.

Some of the ideas that I propose here have already been suggested, at least fragmentally, by others. In this journal alone, Smidt, in his discussion of investment horizons and performance measurement, asks, "How relevant are conventional risk/reward measures?"[2] and F.H. Trainer et al. state that the "holding period is the key to risk thresholds."[3] In fact, I have previously suggested that the holding periods or time horizons of a "major segment of institutional investors . . . (are) really infinity, at least as infinity is perceived by mortal beings."[4] Levy succinctly summarizes the concerns of those who are troubled by the current risk paradigm when he says that "time horizon is just as important as (return) variability in setting asset mixes" and suggests that "what is needed is an appropriate definition of risk."[5]

Although this journal would seem to be read mostly by academics and practitioners, it is my hope that the messages of this paper may eventually reach portfolio owners, and, specifically, their chief executive officers and governing boards who, in the last analysis, are solely responsible for determining the measure of risk that is appropriate to their respective situations. On a more ambitious level, I suggest that the concepts here are relevant to *all* owners of assets, not just financial assets, and to all types of portfolios, not just those of institutions.

The conclusion that the acceptance of a new risk paradigm may prove rewarding for many portfolio owners stems from a belief that the current misunderstanding of what truly constitutes risk in a given situation often leads to portfolios with less than optimal equity contents and, therefore, lower long-term returns than might otherwise be achieved.[6] Furthermore, the failure to understand explicitly how much volatility risk can actually be tolerated in a given situation all too often encourages owners to dampen volatility by attempting to time the market, which, as I—among others— have noted elsewhere, typically leads to mediocre long-term performance results.[7]

The utility of developing a concept of risk that is more intuitively under- standable to all portfolio situations becomes more apparent when we accept the following three premises (of which only the third may be unfamiliar):

- To the extent that the market is mostly efficient, we can expect only mod- est improvements in portfolio returns from active asset management.
- To the extent that well-diversified portfolio returns do vary directly with volatility over long periods of time, returns are indeed a function of risk as risk is presently defined.
- Prudent portfolio owners, when confronted with uncertainties as to what constitutes an appropriate level of risk, will usually err on the side of accepting too little volatility rather than too much.

Given the first two premises, it follows naturally that the most effective way to enhance returns is to determine the extent to which volatility does indeed affect the portfolio owner's true risk situation and to select a port- folio that provides the maximum level of tolerable volatility and thus the highest possible return, given the attendant risk. Since uncertainties con- cerning appropriate levels of risk usually result in overstatements of the impact of volatility, any change in the rational model that reduces portfolio owners' uncertainty of what truly constitutes risk in their particular situa- tions should have a positive effect on future returns.

THE PROBLEM WITH VOLATILITY AS A PROXY FOR RISK

The problem with equating portfolio risk solely to the volatility of portfolio returns is simply that the proposition says nothing about what is being risked as a result of the volatility. For purposes of analogy, consider the most com- mon example in our daily lives—the weather. The risk implications of weather volatility are usually minimal for the vast majority of the popula- tion, who are not farmers, sailors, outdoor sports promoters, or backpack- ers undertaking a winter hike in the mountains. Feeling rewarded by not having the daily burden of carrying a raincoat, many commuters are content to bear the nominal risk of occasionally getting slightly damp on their short walk to the office. However, on a long backpack in the mountains, where one of the rewards is clearly carrying as little weight as possible, prudent hikers will nonetheless hedge their risk of serious discomfort or worse by toting several pounds of raingear and perhaps a tent.

Volatility per se, be it related to weather, portfolio returns, or the timing of one's morning newspaper delivery, is simply a benign statistical probability factor that tells nothing about risk until coupled with a consequence. Its measurement is useless until we describe that probability in terms of the probability of what. If the what is of no concern to the given individual or group, then the probability of what's occurring is also of no concern, and vice versa. This also applies to all the gradations in between. As the editor of this journal reminded his clients some years ago, "The determining question in structuring a portfolio is the *consequence* of loss; this is far more important than the *chance* of loss."[8]

What then is the specific consequence whose probable occurrence should concern us?

RISK IS THE PROBABILITY OF NOT HAVING SUFFICIENT CASH WITH WHICH TO BUY SOMETHING IMPORTANT

Since an investment portfolio is, etymologically, a collection of noncash pieces of paper (see the note for the literal meaning of portfolio),[9] and since nearly everything we buy or every obligation we retire requires outlays of cash, the real risk in holding a portfolio is that it might not provide its owner, either during the interim or at some terminal date or both, with the cash he or she requires to make essential outlays, including meeting payments when due. (In the case of pension funds, such purchases include deferred payments for services previously rendered.) As Smidt aptly points out, "Investors are ultimately interested in the future stream of consumption they will be able to obtain from their portfolios" by converting noncash assets into cash.[10]

Nevertheless, since a portfolio's cash convertibility varies so directly with the volatility of its returns that the two terms are typically used interchangeably, one might argue that this emphasis on cash requirements in no way affects the usefulness of volatility as a proxy for risk. To argue this, however, overlooks the critical fact that *different portfolio owners have different needs for cash*, just as the commuter and the backpacker have different needs for protective clothing.

The ability to purchase, which varies directly with portfolio volatility, should not be confused with the need to purchase. The latter . . . as Smidt suggests, is the portfolio's raison d'être, and is, or should be, the governing factor in determining the division of the portfolio's asset mix of holdings between those that are readily convertible into predictable amounts of cash and those that are not. By developing a risk paradigm that places the emphasis on the need to purchase rather than the ability to purchase, each port-folio owner is encouraged to make a conscious decision as to whether or not to carry a raincoat (that is, low-volatile, nearer-to-cash assets). To carry a raincoat because others are carrying raincoats is simply being fashionable, and being fashionable in investment decisions typically leads to mediocre results or worse.

From this, we can readily see that, strictly speaking, the widely used term *portfolio risk* when standing by itself is meaningless because "the possibility of loss or injury," which is Webster's definition of *risk*, has no abstract significance. Like the weather, portfolios feel no pain; it is only travelers in the weather and owners of portfolios who bear the attendant risk. What then is *owner's risk*?

Owner's risk is measured by the degree of *fit* that appears when a portfolio's minimum projected cash flows from income and principal conversions into cash are superimposed by the time period on the owner's maximum future cash requirements for essential payments. This juxtaposition provides a continuous series of pro forma cash flow statements. The periodic differences between the expected future cash conversion values of the assets, including their income flows, and the expected future cash requirements of the liabilities show up on the pro forma statements either as surpluses, connoting negative risk, or as deficits, connoting positive risk. As in all pro forma statements, however, the problem is not in the arithmetic, but in the accuracy of the assumptions used in projecting the cash flows.

A great deal of useful research has been done on the predictability over varying timeframes of the cash conversion values of various arrays of portfolio assets. In this context, *predictability* can be roughly translated as *volatility* and *cash conversion value* as *total return*. What is typically left undone, however, is an equally thorough analysis of the liability side of the equation, that is, of the essentiality, timing, magnitude, and predictability of the portfolio owner's future cash requirements.

SUMMARY: THE NEED FOR CASH DRIVES THE PROCESS

In the last analysis, risk is the likelihood of having insufficient cash with which to make essential payments. Although the traditional proxy for risk, volatility of returns, does reflect the probable variability of the cash conversion value of a portfolio owner's assets, it says nothing about the cash requirements of his or her liabilities or future obligations. Since fund assets exist solely to service these cash obligations, which vary widely from one fund to another in terms of magnitude, timing, essentiality, and predictability, portfolio owners are being seriously misled when they define risk solely in terms of the asset side of the equation.

Specifically, since both history and theory demonstrate that diversified portfolio returns historically and theoretically increase as return volatility increases, owners should be explicitly encouraged to determine in their own particular situations the maximum amount of return volatility that can be tolerated, given their own respective future needs for cash. Although the theoreticians are presumably correct in directly relating volatility and returns, the owner's future need for cash determines how much volatility he or she can tolerate and, therefore, the level of portfolio return that can theoretically be achieved.

My intention for emphasizing the need for cash has been to purposely shift responsibility for the risk-determination process from the asset manager to the portfolio owner. As J.P. Williamson and H.A.D. Sanger remind us, "Spending decisions (and thus future needs for cash) are the one input to the portfolio management equation that is totally controllable by the owner."[11] Furthermore, the cumulative effect of the owner's prior spending decisions on future needs for cash can, in most cases, best be fathomed and thus planned for, conceivably modified, and insured against within the owner's own shop and not by an outside agent.

Finally, by letting the need for cash drive the portfolio management process, the owner can make future spending decisions more wisely. Over time, he or she can develop and sustain an understandable and defendable asset mix policy that will provide him or her with an optimum portfolio return given the owner's particular cash requirement situation. In one sentence, the traditional, narrow definition of portfolio risk based solely on volatility encourages owners to apply a universal risk measurement standard for which they accept little personal responsibility to what is essentially a highly parochial problem.

NOTES

[1]T. Kuhn, *The Structure of Scientific Revolutions*, (Chicago: University of Chicago Press, 1970), as quoted in T.J. Peters and R. H. Waterman, Jr., *In Search of Excellence*, (New York: Harper & Row, 1982), 42.

[2]S. Smidt, "Investment Horizons and Performance Measurement," *The Journal of Portfolio Management* (Winter 1978): 18.

[3]F.H. Trainer, Jr., J.B. Yawitz, and W.J. Marshall, "Holding Period Is the Key to Risk Threshholds," *The Journal of Portfolio Management* (Winter 1979): 48.

[4]R.H. Jeffrey, "Internal Portfolio Growth: The Better Measure," *The Journal of Portfolio Management* (Summer 1977): 10.

[5]R.A. Levy, "Stocks, Bonds, Bills, and Inflation over 52 Years," *The Journal of Portfolio Management* (Summer 1978): 18.

[6]Although this is presumably unnecessary for readers of this journal, we note here (using Ib-botson and Sinquefield data through 1981) that the annualized total return of the S&P 500 from 1926–1983 was 9.6 percent versus 3.2 percent for 90-day Treasury bills.

[7]R.H. Jeffrey, "The Folly of Market Timing," *Harvard Business Review* (July–August 1984).

[8]P.L. Bernstein, "Management of Individual Portfolios," *The Financial Analyst's Handbook*, edited by S. Levine, (Homewood, Illinois: Dow Jones-Irwin, Inc., 1975), 1,373–1,388.

[9]Portfolio derives from the Latin words *portare* (to carry) and *wd foglio* (leaf or sheet). Since the Romans had a perfectly good word for cash, *moneta,* which they could have used for cashbox, we can thus infer that *foglio* refers to noncash forms of paper. Etymologically, therefore, a portfolio, or even a so-called investment portfolio, is not and should not be confused with cash, a distinction that most investors fail to make in the mark-to-market world in which we live.

[10]Smidt, op. cit., p. 21.

[11]J.P. Williamson and H.A.D. Sanger, "Educational Endowment Funds," *Investment Manager's Handbook*, (Homewood, Illinois: Dow Jones-Irwin, Inc., 1980), 839. The actual quotation is, "The spending rate is totally controllable."

.

CHAPTER 4

The Likelihood of Loss

Mark Kritzman

This paper is a superb primer on the mathematics of risk.

What is the likelihood that a particular investment strategy will lose money? This question seems rather straightforward and indeed is one of the most common standards against which alternative investment strategies are evaluated. It turns out upon reflection, however, that this question is surprisingly complex, and its answer may vary from one extreme to the other depending upon how the question is framed. Let's begin with perhaps the most basic formulation of the question. What is the likelihood of a single period loss?

SINGLE PERIOD LOSS

The value we wish to estimate is the probability that our investment will depreciate by some fraction from the beginning of the period to the end of the period after accounting for the income it generates. To get started, let's assume our investment has an expected return of 10% and a standard deviation of 20% and that we wish to estimate the likelihood of a 10% loss over the course of a year. Let's also simplify the analysis with the assumption that investment returns are normally distributed. Later we will consider the effect of compounding.

The assumption of a normal distribution arises from the belief that surprises are independent and come from the same underlying distribution. Statisticians refer to this notion as independent and identically distributed or "iid" for short. There is a simple thought experiment to illustrate the intuition of a normal distribution. Consider the potential outcomes for a single toss of a die. There is 1/6 chance for each outcome—hardly a normal distribution. Now consider the distribution of the average of two tosses. There is only one way to average a one—by tossing a one on both tries, which has a likelihood of 1/36. There are five ways, however, to average a three: a three on both tosses, a two and a four, a four and a two, a one and a five, and a five and a one. Because each combination has a 1/36 likelihood, the probability of averaging a three equals the sum of the five probabilities, 5/36. It turns out that the distribution of the average of many tosses approaches a normal distribution even though the distribution of the potential outcomes for a single toss is distributed uniformly.

Now let's apply this insight to investment returns. Suppose there is an equal chance of a favorable or unfavorable surprise on any given day that influences the return of an investment. A long string of favorable or unfavorable surprises would be unusual. More likely, favorable and unfavorable surprises would tend to be offsetting. Therefore, we should expect to observe more returns that are closer to what we might consider average than extreme returns in either direction. As these surprises accumulate through time, the resultant distribution of returns will conform roughly to a normal distribution.

A normal distribution has several convenient properties. First of all, the mean, the median, and the mode are all the same; hence the distribution is symmetrical around these values. Second, we can infer the entire distribution from just two values, the mean and the standard deviation or its squared value, the variance. For example, 68% of a normal distribution's returns fall within the range of the mean plus and minus one standard deviation, and 95% of the returns are between the mean plus and minus two standard deviations. Based on our assumption of a 10% mean and a 20% standard deviation, 68% of the possible returns lie within a range of −10% to 30%, and 95% of the returns are between −30% and 50%. From these facts, we infer that the likelihood of at least a 10% loss equals 16% because 32% of the outcomes (16% on either side) lie outside the one standard deviation range.

This calculation works out very conveniently because a 10% loss is precisely one standard deviation below the mean. How do we estimate the probability of a 5% loss? This value is not located at a convenient distance from the mean for which the probabilities are commonly known. It lies somewhere between zero and one standard deviation below the mean. Precisely, it is 0.75 standard deviation units below the mean, which is found by dividing its distance from the mean by the standard deviation [$(-5\% - 10\%)/20\% = -0.75$]. The value -0.75 is referred to as a standardized variable or a normal deviate. Most spreadsheets have functions for converting standardized variables into probabilities, and statistics books have tables that map standardized variables onto probabilities. It turns out that 22.66% of a normal distribution is more than 0.75 standard deviations below the mean, which makes sense given that 16% of a normal distribution is more than one standard deviation below the mean. Thus an investment with a 10% expected return and a 20% standard deviation has a 22.66% chance of generating a 5% loss over the course of a year, *assuming its returns are normally distributed.*

Now let's consider the effect of compounding. Suppose we allocate $100,000 to an investment that has an equal chance of returning 30% or losing 10% each year. There are three possible values for our investment after two years. It can increase 30% per year to $169,000. It can increase 30% in the first year and fall 10% in the second year or reverse this performance, which in both cases will lead to an ending value of $117,000. Finally, it can lose 10% in both years resulting in a final value of $81,000. The expected annual return is equal to the average of the two possible returns, which is 10%, and the expected terminal value is the average of the three possible values, $121,000. (Remember to count $117,000 twice.) The distribution of the possible ending values is skewed in the sense that the high value is further above the middle value ($52,000) than the amount by which the low value is below the middle value ($36,000). Clearly, the distribution of ending wealth is asymmetric. If we were to extend this investment over many periods, the distribution of ending wealth would conform to a lognormal distribution, which simply means that the natural logarithms of the potential ending values are normally distributed. This result arises from the fact that compounding increases the impact of favorable surprises and reduces the impact of unfavorable surprises. The corresponding logarithms of the ending values are shown below:

Ending Values	Logarithm
169,000	12.038
117,000	11.670
81,000	11.302

Note that these logarithms are perfectly symmetric even though the corresponding wealth values are not. Because the logarithms of ending values are normally distributed, we calculate the probability of a loss by applying the normal distribution to logarithmic units. In order to calculate the probability of loss assuming a lognormal distribution, we start by converting the target return and the expected return into logarithmic units, which are commonly referred to as continuous returns. The target return of −10% corresponds to a continuous return of −10.5361% $ln(0.90)$. The conversion of the 20% standard deviation of periodic returns into its continuous counterpart is more complicated. It equals the square root of the following quantity: $ln(0.20^2/(1.10)^2 + 1)$, which is 18.0342%. The conversion of the 10% periodic mean into a continuous mean is also tricky. It equals: $ln(1.10) - 0.180342^2/2$, which is 7.9049.

With these transformations the normal deviate of continuous returns equals −1.023, which corresponds to a 15.33% probability of a 10% loss over a single year. Now let's review how to estimate the likelihood of an average annual loss over a multi-year horizon.

MULTI-PERIOD ANNUALIZED LOSS

The specific probability we wish to estimate is the likelihood that our investment will depreciate, on average, by 10% per year over several years. This particular standard does not require that our investment achieve a rate of return greater than −10% each and every year. It permits annual returns below −10% as long as they are offset by sufficiently high returns to produce an annualized return greater than −10%. Let's assume a 10-year horizon to illustrate the point. The relevant normal deviate is calculated by multiplying the annualized continuous returns by the number of years in our horizon and the standard deviation of continuous returns by the square root of the number of years, as shown below:

$$[(-0.105361 \times 10) - (0.079049 \times 10)] / (0.180342 \times \sqrt{10}) = -3.234$$

This normal deviate corresponds to a probability of 0.06%, which I imagine most investors would consider comfortably remote. If we shorten our horizon to five years the normal deviate increases to −2.286 and the probability rises to 1.11%, still not a particularly worrisome situation for most investors.

Now let's investigate the likelihood of a cumulative loss over a multi-year horizon.

MULTI-PERIOD CUMULATIVE LOSS

The likelihood that our investment will generate a 10% cumulative loss over 10 years corresponds to an annualized loss of 1.0481%. The only adjustment we need to make to our previous calculation of the normal deviate is to leave the target continuous return as −0.105361 instead of multiplying it by 10. In this case the normal deviate is −1.571, which corresponds to a 5.81% probability of occurrence. If we again shorten the horizon to five years the probability increases to 13.33%.

In general, if our investment's continuous return is expected to produce a gain or less of a loss than the loss we are focused on, a longer time horizon will reduce the probability of a multi-period loss. Now let's explore the likelihood of experiencing a loss, not on average over our horizon, but in at least one of the years during our horizon.

AT LEAST ONE PERIODIC LOSS

The probability of a loss in one or more of the next 10 years is precisely equal to one minus the probability of not experiencing the loss in every one of the next ten years. In our earlier example of a single period loss, we estimated the probability of a 10% loss to equal 15.33%. It follows, therefore, that the likelihood of not experiencing a loss in a single year is 84.67%, and assuming year-to-year independence, the likelihood of avoiding a 10% annual loss for 10 consecutive years equals 84.67% raised to the 10th power, which is 18.94%. Thus there is an 81.05% chance that our investment will lose 10% or more in at least one of the next 10 years. If we shorten our horizon to five years, the likelihood falls to 56.47%. In this case, the duration of our investment horizon has the opposite effect on the likelihood of loss. A shorter horizon reduces the number of opportunities for a single period loss.

This standard is much stricter than the earlier standards I described, but it is not unreasonable. A significant single period loss, even if it is likely to be reversed in time, may prompt an investor to react differently than had the investor focused only on the final result. It may be overly heroic to assume that we can ignore intermediate outcomes and stay focused on the long run. This line of reasoning leads to a final variation on the likelihood of loss—the probability that at some point an investment will fall to 90% of its original value, even if it subsequently recovers.

LIKELIHOOD OF REACHING A CRITICAL VALUE

In some cases, we wish to measure the likelihood of breaching a threshold at any point throughout our investment horizon and not just at its conclusion, irrespective of whether or not our investment subsequently recovers. In order to assess the likelihood of such an event, we apply a formula known as a first passage time probability. This formula is also quite messy. The probability that an investment will depreciate to a particular value over some horizon during which it is monitored continuously equals:

$$N[(ln(C/S) - \mu T)/(\sigma\sqrt{T})] + (C/S)^{2\mu/\sigma^2} N[ln(C/S) + \mu T)/(\sigma\sqrt{T})]$$

where

   $N[\ ]$ = cumulative normal distribution function
   ln = natural logarithm
   C = critical value
   S = starting value
   μ = continuous return
   T = number of years in horizon
   σ = continuous standard deviation

Our investment, which has a 7.9049% continuous return and an 18.0342 continuous standard deviation, has a 58.85% chance of falling to 90% or less of its initial value at some point during a 10-year horizon.

SUMMARY

The likelihood of loss depends critically on how we frame the question. I have answered this question five different ways, all for the same investment, the same underlying distribution, and the same loss, and the answers range from 0.06% to 81.05%. These results are summarized in the following:

Likelihood of Loss		
Expected Return:	10%	
Standard Deviation:	20%	
Loss Amount:	10%	
Likelihood of a single year loss:		15.33%
Likelihood of an average annual loss over 10 years:		0.06%
Likelihood of a cumulative loss over 10 years:		5.81%
Likelihood of a loss in one or more of the next 10 years:		81.05%
Likelihood of a cumulative loss at some point over the next 10 years (monitored continuously)		58.85%

It pays to know what you are asking.

Measuring Risk

CHAPTER 5

Measuring and Managing Investment Risk

Roger G. Clarke

An essential component of effectively managing risk is the ability to measure it with relative precision. A conceptual understanding of the mathematical expressions of risk measurements is thus a necessary analytical tool for effective risk management. This chapter overviews the formulaic structure and applicable functions of some commonly used measures of risk.

One of the most common ways to describe investment risk is to relate it to the uncertainty or volatility of potential returns from an investment over time. For example, an investment whose returns could range between 4 and 6 percent is less volatile than an investment whose returns could range between −20 and +40 percent. The source of the uncertainty and the degree of its impact depend on the type of investment. The most common sources of investment risk are financial exposure to changes in interest rates, equity markets, inflation, foreign exchange rates, credit quality, and commodity prices. Effective risk management involves identifying the risk, estimating its magnitude, deciding how much risk will be assumed, and building structures to reduce unwanted risk. This chapter describes the commonly used measures of risk, reviews the most typical ways to describe risk in equity and fixed-income markets, and examines methods to manage risk in the financial markets.

Effective risk management requires a decision as to how much of the risk should be hedged and at what cost. Analytical tools are required if one wants to be most precise about measuring risk. As a result, we frequently

Reprinted from *Portable MBA in Investment*, John Wiley & Sons, 1994, pp. 243–252.

resort to mathematical expressions to capture the central concepts. Understanding these concepts is critical if the investor wants to apply risk management techniques in practice. In fact, the rigor of the mathematics makes the subject easier to understand and apply, not more difficult. For readers who are less comfortable with the algebra, each important mathematical expression is followed by an explanation.

COMMONLY USED MEASURES OF RISK

The primary building block for discussing risk is the concept of a probability distribution of prices or returns. Figure 5.1 illustrates this concept. Figure 5.1 is a bar graph of the return possibilities for an investment. Suppose the investor purchases a security for $100. At the end of a year, the security could take on one of three values: $90, $100, or $120. The probability of each price occurring is given by the height of the bar in Figure 5.1. The *mean return* on the investment of $100 is calculated by multiplying the probability of each occurrence by the corresponding percentage return. Equation 5.1 shows the mathematical equivalent of the concept, indicating that the expected return is equal to the sum of the possible individual returns times the probability of each occurring:

$$E(R) = p_1 R_1 + p_2 R_2 + \cdots + p_n R_n$$

$$= \sum_{i=1}^{n} p_i R_i \qquad (5.1)$$

where $E(R)$ equals the expected or mean return and R_i represents the specific return outcome with probability p_i.[1] Table 5.1 shows that the mean return in the simple example illustrated in Figure 5.1 is equal to 4.0 percent.

Standard Deviation (Variance)

One measure of risk is the variance of the probability distribution. The variance is calculated by squaring the deviation of each occurrence from the mean and multiplying each value by its associated probability. The sum of these values is equal to the variance of the distribution. The square root of the variance is referred to as the *standard deviation*. Equation 5.2 shows that the standard deviation is calculated by first summing the probability-weighted squared deviations of each outcome versus the mean and taking the square root of the sum:

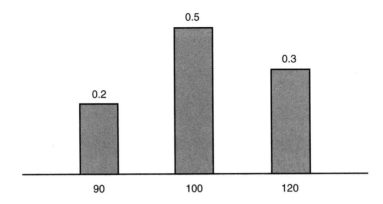

FIGURE 5.1 Probability of security price at year end.

TABLE 5.1 Expected Return and Risk for a Simple Investment

Price at Year End	Percentage Return on Original Investment	Probability	Probability-Weighted Return	Differential Return from the Mean	Prtobability-Weighted Differential Return Squared
90	−10.0	0.2	−2.0	−14.0	39.2
100	0.0	0.5	0.0	−4.0	8.0
120	20.0	0.3	6.0	16.0	76.8
Totals		1.0	4.0		124.0

Notes: Mean return = 4.0%, variance = 124.0%,
      standard deviation = $\sqrt{124.0}$ =11.1%

$$\sigma = \sqrt{p_1[R_1 - E(R)]^2 + p_2[R_2 - E(R)]^2 + \cdots + p_n[R_n - E(R)]^2}$$

$$= \sqrt{\sum_{i=1}^{n} p_i[R_i - E(R)]^2} \tag{5.2}$$

Table 5.1 shows that the variance is equal to 124.0 (last column), whereas the standard deviation is equal to 11.1 percent. The variance or

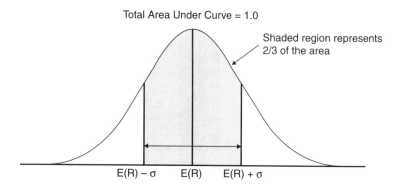

FIGURE 5.2 Normal probability distribution.

standard deviation is a common measure of risk and represents the variability of the returns around the mean. The higher the level of standard deviation, the more variability there is in the probability distribution.

A more complete probability distribution is shown in Figure 5.2, which shows its mean and standard deviation. If the distribution is normally distributed (producing the common bell-shaped curve), about two-thirds of the area will fall between the plus and minus one standard deviation from the mean. The shaded area in Figure 5.2 represents the probability of returns falling within the delineated range of returns.

Other things being equal, most investors prefer less volatile returns to more volatile returns. Other things, however, are usually not equal, which is when the deficiencies of standard deviation as a risk measure begin to appear. The first thing to note about the calculation of standard deviation is that the deviations above and below the mean return are given weights equal to their respective probability of occurring, yet most investors are more averse to negative deviations of the same probability than they are pleased with positive deviations of the same magnitude. Research in an area called *Prospect Theory* indicates that investors treat absolute gains and losses quite differently. (For example, see D. Kahneman and A. Tversky. "Prospect Theory: An Analysis of Decision under Risk." *Econometrica* [1979]: 263–291.) Consequently, if two investments have the same absolute deviations about the mean (giving the same standard deviation), but one has more negative returns, investors often view the distribution with the lower mean as riskier.

Second, standard deviation as a measure of risk tends to work better when the probability distribution of returns is symmetric. If one distribution is skewed to one side or the other while another is symmetric around

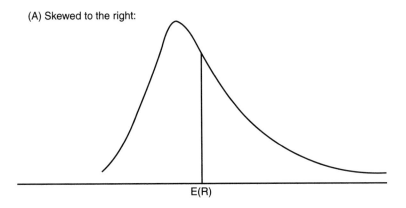

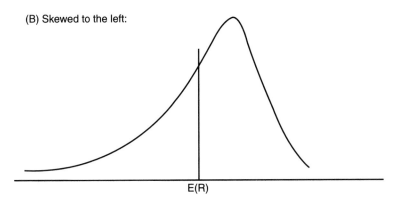

FIGURE 5.3 Skewed probability distributions: equal means and variances but different downside risk.

the mean, both might have the same standard deviation, but be perceived as having quite different levels of risk. This phenomenon is illustrated in Figure 5.3. Both distributions have identical means and variances. The variances are identical because the two distributions are mirror images of each other rotated around the mean. One of the important differences between the two is that the distribution skewed to the left (B) is characterized by less likely but larger losses and more likely but smaller gains than the distribution skewed to the right (A). Our intuitive notion of risk is often related to the possibility of *bad surprises*. The bad surprises in A are more likely but smaller and limited in magnitude, whereas the bad surprises in B are less likely but potentially much larger in magnitude. A risk-averse investor would generally prefer A to B on these grounds, although they have the same standard deviation.

The conceptual underpinning for the use of standard deviation (or variance) as a measure of risk is related to the theory of utility functions. *Expected utility* is a concept developed by Daniel Bernoulli, a famous Swiss mathematician in the 1700s, to explain the *St. Petersburg Paradox*. Bernoulli noted that a particular coin toss game led to an infinite expected payoff, but participants were willing to pay only a modest fee to play. He resolved the paradox by noting that participants do not assign the same value to each dollar of payoff. Larger payoffs resulting in more wealth are appreciated less and less, so that at the margin, players exhibit decreasing marginal utility as the payoff increases. The particular function that assigns a value to each level of payoff is referred to as the *investor's utility function*. Von Neumann and Morgenstern applied this approach to investment theory in 1944 in a volume that formed the basis for Markowitz's article in 1952 on how to form an efficient portfolio of securities using expected return and variance.

Consider an unspecified function, $U(R)$, which represents the utility of investment returns to a particular investor. Mathematicians have shown that the value of a particular function when its random input is close to its mean can be approximated by terms related to the expected value of the random input (called a *Taylor series expansion*). As a result, the expected utility of investment returns can be written as the desirability of the expected random return plus the rate of change in the utility of returns times the variance of returns plus some smaller-size terms, as shown in Equation 5.3.

$$E[U(R)] = U[E(R)] = U''[E(R)]\sigma^2/2 + Higher - Order\ Terms \qquad (5.3)$$

The term $U''[E(R)]$ represents the rate of change in the utility of investment returns when returns are about average. In mathematical terms, $U''[E(R)]$ represents the second derivative of $U(R)$ with respect to R.

If the returns are normally distributed, the higher-order terms are identically zero and the expected utility is

$$E[U(R)] = U[E(R)] + U''[E(R)]\sigma^2/2 \qquad (5.4)$$

Equation 5.4 indicates that the expected utility of an investment's returns is equal to the utility of the expected return plus a term related to the variance of returns.[2] It suggests that the investor would be concerned with only the mean and the variance of the investment return. It is this analysis that in part laid the foundation for the use of variance as a measure of risk in analyzing investment returns.

Equation 5.4 also serves to point out the weaknesses in using variance as a complete measure of risk. Students of mathematics know that a Taylor series expansion is only approximately true in the neighborhood of the expansion point (in our case, the mean return), and it is not in the neighborhood of the mean where investors' questions about risk usually lie. Investors are often concerned about downside returns, which may lie distant from the mean. Thus, investors are usually concerned about returns in a region where the expansion in Equation 5.4 is known to be less accurate. Using variance as the only measure of risk under these circumstances can lead to difficulties.

Furthermore, when returns are not normally distributed (because of the use of options or nonlinear trading strategies, for example), the higher-order terms in Equation 5.4 are nonzero, and overlooking this can distort the assessment of risk. Bookstaber and Clarke (in "Problems in Evaluating the Performance of Portfolios with Options," *Financial Analyst Journal* [January/February] 1985: 48–62) present examples where "if one used standard deviation or variance as a proxy for risk, it would appear that covered call writing is preferable [for reducing risk] to buying puts," and where "buying puts [for reducing risk] is inferior to the stock-only portfolio." Yet the purchase of puts eliminates most of the undesirable downside risk, whereas the sale of call options eliminates the desirable upside potential. Bookstaber and Clarke conclude that "variance is not a suitable proxy for risk in these cases because options strategies reduce variance asymmetrically." The asymmetric shape of the probability distribution distorts the conclusions that come from using variance as the only measure of risk.

In summary, variance or standard deviation is a commonly used measure of risk, but it can lead to misleading results under some circumstances:

- The probability distribution of returns is not symmetric. This could be inherent in the asset itself or could be induced by the use of options or nonlinear trading rules in the portfolio.
- A significant portion of the distribution lies in a range yielding negative returns. Investors often prefer to value gains differently from losses. This asymmetry is not reflected in the equal weighting treatment implicit in calculating standard deviation.

Tracking Error Variance

A modification of variance as a measure of risk is the calculation of tracking error variance relative to an underlying benchmark. Tracking error is defined as the difference between the investment return and a specified benchmark or target position, as shown in Equation 5.5. The tracking error is defined as

$$\Delta R = R - B \tag{5.5}$$

where B represents the benchmark or target return. The variance of the tracking error is sometimes used as a measure of risk when the investor is interested in seeing how closely a position tracks a particular desired result. In actuality, the variance of the total return can be thought of as a special case of the more general tracking error variance that results when the benchmark is equal to the expected return of the investment. In the example in Table 5.1, the standard deviation of the tracking error relative to the mean return is 11.1 percent and rises to 11.8 percent if zero is used as the target return.

In the more general case, the tracking error is calculated relative to a risky benchmark or index and represents how closely the investment tracks the desired result. Tracking error variance typically suffers from the same drawbacks as the normal variance, however. The tracking error variance calculation will treat deviations above the benchmark no differently from deviations below the benchmark return. If the consequences of deviations on the downside are more serious than the benefits of deviations on the upside, tracking error variance will not give a complete measure of risk.

Probability of Shortfall

Another measure of risk proposed by Leslie A. Balzer (in "Measuring Investment Risk: A Review," *Journal of Investing* [Fall 1994] among others is the probability of shortfall. The probability of shortfall measures the chance that returns from the investment may fall below some reference point. The reference point is often set at zero, but it could be set at any other meaningful level to reflect the minimum acceptable return. This measure of risk is captured in Equation 5.6.

$$\text{Shortfall probability} = \text{Probability } (R < B) \tag{5.6}$$

where R = the return on the investment and B = the benchmark or reference return.

In the case of the simple example in Table 5.1, the probability of shortfall below a return of 0 percent would be 20 percent. Figure 5.4 illustrates the probability of shortfall using a more general probability distribution. The

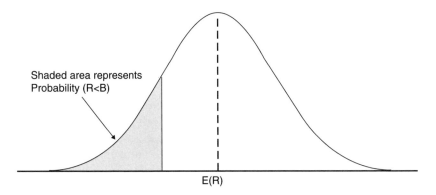

FIGURE 5.4 Shortfall probability.

shaded area to the left of the benchmark return represents the probability of shortfall. The benchmark return could also represent a risky asset or index return. In this case, the probability distribution would represent the distribution of tracking error relative to the index instead of the distribution of total return.

The risk measure in Equation 5.6 gives the probability that an undesirable event might occur, but gives no hint as to how severe it might be. For example, an investor might have two possible investment choices. In one case, the investor has a 10 percent probability of losing 20 percent, whereas in the other case, the investor has a 10 percent chance of losing 100 percent. The probability of shortfall ranks each investment as equivalent from a risk perspective, but most investors would clearly not be indifferent between the two. The second investment presents a much more serious loss if it does occur, even though the probability of losing is the same. Hence, even though the probability of shortfall may be of considerable interest, it is insufficient as a measure of risk.

Expected Shortfall

An alternative to the probability of shortfall is the *expected shortfall*. This measure incorporates not only the probability of shortfall, but also the magnitude of the potential shortfall if it does occur. Equation 5.7 represents this notion, measuring the expected shortfall as the difference between the actual return and the benchmark over the range of returns when there is a shortfall.

Expected shortfall = $E[R - B]$, over the range where $R - B < 0$ (5.7)

In the simple example in Table 5.1, the expected shortfall below a 0 percent return is −2 percent. The expected shortfall represents the magnitude of the shortfall times the probability of it occurring. This measure is influenced by the entire downside portion of the probability distribution and is a more complete measure of downside risk than just the probability of shortfall itself.

A major problem with the expected shortfall measure is that it treats a large probability of a small shortfall as equivalent to a small probability of a large shortfall. We argued earlier, however, that investors tend to view losses differently from gains. The expected shortfall measure has drawbacks if investors view the consequences of large losses per unit differently from small losses. This is often the case. Consider that most people insure their houses, but do not insure many minor items that may have a higher probability of loss than the house.

Lower Partial Moments (LPMs) and Semivariance

Another class of risk measures is termed *lower partial moments* (LPMs) by Harlow (in "Asset Allocation in a Downside Risk Framework," *Financial Analysts Journal* [Sep/Oct 1991]). The term *partial* is used to reflect the fact that the measures relate to only one side of the return distribution relative to a target level. *Lower* indicates that the side of interest is the downside, where most investors are the most sensitive to volatility. The LPMs defined by Harlow can also be expanded to incorporate a risky benchmark as the target return in place of a fixed target return. This more general formulation enables these risk measures to incorporate the tracking error concept as well as the standard interpretation below a fixed return. A set of *relative* LPMs can be defined as the expected value of the tracking error raised to the power of

$$RLPM_n = E[R - B)^n], \text{ over the range where } R < B$$

$$= 0, \text{ over the range where } R \geq B \qquad (5.8)$$

where n represents the order or ranking of the relative LPM.

This concept captures several of the measures referred to earlier. If $n = 0$, the relative LPM is equivalent to the probability of shortfall in Equation 5.6. If $n = 1$, the relative LPM is equal to the expected shortfall in Equation 5.7. Finally, if $n = 2$, the lower partial is equal to the relative lower partial variance. A special case of the lower partial variance when the benchmark is equal to the expected return of the distribution is termed the *semivariance* by Markowitz. The term *relative semivariance* (*relative semideviation* is the square root of the relative variance) is sometimes used in place of the term *lower partial moment* variance when the target return is not the mean of the distribution. In the example in Table 5.1, the *semideviation* is equal to 6.9 percent (calculated relative to the mean return), whereas the semideviation calculated relative to a 0 percent return is 4.5 percent.

Relative semivariance avoids many of the shortcomings that plague other measures of risk. It is an asymmetric measure that focuses on the downside of the probability distribution and avoids penalizing outperformance. It is a relatively complete measure in that it uses all values of the shortfall with their associated probabilities. It is also nonlinear in that it penalizes larger values more than smaller values because of the squaring of the tracking errors in the calculation. This is more consistent with observed investor behavior because most investors perceive infrequent but large losses as more risky than more frequent but small losses.

Nevertheless, there are some disadvantages in using relative semivariance as a measure of risk. Most are not so much conceptual as they are operational in nature. The first is a general lack of understanding of relative semivariance as a measure of risk. Variance and standard deviation are more well known and more integrated into the theoretical structure of investment decision making. Consequently, using semivariance as a measure of risk generally requires some additional education for the user. Second, mathematical optimizers used by most practitioners to make trade-offs between risk and return are generally not set up to construct portfolios of securities using semivariance as a measure of risk. This makes it more difficult to use relative semivariance as a practical tool without some changes in software. Third, there is no clear way to choose the target or benchmark return that is best to use when calculating the relative semivariance. A different benchmark will produce a different set of trade-offs between risk and return. Risk can be measured relative to any benchmark, but there are few guidelines in deciding which benchmark to use. Finally, the analytics for mixing individual securities in a portfolio are more difficult using relative semivariance than they are using variance as a measure of risk. That is, the interactions of securities are not easily decomposed into the individual securities risk measures as in the case of the calculation of variance. As a result, the portfolio has to be treated as a whole rather than building up the risk measures from its individual parts.

NOTES

[1]The symbol $\sum_i$ is a shorthand notation called a *summation*, which represents the sum of the terms following it.

[2]The use of mean and variance can also be motivated by the use of a quadratic utility function. If quadratic utility describes how the investor evaluates the utility of wealth, the only measures that make a difference are the mean and variance of the distribution of wealth. Quadratic utility functions have some severe limitations, however, and don't describe the way people behave very well for extreme wealth values.

CHAPTER 6

An Assessment of Alternative Models of Financial Market Volatility

John F. O. Bilson

Financial models for portfolio optimization, option valuation, and risk analysis all require forecasts of the volatility of asset returns. A large number of alternative models are available, most of which are variants of the (G)ARCH framework originally developed by Engel and Bollerslev. However, the forecasts of the different models are very similar and it is not clear how a practitioner would decide between them for a particular application. This chapter provides three alternative assessment procedures that may be of assistance in this task.

INTRODUCTION

The estimation of the variance of the return on an asset is a crucial issue in modern applied finance. Volatility was first introduced into the financial world in Markowitz's (1952) mean-variance model of portfolio selection. It was later demonstrated to play a crucial role in option pricing in the Black-Scholes (1973) model. In economic terms, however, the most significant role for volatility forecasts in modern financial markets is in the estimation of Value at Risk (VaR). The use of VaR as a standard for determining capital adequacy in the banking system has resulted in a system where extremely large sums of money are dependent upon the volatility forecast. A volatility forecast that is too high will result in excessive capital charges while a forecast that is too low will result in VaR violations that will attract the attention of regulators and capital markets. Seen in this light, the choice of a volatility model is an economic rather than a statistical issue. If the penalties for violating VaR estimates are high relative to the cost of capital, a rational banker would be induced to select a more conservative (that is higher) forecast.

On the basis of this idea, three nontraditional procedures for evaluating volatility forecasts are developed in this chapter. The first is based upon a market in which traders speculate upon the value of the absolute return on the asset at the close of the next day. The second is based upon a market in a "crash" option that pays off if the market declines by more than 2 percent on a given day.[1] The crash option is an instrument that mimics the economic trade-off implicit in the VaR methodology. A trader who is long the option will pay a small price each day to avoid the prospect of a large loss on any given day. Finally, the third procedure introduces some other aspects of the volatility forecasts that should be considered in evaluating alternative models.

Throughout the chapter, five different volatility forecasts will be considered. The underlying asset considered is the Standard & Poor's (S&P) 100 index. The first forecast is the implied volatility of OEX 100 options, or the VIX index, an index of the implied volatility of a standardized, 20-day, at-the-money option on the S&P 100 index published by the Chicago Board Options Exchange (CBOE).[2] The second forecast is an internally developed approach based upon the range estimators originally created by Garman and Klass (1980) and Parkinson (1980). This estimator will be referred to as the LGK, for Logarithmic Garman Klass, estimator. The final three models are the familiar generalized autoregressive conditional heteroscedasticity (GARCH)(1,1) model of Bollerslev (1987), the exponential GARCH (EGARCH) model of Nelson (1991), and the GJR model of Glosten, Jagannathan, and Runkle (1993). The data for the study consist of daily observations on the S&P 100 index and the VIX index over the period from January 2, 1986 to May 20, 2002. The data is divided into a presample period from January 2, 1986 to December 30, 1989; a sample period from January 2, 1990 to December 30, 1999; and a postsample period from January 2, 2000 to May 20, 2002. The models are estimated using the sample period data and tested using the pre- and postsample observations.

THE VOLATILITY FORECASTING MODELS

The VIX index is a widely followed estimate of the implied volatility on the S&P 100 index. It is computed on a real-time basis during the trading day, and the CBOE provides a history of the series going back to 1986. The index is created by calculating the implied volatilities of 4 options that bracket an at-the-money, 22-trading-day option. Professor Robert Whaley, the creator of the index, has referred to it as "the investor fear gauge" in recognition of the empirical regularity that the index tends to be high when the market has declined significantly. However, it is also possible to interpret this regularity as a rational forecast of future volatility rather than as a purely psychological phenomenon. If the VIX is a psychological gauge rather than a volatility forecast, then other forecasting models that avoid psychology should be able to outperform the VIX in forecasting future volatility. The results reported in this chapter suggest that this is not that easy to do. The VIX is a forecast of the volatility over the next 20 trading days. If volatility is mean reverting, the 20-day forecast may be different from the 1-day forecast. However, rather than attempt to make arbitrary adjustments, this study will assume that the VIX is a forecast of 1-day volatility. Specifically, we take the published VIX number, correct it for the day count convention, and then express it as a 1-day forecast by dividing through by 252, the average number of trading days in a year:

$$s^1 = \sqrt{\frac{5}{7}} \, VIX \, \frac{1}{\sqrt{252}} \tag{6.1}$$

The LGK model is based upon a volatility metric that measures the volatility during a given trading day on the basis of the previous close and the open, high, low, and close during the day. Based upon the original contributions of Parkinson (1980) and Garman and Klass (1980), as updated in Garman and Klass (2001), the volatility metric is defined as:

$$v_t = \ln\left(\frac{O_t}{C_{t-1}}\right) + .5 \times \ln\left(\frac{H_t}{L_t}\right)^2 - .39 \times \ln\left(\frac{C_t}{O_t}\right)^2 \tag{6.2}$$

In Equation 6.2, O, H, L, and C refer to the open, high, low, and close respectively. The studies referred to previously demonstrate that this volatility metric has a sampling variance that is considerably smaller than the sampling variance of a metric based solely on the closing prices. The metric also has the advantage that it is always positive. This feature enables us to model the log of the volatility metric rather than the level. The log volatility metric is less influenced by outliers and results in a more stable forecast.

The time series model distinguishes between a long-run trend volatility and the short-run dynamics around the trend. Long-run volatility, *g*, is assumed to follow a simple exponential moving average:

$$g_t = \alpha \ln(v_{t-1})(1 - \alpha) \, g_{t-1} \tag{6.3}$$

The short-run conditional volatility, h, is assumed to exhibit persistence, mean reversion, and a relationship to the return on the underlying asset:

$$h_t = h_{t-1} + \delta_1(\ln(v_{t-1}) - h_{t-1}) + \delta_2(g_t - h_{t-1}) + \delta_3 r_{t-1} \quad (6.4)$$

In Equation 6.4, r represents the return on the S&P 100 index. If negative returns are associated with increased conditional volatility, the δ_3 coefficient should be negative. To complete the model, we assume that the conditional volatility is an unbiased forecast of the actual log of the volatility metric:

$$\ln(v_t) = h_t + u_t \quad (6.5)$$

The residual series, u, is assumed to be normally and independently distributed with a mean of 0. Although the untransformed volatility metric follows a chi-squared distribution with three degrees of freedom, the assumption of normality appears justified for the log of the series since this series exhibits very little skewness or kurtosis. Finally, we retrieve a forecast of the volatility metric from the expectation of Equation 6.5:

$$s^2 = \sqrt{\exp(h + \sigma_u^2/2)} \quad (6.6)$$

The model described in Equations 6.3, 6.4, and 6.5 will be referred to as the LGK model. The annualized volatility forecast derived from the model is obtained by multiplying the daily variance forecast by the number of trading days in the year:

$$s_{LGK} = \sqrt{s^2 \times 252} \quad (6.7)$$

The LGK model is not a GARCH model. GARCH models are primarily models of the rate of return on the asset with hetroscedastic transformations. The LGK model makes no attempt to forecast the rate of return. Instead, it is concerned with directly estimating a model to forecast the values of the volatility metric. Specifically, the parameters are estimated by the maximum likelihood method under the assumption that the forecast errors are normally distributed. The estimation period runs from January 3, 1986 to May 20, 2002 for 4,127 total observations. The reported results were obtained using the BFGS algorithm in RATS-5.

TABLE 6.1 The LGK Model

Parameter	Estimate	StdError	T-Stat
Alpha	0.0544	0.0071	7.63
Delta-1 (δ_1)	0.0992	0.0150	6.61
Delta-2 (δ_2)	0.2462	0.0388	6.34
Delta-3 (δ_3)	-14.4364	1.1930	-12.1
StdError	0.7882	0.0107	73.41

In Table 6.1, the Alpha parameter measures the speed of adjustment of the long-run moving average. The estimated value of .0544 is roughly equivalent to a simple moving average of 35 days.[3] The Delta-1 parameter measures the short-term persistence effect. Using the same transformation, the short-run moving average is around 19 days. The Delta-2 parameter measures the speed of mean reversion toward the long-run moving average. Approximately 25 percent per day of the difference is made up through changes in the short-run volatility forecast each day. Finally, the Delta-3 parameter measures the sensitivity of the conditional volatility to the rate of return. This effect is strongly negative and statistically significant. This implies that negative returns in the market are associated with large increases in predicted volatility.

The next model that we consider is the standard GARCH(1,1) model originally proposed by Bollerslev (1987). This model is of particular importance in the risk management field because of its close association with the exponentially weighted moving average model employed by the RiskMetrics group in their popular "RiskMetrics Technical Document." The RiskMetrics model is a special case of the GARCH(1,1) model arising from certain restrictions on the coefficients. The version that will be used in this chapter is described in the following two equations:

$$r_t = \beta_o + \beta_1 h_t + \sqrt{h_t}\, \varepsilon_t \tag{6.8}$$

$$h_t = \delta_o + \delta_1 \varepsilon_{t-1}^2 + \delta_2 h_{t-1} \tag{6.9}$$

In the first equation, the conditional mean of the return series is assumed to be a linear function of the conditional variance, h. ε_t is an independently and identically distributed random forecast error. This relationship is consistent with the predictions of modern portfolio theory since the model is applied to the return on the overall market as represented by the S&P 100 index. The conditional variance is related to the square of the lagged residual term and to the lagged conditional variance. The RiskMetrics model is applied when the beta coefficients are 0, δ_0 is 0, δ_1 is .06, and δ_2 is .94. Because the residuals exhibit significant kurtosis relative to the normal distribution, the residuals are assumed to follow a Student t-distribution with N degrees of freedom. The degrees of freedom are considered to be a parameter representing the degree of kurtosis and is estimated along with the other parameters. The resulting estimates are provided in Table 6.2.[4]

Using Equation 6.9, the results in Table 6.2 can be used to describe the GARCH model in terms of persistence and mean reversion components:

$$h_t = h_{t-1} + .027 \times (h \times -h_{t-1}) + 0.39 \times (\varepsilon_{t-1}^2 - h_{t-1}) \quad (6.10)$$

In this equation, $h \times$ represents the steady state volatility forecast. Relative to the LGK model, the GARCH model coefficients are quite small, indicating a slow degree of mean reversion (2.7 percent per day) and a moderate persistence effect (3.9 percent per day). This suggests that the model is picking up longer-term volatility trends but that it is not capturing shorter-term volatility spikes.

The most important limitation of the standard GARCH model is that it does not account for the asymmetric effect of market returns on forecasted volatility. Particularly in the equity markets, negative returns tend to increase market volatility and positive returns tend to decrease market volatility. The LGK model indicates that this effect is very strong and statistically significant. The next two models provide alternative ways of capturing this asymmetry effect.

The first attempt to develop a model that explicitly takes into account the specific features of equity markets was Nelson's EGARCH model. In this formulation of Nelson's model, the conditional mean equation is assumed

TABLE 6.2 The GARCH Model

Parameter	Estimate	StdError	T-Stat
β_0	0.0379	0.0219	1.70
β_1	0.0791	0.0476	1.66
δ_0	0.0050	0.0026	1.89
δ_1	0.0391	0.0084	4.60
δ_2	0.9339	0.0159	58.55
N	5.6054	0.7386	7.58

to be the same as in Equation 6.8. The conditional variance equation is described in Equation 6.11:

$$h_t = exp\left\{\delta_o + \delta_1\left[\frac{abs(\varepsilon_{t-1})}{\sqrt{h_{t-1}}} - \sqrt{\frac{2}{\pi}} - \delta_2\frac{\varepsilon_{t-1}}{\sqrt{h_{t-1}}}\right] + \delta_3 ln(h_{t-1})\right\} \quad (6.11)$$

Nelson's model differs from the standard GARCH approach in three important respects. The first is the use of an exponential function to represent the conditional volatility. The second is that the model is based upon the absolute standardized error, relative to its expected value, as the forcing variable for conditional volatility. The third is the inclusion of the actual standardized error to take into account the asymmetry effect. As in the case of the GARCH model, the residuals are assumed to follow a Student t distribution with N degrees of freedom. The estimation results are reported in Table 6.3.

The δ_2 parameter estimates the impact of the asymmetry effect. This parameter is significantly different from zero at standard levels of statistical significance. The δ_3 parameter is estimated to be .9884. This indicates that the model is relatively slow, like the GARCH model, in the sense that it is based upon a relatively long history of the series. Expressed as a simple moving average, the estimated number of days is approximately 170.

The GJR (1993) model offers an alternative procedure for capturing the asymmetry effect. The GJR conditional volatility equation is described in Equation 6.12:

$$h_t = \delta_0 + \delta_1\varepsilon_{t-1}^2 + \delta_2 D_{t-1}\varepsilon_{t-1}^2 + \delta_3 h_{t-1} \quad (6.12)$$

TABLE 6.3 The EGARCH Model

Parameter	Estimate	StdError	T-Stat
β_0	0.0268	0.0235	1.14
β_1	0.0748	0.0525	1.42
δ_0	−0.0218	0.0067	−3.24
δ_1	0.0889	0.0162	5.45
δ_2	0.5131	0.0901	5.69
δ_3	0.9884	0.0060	165.08
N	5.2341	0.9262	5.65

TABLE 6.4   The GJR Model

Parameter	Estimate	StdError	T-Stat
β_0	0.0241	0.0214	1.12
β_1	0.0808	0.0418	1.93
δ_0	0.0089	0.0043	2.05
δ_1	0.0171	0.0059	2.9
δ_2	0.0597	0.0217	2.74
δ_3	0.9163	0.0211	43.39
N	6.0264	0.8786	6.85

The GJR model differs from the standard GARCH model because of the D variable in the equation. This is a dummy variable taking the value of 1 when the lagged residual is negative and 0 otherwise. The impact of a positive lagged residual is given by δ_1, and the impact of a negative residual is given by δ_1 plus δ_2. The δ_2 parameter consequently measures the asymmetry effect. Estimates of the GJR model are provided in Table 6.4.

The GJR model confirms the importance of the asymmetry effect. The impact coefficient of a positive squared residual is .0171, while the same coefficient for a negative residual is .0768. The GJR model is also relatively fast compared to its GARCH cousins with a simple moving average representation of 23 days.

A PRINCIPAL COMPONENTS ANALYSIS

The objective of this study is to determine the best volatility forecast. Before proceeding to this task, it is useful to begin with a discussion of why it is so difficult. The first point to note is that the variable—the squared return on the index—is extremely difficult to forecast. It is unlikely that any of the models would account for more than an extremely small percentage of the variation in the underlying series. The second problem is that all the models are based upon the same set of data and that it is likely, therefore, that the forecasts will be highly correlated. This second point can be illustrated by estimating the principal components of the forecast series. For each model, the estimated annualized standard deviation is calculated and the first two principal components of the resulting time series are calculated. Let X represent the TxK matrix of forecasts, let a represent a Kx1 vector of weights, and let Z represent the Tx1 component vector. Define:

$$Z = Xa \tag{6.13}$$

The principal components procedure selects the vector a to maximize $Z'Z$ subject to the constraint that $a'a$ equals unity. For the second principal component, a second constraint is imposed that requires that the second vector of weights is orthogonal to the first set. The principal component analysis was run over the entire data set. Similar results were obtained from the pre-, in-, and postsample data sets.

Table 6.5 demonstrates that the first principal component is roughly an equally weighted average of the alternative volatility forecasts, because the weights in the principal component calculation are all roughly equal in size. The GARCH and GJR models receive positive weights in the second principle component while the VIX and LGK receive negative weights. Since principal components weights are indeterminant with respect to sign, the second component is simply grouping the forecasts without providing an evaluation. Furthermore, this average accounts for 98.13 percent of the total variation in the forecast series. The second component can be interpreted as an average of the GARCH and GJR models minus an average of the VIX and LGK models. However, this second component only increases the percentage of the variance explained to 99.32 percent. The obvious conclusion to be drawn from this analysis is that there is extremely little independent variation in the forecasts.

It is important to note that the sign of the weights in the principal components analysis is arbitrary. In order to explore the value of the forecasts in more detail, the absolute return on the OEX index was regressed on the first two principle components. The dependent variable in the regression is the absolute value of the return on the stock market index, which is a measure of its observed volatility, and the independent variables are the lagged values of the first two principle components. The results are reported in Table 6.6.

In each sample, the first component is estimated to have a positive and statistically significant relationship to the subsequently observed absolute return. The second component has a statistically significant negative relationship to the absolute return in each period. This suggests that the forecasts that receive a negative weight in the second component, namely the VIX and the LGK, provide superior forecasts to the forecasts that have a positive weight, namely the GARCH and the GJR models.

TABLE 6.5 Principal Components Analysis

	VIX	LGK	GARCH	EGARCH	GJR	Percent Variance
a1	0.51	0.38	0.40	0.52	0.42	0.9813
a2	−0.42	−0.50	0.34	−0.03	0.67	0.9932

TABLE 6.6 Regression Analysis of Principal Components

Presample		Estimate	StdError	T-Stat
	Constant	−0.2448	0.0962	2.54
	Z1	2.8850	0.2425	11.89
	Z2	−3.3179	0.7157	4.63
In-sample				
	Constant	−0.1668	0.0389	4.33
	Z1	2.6093	0.1205	21.64
	Z2	−4.0724	0.6242	6.52
Postsample				
	Constant	−0.6033	0.2060	2.92
	Z1	3.5749	0.4264	8.38
	Z2	−5.7811	1.4138	4.08

A REGRESSION ANALYSIS

The multiple regression model is another popular method for evaluating alternative forecasts. In this approach, the variable to be forecast, in this case the absolute return on the series, is regressed upon the alternative forecasts. If the return series is normally distributed with mean 0 and standard deviation of σ_t, the relationship between the expected absolute return and the daily standard deviation can be shown to be:

$$E(|r_t|) = \sqrt{\frac{2}{\pi}}\,\sigma_t \qquad (6.14)$$

In Table 6.7, results are reported from a multiple regression analysis relating the observed absolute return to the absolute return forecasts generated by the various models.

The VIX and LGK forecasts add up to 1.27 in both the pre-sample and postsample data sets. The in-sample sum is 1.47. The combination of these two forecasts exhibits a statistically significant positive relationship to the observed outcome in all the data periods. However, the GARCH forecast receives a negative weight in all periods. Since the GARCH is closely related to the GJR, it is tempting to interpret the results as a combined forecast that is long GJR and short GARCH. The difference between these two models is the allowance for asymmetry in the GJR model. The EGARCH model is statistically insignificant in all periods.

TABLE 6.7 Regression-Based Composite Forecasts

	Presample Estimate	T-Stat	In-sample Estimate	T-Stat	Postsample Estimate	T-Stat
Constant	0.0008	0.50	-0.0009	2.17	−0.0001	0.02
VIX	0.9064	3.68	0.8656	6.07	−0.0746	0.21
LGK	0.3709	2.01	0.6138	3.55	1.3305	4.62
GARCH	−2.1055	−.46	−1.1773	4.18	−1.7479	−3.06
EGARCH	0.1383	0.39	−0.1084	0.49	0.3053	0.62
GJR	1.3600	2.68	0.8343	4.04	1.2231	2.51

When the results of the principal components analysis and the regression analysis are combined, the results suggest that the best forecast is an equally weighted average of the VIX and LGK forecasts. The GARCH and GJR models appear to have some forecasting value as a spread, and the EGARCH doesn't appear to have any forecasting value at all. EGARCH receives a very small weight in the second principal component and it also receives small and statistically insignificant weights in the multiple regression analysis. However, it is not clear that either statistical procedure provides a complete answer to the best forecast issue. Most practitioners argue that the correct forum for determining the best forecast is the market. In the next two sections of this chapter, two market-based evaluation procedures will be presented.

THE DAILY ABSOLUTE RETURN CONTRACT

It is somewhat surprising that the futures industry has not developed contracts that relate to the forecasting needs of the risk management industry. The two most pressing needs are for a futures contract that directly reveals the market's estimate of daily volatility and for an option contract that can be used to hedge VaR exposures. The CBOE has partially addressed the first need with its VIX and VXN volatility contracts, but these contracts are specified in terms of a standardized, 22-day, at-the-money option contract. It is not clear that the resulting implied volatility forecast is the market's best estimate of volatility during the next trading day.

The contract that will be considered in this paper is based upon the absolute return on the index. The contract is a variant of the rolling spot contract on foreign currencies introduced by the Chicago Mercantile Exchange, but it is a purely hypothetical construct at the present time. The contract has a face value of $200,000 for reasons that will be presented. The payoff on the contract is the absolute return on the index from the previous day's settlement to today's settlement multiplied by the face value. If the market rose or fell by 1 percent, the long position would receive 1 percent of $200,000, or $2,000. The contract can be purchased or sold at any time prior to the settlement, but we shall focus on trading centered upon the previous close. Suppose that the contract is trading at a price of 1 percent. A purchaser of the contract would pay $2,000 today in order to receive the absolute return on the index times $200,000 tomorrow.

If the underlying return series is normally distributed with mean zero and standard deviation σ_t, the expected value of the absolute return and its variance can be found to be:

$$E(|r_t|) = \sqrt{\frac{2}{\pi}}\,\sigma_t = .7979\,\sigma_t \tag{6.15}$$

$$E[|r_t| - E(|r_t|)]^2 = \left(1 - \frac{2}{\pi}\right)\sigma_t^2 = .3634\,\sigma_t^2 \tag{6.16}$$

If we ignore the fact that the payment for the contract occurs 1 day before the payout, these two equations demonstrate that the mean and variance of the rolling volatility contract are simple functions of the variance of the return series.

Equation 6.15 also provides a rationale for setting the face value of the contract equal to $200,000. The expected absolute return is approximately 80 percent of the standard deviation so that the standard deviation is approximately 125 percent of the expected absolute return. The annual standard deviation is equal to the square root of 252 (the number of trading days) times the daily standard deviation. Consequently, the relationship between the expected absolute change and the annual standard deviation is:

$$\sigma_A = \sqrt{252} \times 1.25 \times E(|r|) = 19.8\,E(|r|) \tag{6.17}$$

If the expected absolute return is 1 percent, the contract cost would be $2,000 and the predicted annual standard deviation would be 19.83 percent. Choosing the nominal contract size at $200,000 therefore allows the price to be an approximate representation of the annualized volatility.

In order to generate demand functions for the contract, it is assumed that each trader maximizes a mean-variance utility function:

$$E(U) = [E(|r_i|) - |r_m|]q_i - \frac{1}{2\lambda}q_i^2 \, E(\sigma_i^2) \qquad (6.18)$$

In this equation, q represents the dollar value of the position and λ is a coefficient of the absolute risk aversion. Maximizing $E(U)$ through the choice of q, the demand for the asset by the i'th trader can be found to be:

$$q_i = \frac{\lambda[E(|r_i|) - |r_m|]}{E(\sigma_i^2)} \qquad (6.19)$$

The model assumes that each trader starts each period with notional capital of $1 million and a relative risk aversion parameter of .2. The absolute risk aversion parameter is consequently $200,000. This assumption enables us to express the demand function in terms of the number of contracts as:

$$Q_i = \frac{q_i}{\lambda} = \frac{E(|r_i|) - |r_m|}{E(\sigma_i^2)} \qquad (6.20)$$

The market equilibrium condition is that the sum of the positions should be zero. This condition is used to determine the market price:

$$|r_m| = \frac{1}{\Sigma(1/E(\sigma_i^2))} \, \Sigma \, \frac{E(|r_i|)}{E(\sigma_i^2)} \qquad (6.21)$$

This equation states that the market clearing price will be a variance-weighted average of the individual expected absolute returns. The rationale behind the variance weighting is that traders with a large forecasted variance will take smaller positions and hence will have a smaller impact on the market price. It is also possible to interpret the market price as the first principal component of the individual forecasts. The positions taken by the traders are all relative to this market price. In essence, the second principal component consists of a static allocation across the traders, whereas the market model enables variations across traders in each period. Similarly, the multiple regression model is a static weighting of the forecasts, resulting in a single optimal composite forecast. This composite forecast is based upon the covariance matrix of the forecasts.

In Table 6.8, the average daily returns for the forecasting systems are reported. In each of the sample periods, the VIX and EGARCH models are found to have positive returns that are significantly different from zero using

TABLE 6.8 Absolute Return Contract Results

	Presample Return	T-Stat	In-sample Return	T-Stat	Postsample Return	T-Stat
VIX	0.73%	3.33	0.50%	4.74	0.65%	3.53
LGK	−0.16%	−0.62	0.04%	0.40	0.32%	1.90
GARCH	−0.50%	−3.00	−0.52%	−5.36	−1.28%	−5.00
EGARCH	0.50%	2.58	0.29%	2.86	0.80%	3.74
GJR	−0.57%	−3.08	−0.31%	−3.59	−0.48%	−2.44

standard confidence limits. The positive returns from these forecasts are offset by statistically significant negative returns on the GARCH and GJR models. The LGK model is basically neutral in this market, with negative returns in the presample period and slight positive returns in the in-sample and postsample periods. The results consequently support the view that the implied volatility from option markets is an efficient forecast of future observed market volatility and that the EGARCH model provides the best forecasts of the standard time series approaches.

It is interesting to compare the results of the market experiment with the multiple regression evaluation provided earlier. In the regression framework, the EGARCH model did not make a statistically significant contribution to the composite forecast in any of the sample periods. The LGK model, which did receive statistically significant weights in the composite forecast, does not provide a significant contribution to trading performance. The answer to the puzzle lies in the fact that a market requires a trader to lose money in order for another trader to make money. In the market experiment, most of the profits earned by the VIX and EGARCH models occurred when the GARCH and GJR volatility forecasts were relatively low. If the GARCH and GJR models are removed from the market, the LGK returns become significantly negative. If the LGK model is removed, we are left with positive returns on the VIX and negative returns on the EGARCH. The trading model consequently offers an unambiguous choice of the best volatility forecast using the absolute return contract.

A CRASH OPTION CONTRACT

Although the absolute return contract is a valuable tool for the assessment of volatility forecasts, it is not directly related to the types of decision problems faced by risk managers. A *crash option* is an option that pays off if the market falls by more than a certain strike amount in a single day.[5] For example, a 2 percent crash option with a $1 million face value would pay

$(r_t - 2\%) \times \$1m$ if the market fell by more than $2 on a given day. Crash options can be specified in terms of both the strike rate of return and the time horizon. A bank facing compliance with the Basle accords may purchase crash options at the 99 percent confidence level over a 2-week horizon. The crash option would be a very effective tool for traders facing VaR constraints.

For the crash option trader, the primary forecasting issue is whether the use of a volatility forecast can be used to time the purchase or sale of the option. This is the issue that we will explore in this section. The analysis is based upon the assumption that the VIX index represents the market price of volatility and that the traders using the time series models can purchase or sell at the market price without influencing the price. This assumption, which is consistent with the results in the previous section, removes the difficulty of defining a market equilibrium price for instruments that have highly nonlinear payoff structures.

For the purpose of this discussion, the crash option will be defined with a 1.75 percent strike and a 1-day time horizon. The average daily standard deviation of the VIX over the 1990 to 2002 sample period is 1.05 percent, so the 1.75 percent is close to the 5 percent critical value at the 1-day horizon that is most often used in VaR reports. This value also yields option valuations that match the values obtained from the actual distribution. Because the distribution of returns is kurtotic (that is, fat-tailed) relative to a normal distribution, too many extreme observations and too few moderate observations exist. A well-known empirical regularity states that the cumulative densities of the normal and actual distributions are similar at the 5 percent level.

As a first step, the value of the option will be evaluated from the perspective of the VIX market maker. The market maker has an estimate of the daily standard deviation. Dividing the strike return by the daily standard deviation expresses the strikes in standardized variables that are assumed to be normally distributed. The market maker then calculates:

$$F(A) = \int_{-\infty}^{A} f(z)\, dz \tag{6.22}$$

and

$$E(P) = \frac{\int_{-\infty}^{A} z f(z)\, dz}{\int_{-\infty}^{A} f(z)\, dz} = \frac{-f(A)}{F(A)} \tag{6.23}$$

Equation 6.22 defines the probability that the option will end in the money and Equation 6.23 defines the expected payout if the option ends in the money.[6] The expected value of the option is consequently:

$$V = -F(A)E(P) = f(A) \qquad (6.24)$$

Here is an example. Suppose that the daily standard deviation is 1 percent so that the Z-score is -1.75. From the properties of the standard normal distribution, $F(Z) = 4.01$ percent and $f(Z) = .0863$. The conditional expectation of Z is consequently $-.2420/.1587$ or -2.15 or, multiplying back by the standard deviation, -2.15 percent. However, since the option only pays the excess over the strike, the payout will be 0.40 percent times $1 million, or $4,000. The value of the option is equal to the probability of the payout times its expected value or $162. The VIX market maker offers a two-sided market in crash options at $162 per day per million. If the same price held for all future days, an investor could protect his or her portfolio against a crash for 1 year for approximately $40,000 per million or 4 percent per year.

The crash option value is also purely a function of the volatility forecast if time discounting is ignored. The relationship between the level of implied volatility and the price of the option is described in Table 6.9.

The option values are modest when implied volatility is in its normal range of 10 to 20 percent. However, the values increase rapidly at higher volatilities, reflecting both the greater probability of the option ending in the money and the greater expected payoff when it does. The largest value for the crash option occurred on October 19, 1987 when implied volatility

TABLE 6.9 Crash Option Valuation

Implied Volatility	Option Value	Annual (Percent)
5%	0	0%
10%	5	0%
15%	118	3%
20%	473	12%
25%	1,057	27%
30%	1,809	46%
35%	2,680	68%
40%	3,634	92%
45%	4,648	117%
50%	5,707	144%

TABLE 6.10 Premiums and Payouts

	Average Premium	Average Payout
Full	448	448
Presample	646	786
In-sample	290	216
Postsample	754	715

closed at 162 percent. A 1-day 1.75 percent crash option was valued at $23,000 on this day. (It didn't pay off! The market rose 7.48 percent on the next day.) In Table 6.10, the average premium and the average payout are presented for the full-sample and subsample data sets.

The premium is the amount that the trader pays today for the contract. The payout is the amount received if the option ends in the money or zero. Over the full-sample period, the two values are virtually identical. The VIX market maker is consequently making a fair price in the contract over the whole sample. As one would expect, the premium is less than the payout in the volatile period from 1986 to 1990. A large part of the difference is the $220,000 payout on October 19, 1987. In the second two periods, the premium is a little higher than the payout.

Now consider an active manager who is trading in the cash option market. For this manager, the volatility forecast is important because it enables an assessment of the anticipated cost of the crash option. Using the same methodology as the market maker, the trader calculates the expected payout on the option and compares this expectation to the market premium. Because the payoff structure is asymmetric, a mean-variance trading model is inappropriate. In the mean-variance model, the long and short positions are considered to be of equal risk, whereas the risk of a short position is far larger than the risk of a long position. For this reason, a simple asymmetric trading rule is proposed:

$$Q = K \frac{E(V) - V}{E(L)} \tag{6.25}$$

The trader compares the expected value of the option $E(V)$, based upon the volatility forecast, with the value posted by the market maker, V, and expresses the difference as a function of the expected loss, $E(L)$. The position, Q, is a multiple, K, of the resulting variable. If the position is long, the

TABLE 6.11   Relative Performance

	LGK	GARCH	EGARCH	GJR
Presample	11.5%	−0.4%	14.3%	13.7%
In-sample	3.7%	1.4%	-1.6%	1.8%
Postsample	4.2%	−5.3%	-7.0%	−1.3%

expected loss is the premium. If the position is short, the expected loss is the conditional mean of the payout function. Since the second factor is 10 times the size of the first factor, short positions will be very small relative to long positions. The scale factor, K, is set equal to 10. The standard deviation of the position vector over the 1990 to 2002 position for the LGK model is around .7. So a trader with $1 million in capital would have, on average, a long or short position of around $700,000.

The performance of the different forecasting models is evaluated in terms of the return on capital. Each trader begins each day with $1 million in equity. The profit or loss on the position is calculated and the average value determined. This number is then multiplied by 252 in order to obtain an annual number and is divided by the capital. The results are reported in Table 6.11.

In this test, the LGK model is the clear winner. Although it underperforms the EGARCH and GJR models in the volatile 1980s, it is the only model that is profitable in all three periods. The incremental return from the LGK strategy is about 4 percent per year in the last 2 sample periods. Since this is a pure gamble, this return should be considered as a return in excess of the benchmark.

SOME OTHER FACTORS TO CONSIDER

Although statisticians may prefer forecast accuracy and traders prefer profitability as criteria for evaluating alternative models, management is most likely to be concerned with other issues. When the previous results have been presented to practicing risk managers, the following questions have arisen during the discussion period:

1. Which model requires the highest average level of regulatory capital?
2. Which model has the widest range of capital requirements?
3. Which model has the largest number of violations of the VaR limit?
4. Which model has the largest daily variation in capital requirements?

TABLE 6.12   VaR

	LGK	GARCH	EGARCH	GJR
Average	−1.36%	−1.38%	−1.87%	−1.42%
StDev	0.60%	0.68%	0.73%	0.85%
Max	−0.57%	−0.64%	−0.75%	-0.62%
Min	−18.91%	−8.47%	−7.90%	−11.47%

To explore these issues, we use the different models to estimate the 5 percent confidence limit VaR over the 1-day horizon. Table 6.12 reports the summary statistics on the VaR calculations for the different models over the full-sample period.

The LGK model has the lowest average VaR, at −1.36 percent. It also has the lowest standard deviation of the VaR over the 1-day horizon. This result is somewhat surprising since the LGK is a relatively fast model in comparison with the alternatives. These two features of the model make it a preferable forecast from a management perspective since it implies that a daily variation in the VaR report will primarily reflect changes in position rather than changes in the volatility forecast. However, despite its stable volatility, the model also has the largest spread in VaR calculations over the sample period. This feature of the model reflects the sensitivity of the model to negative returns. The EGARCH model has the highest average VaR, which by itself is not a desirable characteristic, but it also has the smallest range between the maximum and minimum values. It is again important to stress that the primary concern of management is that the VaR report reflects changes in positions rather than changes in volatility forecasts. A small range is consequently a very desirable characteristic of the forecast. Management would be prepared to accept a high average VaR if this value results in a small number of failures. This is the second dimension of the forecast that is examined.

A failure refers to the situation when the actual return on the market lies outside the VaR confidence limits. Within the terms of the crash option, a failure corresponds to those situations in which the option ends its life in the money. Management can be presumed to derive negative utility from any failure and can be presumed to derive additional negative utility from a percentage of failures that exceeds the VaR confidence limit. In Table 6.13, the percentage of failures in both the positive and negative tails is recorded. Since the trading group may have a short position in the stock, the forecasting model should be evaluated in terms of both negative and positive failures.

TABLE 6.13   Failure Rates

	LGK	GARCH	EGARCH	GJR
Negative	7.46%	7.73%	3.51%	7.51%
Positive	8.87%	8.85%	3.51%	8.77%

Table 6.13 demonstrates that the EGARCH model is clearly superior to the other models in terms of the failure criterion. The EGARCH model has a 3.51 percent failure rate, which is less than the VaR confidence level, in both the positive and negative tails. All the other models have failure rates that exceed the VaR confidence level in both the positive and negative tails. The superiority of the EGARCH model arises from both the higher average level of the VAR and the smaller range of forecast values. Since it is very difficult to predict failures, a model that results in a high and stable volatility forecast is less likely to result in excessive failures.

Subject to these limitations, the results do suggest that market volatility forecasts derived from option prices do appear to be efficient forecasts of future volatility. The VIX forecast is found to have the highest weight in a composite forecast based upon multiple regression analysis, and it also has the highest rate of return in a market test using absolute returns. This suggests that rather than being an index of market fear, the VIX index is a coldly calculated forecast of the future return volatility.

This chapter also introduced the concept of a crash option as a market representation of the VaR model. If crash options were traded in the market, risk managers could use the instruments to hedge against violations or failures of the VaR limits. If the objective of the time series model is to determine when to undertake this hedge, the LGK model appears to be the best forecast. Although the EGARCH and GJR models outperformed the LGK in the volatile 1980s, they experienced negative returns in trading the crash option in the period from 1990 to 2001.

Finally, the last section recognized that a variety of nonstatistical issues should be considered in evaluating volatility forecasts. Ultimately, the choice of a forecast is an economic issue and a control issue for management. The economic issue concerns the trade-off between having a VaR that is too high, and consequently consumes too much capital, and a forecast that is too low so that it results in excessive failures. The control issue is that management would prefer that variations in the VaR reflect changes in positions rather than changes in volatility forecasts. On the basis of these criteria, the best model appears to be the EGARCH model since its forecasts were relatively stable and its failure rate was considerably smaller than the alternatives.

NOTES

[1]Bilson (1996).

[2]The construction of the VIX index is discussed in Whaley (1993) and Whaley (2000). A Salomon Smith Barney report from the Equity Derivatives Sales group (2001) demonstrates that the published estimates of the VIX are subject to a day count error. This chapter employs the adjusted VIX series that is obtained by multiplying the published series by the square root of 5/7.

[3]If α is the parameter in an exponential moving average and N is the number of observations in a simple moving average, then the approximate relationship between the two is $\alpha = 2/(N + 1)$.

[4]All the time series models were estimated using the RATS-5 routines written by Robert Trevor and distributed on the RATS Web site at www.estima.com.

[5]For further details on crash options, see Bilson (1996).

[6]See Jorion (2001), p. 97.

REFERENCES

Bilson, J. F. O. "Perpetual 'Crash' Options: A New Tool for Risk Management," 2:4 (Summer 1996).

Black, F. and M. Scholes. "The Pricing of Options and Corporate Liabilities," *Journal of Political Economy* 81 (1973): 637–654.

Bollerslev, T. "Generalized Autoregressive Conditional Hetroscedasticity," *Journal of Econometrics* 31 (1986): 307–327.

Engel, R. F. "Autoregressive Conditional Hetroscedasticity with Estimates of the Variance of the U.K. Inflation Rate," *Econometrica* 50 (1982): 987–1008.

Garman, M. B. and M. J. Klass. "The Estimation of Security Price Volatility from Newspaper Data," Financial Engineering Associates, 1992.

———. "On the Estimation of Security Price Volatilities from Historical Data," *Journal of Business* 53:1 (1980): 67–78.

Glosten, L., R. Jagannathan, and D. Runkle, "On the Relation between the Expected Value and the Volatility of the Nominal Excess Return on Stocks," *Journal of Finance* 48 (1993): 1779–1801.

Markowitz, H. "Portfolio Selection," *Journal of Finance* 7 (1952): 77–91.

Morgan, J. P. *RiskMetrics Technical Document*, 4th edition, 1997.

Nelson, D. "Conditional Hetroscedasticity in Asset Returns: A New Approach," *Econometrica* 59 (1991): 347–370.

Parkinson, M. "The Extreme Value Method for Estimating the Variance of the Rate of Return," 53:1 *Journal of Business,* 61–65.

Salomon Smith Barney. "Nasdaq Volatility Indices, Why Is the VXN 10 Points Higher," SSB Equity Derivatives Sales, February 2001.

Whaley, Robert E. "Derivatives on Market Volatility: Hedging Tools Long Overdue," *Journal of Derivatives* 1 (1993): 71–84.

———. "The Investor Fear Gauge," Working Paper, Duke University, 2000.

CHAPTER 7

The Case for the Relevancy of Downside Risk Measures

David Nawrocki

The author attempts to bridge the gap between the limitations of the Capital Asset Pricing Model (CAPM) and actual investor behavior. He argues that downside risk measures more accurately reflect the non-normality of capital markets and the tendency of investors to vacillate between risk aversion and risk-seeking behavior. He then presents a number of candidates for measuring downside risk, including the compartmentalization of utility concept and the lower partial moment (LPM).

Why do we need downside risk measures like the semivariance and the lower partial moment (LPM) in investment analysis? Very simply, we need these measures to cope with the complexity (and reality) of the financial markets. The simple reason given in many articles on downside risk measures is that they are needed to deal with the skewness found in the non-normal distributions of security returns.[1] This answer is too simplistic. We need downside risk measures because they are a closer match to how investors actually behave in investment situations. The theory of economic behavior is known as *utility theory*. It states that economic units will act to maximize their economic satisfaction (or utility). Utility theory has rarely been taught in finance courses in the past 30 years because the market theories developed in the 1960s effectively eliminated the need for economic utility theory. The main culprit is the Capital Asset Pricing Model (CAPM), which makes beautiful intuitive sense, but, unfortunately, has no grounding in the reality of how financial markets actually work. The past 30 years have provided no empirical support for the CAPM. In fact, the academic finance profession has known since Richard Roll's pivotal article in 1977 that it was not feasible to test the CAPM.[2] Fortunately, CAPM is only one small part of a body of knowledge known as *modern portfolio theory*. We can still use portfolio theory without tying ourselves to the limitations of the CAPM model.

Having said this, it is still important to bridge the gap between modern portfolio theory (quantitative theory) and actual investor behavior (behavioral theory). Theories are useless unless they can be put into practice.

Imagine Monty Python's famous "parrot sketch," which presents a conversation between a finance academic and a finance practitioner. John Cleese plays the part of a finance practitioner and Michael Palin plays the part of a finance professor.

THE CAPM SKETCH

John Cleese (entering a large university): "Excuse me. I would like to register a complaint about this financial market theory which I purchased from this very boutique."

Michael Palin: "Ah, the CAPM, a remarkable theory. What's wrong with it?"

John Cleese: "I will tell you what is wrong with it. It's dead."

Michael Palin: "Nah, nah. It's resting. It will be up and about shortly. Haven't you been reading *The Journal*?"

John Cleese: "Never mind that. I know a dead theory when I see one and I'm looking at one right now."

Michael Palin: "Nah, it's not dead. It's resting."

John Cleese (incredulous): "Resting?"

Michael Palin: "Yeah, resting. A remarkable theory, the CAPM. Beautiful plumage."

John Cleese (raising his voice): "Beautiful plumage? It's stone dead."

Michael Palin: "No, it's just resting."

John Cleese: "This theory is definitely deceased. This theory wouldn't move if you put 4,000 volts through it. It's bleeding demised. It's passed on. This theory is no more. It has ceased to be. It has expired and gone to meet its maker. This is a late theory. It's bereft of life. It rests in peace. If you weren't still trying to salvage it, it would be pushing up the daisies. It has rung down the curtain and joined the choir invisible. This is an ex-theory."

Michael Palin: "Well, then we'll have to replace it." (After rustling around the university for a few moments, he returns.) "I'm sorry, but we don't have any more financial market theories left."

Let's leave John Cleese and Michael Palin and ponder the following question: Why is the CAPM still taught in finance textbooks and certified financial planner (CFP) courses? The answer is that it reduces the complexity of the market down to a few rules. All-encompassing theories like the CAPM make the markets easier to understand. The problem is that the CAPM model does not mirror reality. The price of simplicity is that the model is not relevant to the real world. If the financial markets operated according to CAPM, we would simply purchase the market index portfolio and manage risk and return by mixing risky stock portfolios with risk-free Treasury bills. (You may argue that indexing is working best right now, but it is only the indexes that measure a narrow segment of the market. The broad indexes performed poorly the past year (1998). Indexing also did not work during the 1980s. We need a framework that is flexible enough to work during different market periods.)

Other than the simple rules derived from CAPM, we wouldn't have to have any other substantial knowledge. We wouldn't have to study law, accounting, tax code, macroeconomics, business cycles, human behavior, human decision making, utility theory, psychology, social psychology, socialization, philosophy, product quality, marketing, distribution channels, design, management, and so on. Would a good investment advisor buy a client a market index mutual fund in October that is up 35 percent this year to date and will be distributing a ton of short-term capital gains to shareholders in the near future? It depends on the tax status of the client. Did Gibson Greetings and Procter and Gamble understand the legal contracts (known as *derivatives*) that Bankers Trust was selling to them? In a CAPM financial world, none of this knowledge is relevant. The market magically takes care of these mundane details. (Given the assumptions that are required to have a CAPM world, no practical knowledge as noted previously would be relevant.)

In a CAPM market, how does a financial professional add value in order to justify the fees or commissions charged to customers? It can't be done, given the assumptions of perfect capital markets (no information, costs, no transaction costs, and complete access to information) and rational investors. The financial professional is basically a ticket office charging admission to the financial markets, which is essentially similar to the ticket office at a movie complex. If the market is not efficient and if it does not operate according to CAPM, then the financial advisor can add value by providing knowledge. The financial advisor has to provide substance, that is, something to bring to the table. That substance is knowledge: the knowledge of law, accounting, taxes, economics, human behavior, and so on.[3]

One area of knowledge that opens up when we no longer have CAPM helping us is utility theory. It now has to be applied. The little piece of substance in which this paper is interested is the application of utility theory through the use of downside risk measures.

There are two serious problems with using CAPM to build asset allocation models.

First is the diversification problem. Unfortunately, the investment cannot be in one security as this exposes the investor to default or bankruptcy risk and business risk. The response to this problem is to diversify the investment into many different investments, which will lower the overall return. Diversification using a large number of assets over a long period of time is a very complex multidimensional dynamic programming problem. The probability that an investor can solve this problem without a computer is zero. The problem is the multidimensionality. If the portfolio is going to be built from 100 individual assets, the programming problem will involve 100 dimensions plus additional dimensions to handle the time horizon in the dynamic programming problem.

This results in a very serious problem for the investor. Very simply, humans do not think well beyond three dimensions. Our minds are limited to the three dimensions that we can sense. Therefore, we will have a problem allocating funds to five assets over a 5-year time horizon. The computer does not have this limitation and can mathematically solve a complex multidimensional problem.

The second problem is the ability to instill a complete picture of the investor's goals, aspirations, expectations, and so on into one utility function that can be solved by our multidimensional dynamic programming. The behavior of a human cannot be distilled into one utility function; rather, a multitude of utility functions is required to describe the behavior of an individual. Plus, these functions change over time.

Still, investors do make allocation decisions without resorting to 100-plus dimensional computer programs and aggregate utility functions, and the solutions seem to work. (People have successfully retired or otherwise met their goals.) Why? The major barrier to an understanding of investor behavior is the concentration of attention on the behavior of an idealized investor in a highly constrained environment, that is, the perfectly rational investor. This results in a model of how investors are supposed to behave given numerous simplifying assumptions so that the rational investor can maximize returns and minimize risk.

There is a considerable body of thought that states if every investor in the marketplace behaves according to rational investor return maximization and risk minimization, it would wreak havoc in the marketplace. In his 1948 book, Norbert Wiener states that the market would be highly volatile, careening from overbuying to overselling. The aggregate behavior of rational investors would create a monster roller coaster ride for the markets. In 1992, E.E. Peters describes a market dominated by short-term time horizon investors as highly unstable with huge volatility. Both Wiener and Larry Alan Bear and Rita Maldonado-Bear state that society will have to pass laws to protect society in general from the behavior of these rational investors. Of course, the United States has passed numerous security laws to protect society from rational behavior. If rational behavior is so unacceptable to society in general that it legislates against this behavior, how realistic is it to assume all investors in the marketplace are rational?

The key to understanding the operation of financial markets is to understand how investors actually do behave in the financial marketplace. Since an aggregate (one) utility function is impossible to derive for a human investor, it is pretty certain that investors do not use aggregate utility functions. The alternative to aggregate utility functions was being developed in the 1950s and 1960s when the financial market theories such as CAPM came along and swept away everything in their paths.

It is impossible to derive one all-encompassing aggregate utility function that will work for a person's entire life. As a person goes through life, his or her goals, tax situation, and so on constantly change; therefore, the person's utility function is always a work in progress. (Kurt Godel is featured as one of the 100 greatest scientists and thinkers of the twentieth century according to *Time*'s "The Greatest Scientists and Thinkers of the Twentieth Century" 153, no. 12 [March 29, 1999]. His *incompleteness theorem* states that no system of mathematical equations can completely describe a system, or, in this case, human behavior.)

The first author to address this problem was Herbert Simon, who developed the concept of utility *satisficing* in 1954. Simon states that humans will not optimize their utility, but will accept satisfactory results from a limited search rather than an optimal search. In 1948, Wiener described such behavior. He suggests that humans will group together into cooperatives (savings banks, credit unions, savings and loan, mutual insurance funds, and mutual funds) to reduce the uncertainty of the financial marketplace, protecting the group from the rational investors and providing satisfactory results. Richard M. Cyert and James G. March followed this up in 1963 with probably one of the best books on corporate finance—*The Behavioral Theory of the Firm*. Cyert and March studied human behavior. From these studies, they generated a model of how humans within organizations make decisions. They state that complex problems are solved by breaking down multidimensional problems into a series of mono-dimensional problems and then solving these problems sequentially until a satisfactory solution is achieved.

We also can proceed by breaking the problem into subproblems and achieving satisfactory results with each subproblem. This procedure is going to be controversial with most academics who believe in the possibility of the aggregate utility function, but the practitioner has to be pragmatic and use techniques that are possible. One problem cited by academics is that the process of solving subproblems over time will be myopic, that is, short-sighted. However, this argument is based on the assumption that the person and the market environment is stationary and never experiences change. In reality, with complex changing environments, the investor has to take Wiener's advice and engage in adaptive behavior based on adaptive feedback controls.

This procedure is reflected in the compartmentalization of utility concept. An individual is going to have different financial compartments, each with a different goal, utility function, and solution. When we aggregate the results of the compartmentalization process, we will achieve a satisfactory result, not an optimal result.[4]

The individual's financial situation is broken into compartments. Each compartment has a different goal and time horizon. Each compartment also has a different utility function. Finally, each compartment will have a different solution. As a goal is achieved, this affects the remaining goals. Therefore, the compartmentalization process has to be repeated on the remaining goals. As a person moves through life, his or her financial situation changes and his or her allocation decision will have to be continually resolved. The reader should be reminded that the original Markowitz portfolio theory was developed for a portfolio of individual stocks, that is, for only one compartment.

As a person changes over time, the investment environment also changes. As a result of a changing human being and environment, there is no such thing as a static utility function or a static financial plan. Revising and resolving the compartment problem can help an individual keep up with his or her changing conditions.

The environment changes because economic units go through various life cycles. For example, businesses go through product life cycles. As a result, firms will go through a life cycle from being a startup firm, to a high-growth firm, to a cash cow, and, finally, to a profit-challenged firm heading to liquidation.

Measuring risk under these conditions of the compartmentalization of investment goals and business cycles is not going to be that difficult. First, statistical measures of risk are going to work because the constant revision and resolution of the compartment problem can lead to relatively short-term time horizons. Using statistics like the standard deviation and semivariance measures the liquidity risk of an investment and is only relevant to a short-term investment horizon investor. Does a standard deviation calculated from 20 years of dates provide any useful information? Looking backwards and taking a historic perspective, the standard deviation provides a meaningful interpretation of history. However, looking forward to the next 1, 2, 5, or 10 years, the information in the standard deviation is basically useless because it only measures short-term liquidity risk. If the investor has a long-term investment horizon (say, 20 years), then it is safe to ignore liquidity risk and simply maximize the expected return of the investment.

Second, the risk measure, the allocation of funds in the investor's portfolio, and the measurement of the investment performance have to reflect the investor's utility. For all of these steps, a risk measure that approximates liquidity risk and investor utility can be used. The first candidates for the appropriate risk measure are the beta and the standard deviation. Both, unfortunately, represent only one utility function, which provides a one-size-fits-all approach. The second candidate is the LPM risk measure, which provides a multitude of utility functions that represent the whole range of human behavior, that is, from risk seeking to risk neutral to risk averse.

The LPM is computed using different degrees. The degree, n, represents the investor's utility in terms of risk aversion. When $n < 1$, the investor is a risk seeker. When $n = 1$, the investor is risk neutral. When $n > 1$, the investor is averse to risk. The higher the value of n, the higher the level of risk aversion. Within the utility theory literature, individuals with degrees of risk aversion as high as 4.0 have been identified.[5]

The n-degree LPM and the compartmentalization of utility concept can be used to explain complex and seemingly contradictory human behavior. An example is a man who is approaching retirement age and whose total lifetime savings is $500,000. Our hero has an appointment to see a financial advisor and at the meeting agrees to place the $500,000 in a bond portfolio consisting of AAA-rated corporate bonds and U.S. Treasury bonds. Since the $500,000 represents all of his wealth, the portfolio represents a very high degree of risk aversion (probably $n > 3$). He signs the papers to implement this plan. As our hero leaves the office building where he met with the financial advisor, he stops into a store and buys a daily number lottery ticket for $1 ($n < 1$). Compartmentalization explains that this behavior is not irrational, but each decision is rational within its compartment. In the first compartment, the investor is very risk averse since all of his wealth is at stake. The lottery ticket in the second compartment represents no threat to the investor's wealth as long as it is only $1 every so often. (When a person is buying $2,030 worth of lottery tickets daily, 5 or 6 days a week, then it is probably a matter for Gambler's Anonymous. Again, this depends on the person's total wealth or income.) The investor can be risk seeking in the second compartment because the wealth amount is so low relative to his total wealth. Any entertainment such as movies, theater, sporting events, horse racing, casinos, amusement parks, and so on could be included in this category. In this case, the lottery ticket is entertainment, not an investment.

At this point, the practicing financial planner/investment manager has every right to be confused. For most of the past 20 years, academics have been attempting to have investment managers derive an aggregate solution for clients based on an aggregate utility function. A very extensive asset-class optimization solution (asset allocation) has been recommended as the proper implementation of portfolio optimization programs. The typical mean variance optimization of asset classes assumes that all clients have a short-term quadratic utility function. By changing the slope of the quadratic utility function, different risk-return trade-offs may be chosen for the client. However, the solution is for short-term risk aversion and represents one aggregate utility function for the client. Figure 7.1 represents the utility behavior of three investors. Each investor has a quadratic utility function, the only difference being that their utility curves have different slopes indicating different levels of risk aversion. The slope is the change in the y-axis (return) divided by the change in the x-axis (risk). Investor A is willing to accept larger amounts of risk in exchange for small increases in return. Investor B is balancing risk and return somewhat equally. Investor C is willing to give up larger returns in exchange for smaller amounts of risk. In all of these cases, risks are expressed through the variance measure.

The short-term risk aversion inherent in an efficient frontier analysis is a problem. Actually, the feasible risk-return space is changing over time.

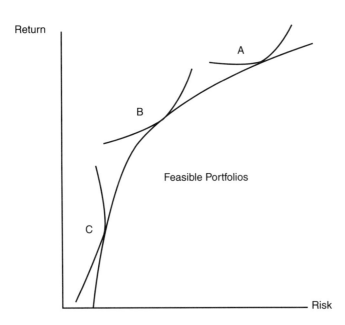

FIGURE 7.1 Traditional risk-return analysis with quadratic utility functions.

Think of the market over time as a stick of pepperoni. Each time a pepperoni slice is sliced off to put on a pizza, the cross section of the slice is a point in time. The markets can be described as a series of cross sections over time, as depicted in Figure 7.2.

Therefore, the traditional analysis is only looking at short-term liquidity risk at one point in time. The variance risk measure cannot handle long-term exposure to risk except through the rather heroic assumptions of stationary expected return and variances over the time period. As this is not realistic in our world of changing expectations and investor utility, it is not a very helpful solution. Asset allocation packages, however, still provide an analysis called *time diversification* where these heroic assumptions are used to develop a long-term investment plan for the client.

It is imperative that the use of asset allocation not be confused and misused. There are two ways to use asset allocation appropriately. First, the

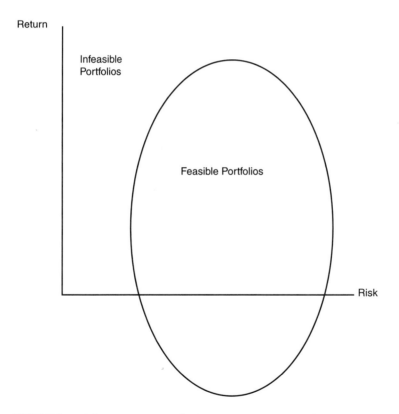

FIGURE 7.2   Risk-return space during one moment in time.

client may segment his or her funds by different goals and optimize within the resulting compartment. Second, a client may segment investments into different segments of the markets depending on the dynamic nature of the market.

Asset allocation may be used with different asset classes to provide a diversified portfolio to meet client needs for a single investment need. Asset allocation should not be used to try to meet multiple goals from different investor utility compartments. The compartmentalization of utility approach enables each compartment to have a different time horizon, a different utility function, and a unique solution. The compartments are assumed to be independent of each other; however, the interrelationships between some of the compartments can be handled within the Cyert and March sequential solution of subproblems framework.

A framework is also needed to handle the dynamic nature of the market environment and help to improve planning. One framework that seems promising is the product life cycle, which is used by many security analysts to study rapidly changing industries. A firm can go through many stages of a product life cycle depending on its product mix. If a firm is a single-product startup or has many new products, it is early in its product life cycle. Next, a successful product will go through a strong growth period. Early in the growth period, there will be large growth rates and low or negative profits. Late in the growth period, the growth rate will start to decline, but the profits will increase. During the cash cow period, the firm experiences growth rates consistent with the general economy's growth rate. However, the firm has a mature product market and generates large profits and high cash flows. Finally, the product profitability turns to losses and if new products do not come along to restart the firm's product life cycle, the firm will move toward liquidation.

The product life cycle (see Figure 7.3) is where the utility functions in the n-degree LPM became important. We would select stocks using their location in a product life cycle and the appropriate investor risk aversion. In the early startup stage, investors will have to exhibit high degrees of risk tolerance and may actually engage in risk-loving behavior, that is, taking on high degree of risk for the small chance of a large return. Although the short-term risk is very high and current returns are negative, these investors are interested in startups because of their long-term potential. When companies start their growth stage, returns are still negative and risk is still high, but the odds of the firm experiencing strong growth to positive cash flows is improving. Again, investors will be willing to exchange short-term risk and negative returns for potentially high future returns. Later, in the growth stage, firms will be profitable and more investors will be attracted to the company because of the high returns and lower risk. The cash cow stage is

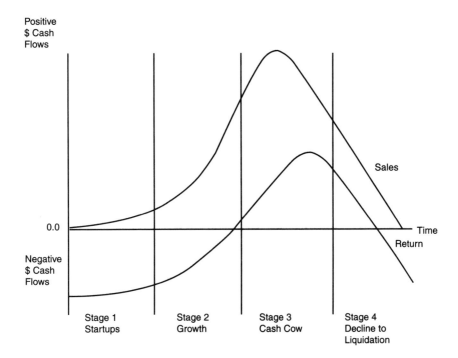

FIGURE 7.3 The four stages of a corporation's product life cycle.

where the company has established its franchise within the marketplace and is generating strong cash flows. Cash cows have typically achieved full market penetration and will experience low growth rates tied to the general population growth rate. Finally, the company's franchise will wear down, profitability will drop, and speculators will start hovering around the company, betting on the liquidation value of the company. Now the firm has entered the last phase of its life cycle—the liquidation phase. If the firm can successfully develop new products to start its life cycle over again, it can remain in business. Otherwise, it will be liquidated.

In order to move forward at this point, an understanding of how LPM portfolios with a different degree n would appear on a graph is necessary. Figure 7.4 demonstrates the use of the n-degree LPM measure. The degree n is a measure of the investor's attitude toward risk. When the efficient frontiers derived from different degrees of the LPM are plotted on one graph, the problem of measuring risk on the x-axis arises. In both graphs, the LPM $n = 2$ measure is used on the x-axis. Therefore, the efficient frontier derived

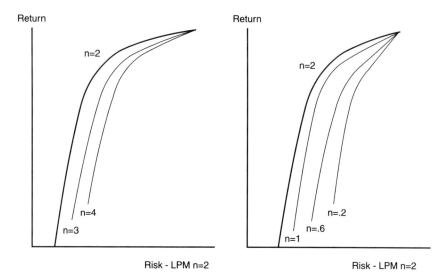

FIGURE 7.4 Efficient frontiers generated by LPM Optimizer using different values of n-degree LPM. All efficient frontiers are graphed using LPM $n = 2$ as the risk measure.

using the LPM $n = 2$ will be the dominant or best frontier. The more risk-averse frontiers ($n = 3$ and $n = 4$) will be less efficient subsets of the $n = 2$ frontier. The risk-neutral ($n = 1$) and risk-loving ($n = .6$ and $n = .2$) frontiers will also be less efficient subsets of the $n = 2$ frontier because their frontiers are being graphed using $n = 2$. Note that the risk-loving frontiers will experience the largest increases in risk as measured by the LPM $n = 2$. Now if we use LPM $n = 4$ on the x-axis, the $n = 4$ frontier will be the dominant frontier and the other frontiers will be less efficient subsets of the $n = 4$ frontier. As we change the risk metric on the x-axis, the dominant frontiers will always be the frontier derived using the same risk measure as the risk measure on the x-axis.

The previous discussion of Figure 7.4 is necessary to understand Figure 7.5. First, the risk measure on the x-axis is the LPM $n = 1$ risk-neutral measure. Next, the feasible frontier is segmented using the product life cycle. High risk and negative returns will typically characterize startups. Growth companies will run the range from high risk and negative returns to high risk and positive returns. Cash cows will be represented in the low risk and positive return section of the graph. Liquidation candidates will be moving toward the higher risk and negative return area of the graph.

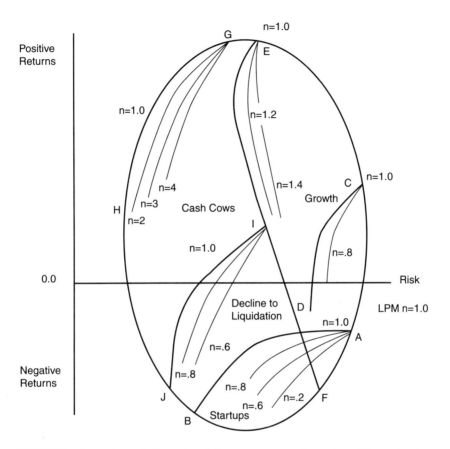

FIGURE 7.5 Location of firms in different stages of product life cycles in a single-period risk-return space.

With startup companies, the appropriate utility function will be a risk-seeking function ($n < 1$). Investors in startup companies typically will invest in a large number of startups over a long period of time hoping to hit one home run. Anyone looking at a startup on a short time horizon risk-return graph is going to see a very risky investment with negative returns. Therefore, a risk-seeking utility function would be used. Although the investor in a startup is usually looking at a long-term investment horizon, the short-term risk-seeking utility function will be used in the risk-return analysis to correct for the short-term nature of a statistical risk measure. If we limit the portfolio optimization to only startup companies, the efficient frontier (AB) for LPM $n = 1$ will be the dominant frontier because the x-axis is measured in units of LPM $n = 1$. Risk-loving frontiers ($n = 0.8$, $n = 0.6$, and $n = 0.2$) will be subsets of the AB $n = 1$ frontier. However, for an investor with a risk-loving utility function of $n = 0.8$, the $n = 0.8$ frontier will be the efficient frontier. From there, the investor will have to pick one portfolio that matches the investor's risk-return profile.

Investors in high-growth companies are looking at firms with high-risk variable returns. Firms early in the growth phase will have negative returns, whereas firms later in the growth phase will have higher returns. Investors will have long-term investment horizons and will be risk loving ($n < 1.0$). They will invest in the early-growth frontier, CD, and its subsets ($n = 0.8$ is one example). Investors who are risk neutral and slightly risk averse will invest in the late-growth frontier, EF, and its subsets ($n = 1.2$ and $n = 1.4$).

When firms are experiencing high growth rates, it's because they are continuing to open new markets to their product. As the industry grows, it will reach saturation points where all markets have access to the product and the market is saturated with the product. At this point, high growth rates cannot continue and will slow down to the general market growth rate. At this point, the firm becomes a cash cow.

Investors purchasing cash cows are interested in current income and liquid investments.

Their utility function will be short term and risk averse ($n > 1.0$). They will invest in the cash cow frontier, GH, and its risk-averse subsets ($n = 2$, $n = 3$, and $n = 4$).

Finally, firms headed for liquidation will attract investors with long-term investment horizons who are betting that the liquidation value of the firm is more than the current market value. Again, these investors will have short-term risk-seeking functions ($n < 1.0$) and will invest in the liquidation frontier, IJ, and its risk-seeking subsets ($n = 0.8$ and $n = 0.6$).

The n-degree LPM enables the investment manager to compartmentalize utility. For example, a portfolio algorithm can be used to solve for a portfolio of startup companies for a value of $n < 0$. A portfolio algorithm can be used to solve for a portfolio of growth companies for a value of $n = 1$. A portfolio algorithm can be used to solve for a portfolio of cash cow companies for some value $n > 2$. There will be a unique efficient frontier for each individual degree n of the LPM measure. Therefore, there is a unique LPM efficient frontier for each compartment of an individual's investment decision.

It is the inherent capability of the n-degree LPM to fit into the process of how investors actually make investment decisions that makes the LPM downside risk measures so important to the investment community. It describes how investors actually do behave rather than how investors are supposed to behave.

This analysis demonstrates that it is fine to use portfolio theory to optimize subgoals that are contained in different compartments of the investor's behavior. The overall result is not optimal, but that is fine since each subgoal is optimized or satisfactory. It is irrelevant that the overall result is not optimal, as it is irresponsible for us to measure this result using utility theory or any other measurement technique.

Traditionally, financial planners would break the financial planning problem into different categories and then design a strategy for each category. The academic models said that was the wrong approach, so it was abandoned. This paper demonstrates that there may be life in that old approach and it probably should be the recommended approach. Looking at the investment decision for a client, the process would be to set up the utility compartments for the individual. These could include retirement, children's college funds, saving for a house, real-estate ownership, and so on, and a specific strategy can be implemented to meet the goals of each compartment.

Another interesting observation is that mutual funds have been moving away from style objectives where they would meet the objectives of a specific compartment. Instead, we are seeing a movement toward indexing. According to the framework presented here, there will continue to be a market for mutual funds that are managed to fit a particular investment objective (or compartment).

NOTES

[1]It would be nice to write an article without a single equation. The LPM measures the downside risk below some target return set by the investor. The equations for the variance and the below-target return LPM are

$$V_i = \frac{1}{m} \sum_{}^{m} (R_t - E(R))^2 \qquad (7.1)$$

$$LPM_{in} = \frac{1}{m} \sum_{t=1}^{m} [Max\,(0,\,h - R_t)]^n \qquad (7.2)$$

Where V is the variance for security i with $t = 1, 2, \ldots m$ observations, R is the return for period t, and $E(R)$ is the expected mean return for security i. The square root of the variance is the standard deviation. The LPM is the lower partial moment for security i and for degree n with $t = 1, 2, \ldots m$

observations. *Max* is the maximization function that selects the larger of two numbers: either 0 or $h - Rt$, and h is the target return for the portfolio. The degree n determines the power exponent of the differences. When $n = 2$, then the LPM is known as the *semivariance*. Taking the square root of the LPM, $n = 2$ will provide a downside risk measure known as the *semideviation*. The LPM can also be raised to the n power and the nth root can be taken. A number of the traditional statistical advantages of the LPM measure can be found in the studies by Leslie Balzer, Briar Rom and Kathleen W. Ferguson, and Frank A. Sortino and Robert Van Der Meer. Harry E. Merriken emphasizes that risk measures such as variance and LPM are appropriate for investors with short-term investment horizons. Finally, Nawrocki provides a history of the development of the LPM risk measures.

[2]Richard Roll wrote one of the first critiques of the CAPM model. His final conclusion was that the CAPM model was not testable; therefore, there is no empirical support for the model.

[3]This section derives from the discussion in George M. Frankfurter's article "Pushing the Epsilon to the Abyss: Post-Modern Finance."

[4]This view, however controversial, is supported by academic research. There is a strong academic body of theory known as *evolutionary economics* that has integrated systems theory and economics. K.E. Boulding was the major proponent of this school of thought. The integration of systems theory and the Cyert and March behavioral theory into evolutionary economics is presented in R.R. Nelson and S.G. Winter's book *An Evolutionary Theory of Economic Change.*

[5]Peter C. Fishburn provides the theoretical support for using LPM to capture the individual utility function of a specific investor.

REFERENCES

Balzer, Leslie A. "Measuring Investment Risk: A Review." *Journal of Investing* 3, no. 3 (1994): 47–58.

Bear, L.A. and R. Maldonado-Bear. *Free Markets, Finance, Ethics, and Law.* (Englewood Cliffs, NJ: Prentice Hall, 1994).

Boulding, K.E. *Evolutionary Economics.* (Beverly Hills, CA: Sage Publications, 1981).

Cyert, Richard M. and James G. March. *A Behavioral Theory of the Firm.* (Englewood Cliffs, NJ: Prentice Hall, 1963).

Fishburn, Peter C. "Mean Risk Analysis with Risk Associated with Below-Target Returns." *American Economics Review* 67, no. 2 (1977): 116–126.

Frankfurter, George M., ed. "Pushing the Epsilon to the Abyss: Post-Modern Finance." Panel Discussion, *International Review of Financial Analysis* 6, no. 2 (1997): 133–177.

Merriken, Harry E. "Analytical Approaches to Limit Downside Risk: Semivariance and the Need for Liquidity." *Journal of Investing* 3, no. 3 (1994): 65–72.

Nawrocki, David N. "A Brief History of Downside Risk Measures," *Journal of Investing*, 1999, V8 (3, Fall), 9–25.

Nelson, R.R. and S.G. Winter. *An Evolutionary Theory of Economic Change.* (Cambridge, MA: Harvard University Press, 1982).

Peters, E.E. *Chaos and Order in the Markets.* (New York: John Wiley and Sons, 1991).

Roll, Richard. "A Critique of the Asset Pricing Theory's Tests; Part 1: On Past and Potential Testability of Theory." *Journal of Financial Economics* 4, no. 2 (1977): 129–176.

Rom, Briar M. and Kathleen W. Ferguson. "Post-Modern Portfolio Theory Comes of Age." *Journal of Investing* 3, no. 3 (Winter 1993, reprinted Fall 1994): 11–17.

Simon, Herbert A. "A Behavioral Model of Rational Choice." *Quarterly Journal of Economics* 69, no. 1 (1995): 99–118.

Sortino, Frank A. and Robert Van Der Meer. "Downside Risk." *Journal of Portfolio Management* 17, no. 4 (1991): 271, 32.

Wiener, Nobert. *Cybernetics.* (Cambridge, MA: The MIT Press, 1948).

CHAPTER 8

Measuring Risk for Asset Allocation, Performance Evaluation, and Risk Control: Different Problems, Same Solution

Christopher L. Culp, Ph.D., and Ron Mensink

This chapter explores the many differences between ex ante risk *(the measurement of risk before a market shock occurs) and* ex post risk *(the analysis after the event). The author argues that any estimate of risk using purely historical data may be appropriate for performance evaluation, but not for risk control. When evaluating risks going forward, managers should consider the characteristics of the financial instruments currently held, regardless of the performance of those utilizing them.*

THE LANGUAGE OF RISK

Risk measurement is easily one of the most confusing phrases in the finance lexicon. A main source of this confusion is the distinction between the identification and measurement of *ex ante* risk versus *ex post* risk. Ex ante risk measurement is the evaluation of risk *before* that risk is actually incurred, and ex post risk measurement is the analysis of risk *after* it has been taken, usually for the purpose of evaluating historical performance on a risk-adjusted

Reprinted from *The Journal of Performance Management* (Fall 1999): 55–73. New York: Institutional Investor, Inc. Copyright © Institutional Investor, Inc. All rights reserved.

basis. In this paper, we explore the similarities and differences between ex ante and ex post measures of investment risk.

Asset allocation, performance evaluation, and risk management (that is, the formal measurement and control of risk-taking activities) are three important—and distinct—components of the investment management process. The latter two are intended primarily to provide a diagnostic check and regular informational feedback mechanism for the refinement of the first. But all are important. As we discuss here, unless risk is measured in a manner appropriate to its specific application, investors can get into trouble—for example, legitimate asset allocation decisions may be called into question by poor estimates of risk for risk-management purposes and other similar problems.

We explain here that the basic building block definitions of risk are essentially the same for ex ante and ex post measures of risk, but the means by which risk is measured (and the data used to do so) depends on the application of the particular measure. In particular, we examine the means by which risk can be calculated and summarized for three purposes: the ex ante measurement of risk for allocating capital into distinct asset classes; the ex post measurement of risk for evaluating risk-adjusted performance; and the ex ante measurement of risk for the management and control of risk and risk-taking trading/investment decisions. These three applications of risk measurement are, of course, strongly interrelated. A poor measure of risk-adjusted performance ex post may result in a lower allocation of capital on the next round of ex ante asset allocations, as may a high ex ante measure of risk for risk-control purposes.

We begin by outlining the basic building blocks by which market risk can be measured. Then we explore how those basic definitions of risk are applied in the allocation of capital into asset classes. Next we show how the building block risk measures are used in measuring risk-adjusted performance ex post. We explore several summary measures of risk that are useful for ex ante risk-control decisions. We show that although these measures are also based on the same basic definitions of risk used for performance evaluation, their calculation and application are fundamentally different.

Building Block Definitions of Risk

Market risk is measured in essentially two distinct ways. The first approach rests mainly on the probability and statistics of returns on asset classes, securities, and/or managers. This approach does not distinguish between the types of risk borne by the manager and looks only at total risk. The second approach, by contrast, uses historical data to analyze the components of total risk—namely, *idiosyncratic risk* and *systematic risk*. The former is risk that is specific to the particular asset in question. The idiosyncratic risk of a share of common stock or a corporate bond, for example, is the specific risk that the financial performance of the security issuer will adversely impact the value of the security. By contrast, systematic risk is the risk that a security's value declines as a result of changes in some risk factor that affects all asset prices in some way.

As we will show in the heart of this paper, despite some popular misconceptions to the contrary, these basic building blocks of risk are essentially the same regardless what the application is. When it comes to differentiating between the risk used to calculate risk-adjusted returns for performance evaluation and the risk used to make risk-control decisions (for example, limits and limits administration), few theoretical and conceptual differences exist between the two. Rather, the distinction comes in how the various building block measures of risk discussed in this section are calculated and applied.

The Total Risk Perspective

The analysis of total risk—whether ex ante for risk measurement or ex post for performance evaluation—involves the quantification of any uncertainty that impacts the value of an asset or portfolio. Consider a single asset j whose return from month $t - 1$ through month t is denoted $R_{j,t}$.[1] This return is a *random variable*—that is, the realized return in any given month is driven by random factors in such a way that the return is unknown until prices are realized at month t. The total risk of holding the asset from time $t - 1$ to time t can be summarized in various ways, all of which involve the application of probability and statistics. The two most common ways of summarizing total risk are discussed in the next two sections.

Volatility   By far the most popular measure of the total risk of asset j for month t is the volatility of the return on that asset during month t. If the return on asset j is drawn from some probability distribution, $f_{j,t}(R)$, the variance of that asset return reflects the possibility that the realized return may be above or below the expected (average) return. Asset or portfolio volatility is commonly measured using variance (or standard deviation, which is the square root of variance). The standard deviation reflects fluctuations below and above the average return. Mathematically, we define variance in terms of the underlying probability:

$$\mathrm{Var}(R_{j,t}) = \sigma^2_{j,t} = \int_{-\infty}^{\infty} (R - E(R))^2 f_{j,t}(R) dR$$

$$(8.1)$$

where $E(R)$ is the expected return on asset j in month t. The expected return is another probabilistic concept that summarizes the average return on the asset in month t:

$$E(R_{j,t}) = \int_{-\infty}^{\infty} R f_{j,t}(R) dR$$

(8.2)

The previous mathematical definitions of variance and expected returns assume that we know the probability distribution from which the random returns are drawn—that is, that $f_{j,t}(R)$ is known. In other words, we assume that we know the exact probability to associate with every possible realizable return. For example, if we know that $f_{j,t}(R)$ is a normal distribution, then we know that there is a 5 percent probability that the actual return in month t will be 1.65 standard deviations below the mean return. But that, in turn, requires that we know the mean and standard deviation of asset j's return in month t.

For practical purposes, we never know the true probability distribution from which an asset's return is drawn. Instead, we use statistics to draw inferences about that probability—in other words, we take observed, historical data and use that to approximate the probability distributions that we cannot directly observe.

A collection of historical data that has been observed over a particular period of time is called a *time series*. If asset j is a share of IBM common stock, for example, a time series of monthly returns on asset j might include the last 5 years of observed monthly returns on IBM common stock.[2] We then could measure the historical variance of returns using the following formula:

$$\sigma^2 = \frac{1}{N-1} \sum_{t=1}^{N} (R_t - \bar{R})^2$$

(8.3)

where $\bar{R}$ is the sample mean over the time series. Because these statistics depend critically on the length of the time series chosen, the particular time period spanned by the time series, and the frequency of the returns (such as daily versus monthly), we refer to the previous process as *sample statistics*.

In practice, sample statistics like the previous one are used to measure the risk of an asset rather than the more mathematical probability-based definitions. Nevertheless, it is important to recognize that there is a direct correspondence between sample statistics and the probability-based definitions that underlie those statistics; the former are simply used as a method of inferring what cannot be directly observed in the latter.

Other Measures of Total Risk   Volatility is often used to measure the risk of an asset for one primary reason—it is easy to compute. In addition, volatility measures in finance are popular because of the way they relate to the normal or bell-shaped distribution. Specifically, the normal distribution is symmetric, which means that a return of −R percent below the mean is just as likely to occur as a return of +R percent above the mean. Thus, the variance of a normal distribution is a *sufficient statistic* to describe fully the risks of the asset or portfolio.

However, when the returns on an asset are not symmetric or normally distributed, variance can be an imprecise measure of risk. Indeed, volatility can actually be misleading in some cases. Consider the two probability distributions shown in Figure 8.1 for Portfolios C and D.[3] The probability that returns will fall below some arbitrarily chosen target is just the area under the curves to the left of the vertical line drawn for that target—such as the gray shaded area for Portfolio D. Portfolios C and D have identical mean returns and the same variance. However, as the figure illustrates, Portfolio D is riskier than Portfolio C because the likelihood of returns falling below the target is much higher for Portfolio D than for C. This results because Portfolio D has an asymmetric return distribution and Portfolio C does not. Specifically, Portfolio D has a return distribution that is negatively skewed —in other words, the probability of realizing a return of −R percent is greater than the probability of achieving a +R percent return.

When an asset's return distribution is asymmetric, variance is no longer a sufficient summary measure of the total risk of holding that asset. Instead,

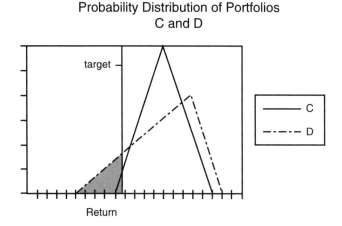

Probability Distribution of Portfolios C and D

FIGURE 8.1   Probability distribution of Portfolios C and D.

other summary statistics describing the presumed distribution of returns must be used to supplement variance.[4] The two most common such summary statistics are *skewness* and *kurtosis*. As noted previously, skewness measures the degree to which a return distribution is asymmetric. Kurtosis measures the *r*-fatness of the tails and the peakedness of the center of the distribution, usually relative to a normal distribution. If a distribution is *leptokurtic*, it has more probability in the tails and around the mean than in the middle. Common in markets like foreign exchange, leptokurtic returns are characteristic of markets that exhibit long periods of trending followed by short periods of volatile trend reversals and adjustments.

One popular measure of risk when portfolio returns are asymmetric is *downside risk*. This summary of the total risk of the portfolio is essentially the risk that portfolio returns will fall below some specific target return level. The general form for downside risk measures is written in terms of actual probability distributions:[5]

$$\int_{-\infty}^{T} (T - R)^z f_{j,t}(R) dR$$

$$(8.4)$$

where T is the prespecified target return and z is a parameter for the particular risk statistic chosen. When $z = 0$, the downside risk measure is called *below-target probability* (BTP) and is just

$$BTP = \int_{-\infty}^{T} f_{j,t}(R) dR$$

$$(8.5)$$

In other words, BTP simply measures the probability of a shortfall in returns below some target T.

BTP is often criticized because it reveals how likely returns are to fall below a chosen target, but it does not reveal the degree to which return shortfalls have occurred. A return 0.01 percent below target T is given just as much weight as a return 1,000 percent below target T. As a remedy for this problem, many focus instead on downside risk when parameter $z = 2$. This results in a measure of total risk called the *below-target variance* (BTV) or *downside semivariance*:

$$BTV = \int_{-\infty}^{T} (T - R)^2 f_{j,t}(R) dR$$

$$(8.6)$$

BTV measures the risk of a return shortfall below the target and gives more weight in the calculation to larger shortfalls. The standard deviation of BTV is called the *below-target risk* (BTR). When the underlying return distribution is symmetric, BTV is equal to traditional portfolio variance.

Just as in the case of traditional variance, the link between probability and statistics requires using actual sample data to draw statistical inferences. The actual calculation of summary risk measures then requires using a sample statistic. The sample statistic for the BTV of a time series with N observations is:[6]

$$BTV = \frac{1}{N+1} \sum_{t=1}^{N} (\max[T - R_t, 0])^2$$

(8.7)

DECOMPOSING TOTAL RISK INTO ITS COMPONENTS

The measures of total risk discussed in this section do not differentiate between the sources of risk—that is why some portfolios and assets are riskier than others. In that connection, the total risk of an asset also can be decomposed into idiosyncratic and systematic components. The former concerns those sources of risk in an asset that are particular to the asset in question, such as issuer-specific credit risk or earnings growth. The latter type of risk refers to movements in the price of an asset that are driven by movements in the market as a whole or by changes in some risk factor that affects all asset prices (for example, the inflation rate).

In order to allocate the total risk of an asset or portfolio into idiosyncratic and systematic components, some set of systematic risk factors must be defined. A systematic risk factor is any economic factor (such as aggregate consumption growth) whose changes drive *all* asset prices. The impact of a change in a risk factor on any particular asset price may be different depending on the asset, but if the risk factor is truly systematic, it affects all asset prices in some way.[7]

The Capital Asset Pricing Model (CAPM)

The best way to understand systematic risk factors is by walking through the most common example—the Capital Asset Pricing Model (CAPM) of Sharpe, Lintner, Mossin, and Black. In the CAPM, the return on any asset j is related to a single risk factor—the return on the market portfolio. Specifically, the CAPM implies that the excess return on any asset j (for example, the return in excess of the risk-free rate) is proportional to the covariance of the return of that asset with returns on the market portfolio and to the excess return on the market portfolio. Although the model involves the true market portfolio of all invested wealth and the true risk-free rate, we usually measure these variables using a broad equity index (such as the S&P 500) and the U.S. Treasury bill rate, respectively.

Mathematically, the CAPM implies the following for any asset j:

$$E(R_j) - R_f = \beta_j[E(R_m) - R_f] \qquad (8.8)$$

where

$E(R_j)$ = Expected return on asset j
R_f = Risk-free rate (that is, Treasury bill rate)
$E(R_m)$ = Expected return on the market

where

$$\beta_j = \frac{\text{Cov}(R_m, R_j)}{\text{Var}(R_m)} \qquad (8.9)$$

The parameter β_j measures the degree to which changes in the systematic risk factor (the market) impact changes in the expected asset returns. In other words, the expected excess return on the market portfolio is the risk factor, and β_j is the price of that risk factor in asset j. The price of market risk may be different for different assets, because both β_j and $E(R_j)$ differ for different assets and portfolios. Nevertheless, the characterization of expected excess returns on the market as a systematic risk factor means that the excess return on the market always affects excess returns on assets somehow.

The CAPM is called a *single-factor model* because excess returns on all assets are systematically affected by only one factor—the excess return on the market portfolio. In the CAPM, all systematic risk is reflected in the relation between expected asset returns and expected market returns, and the price of this systematic risk—that is, the degree to which it affects returns on a particular asset—is reflected fully in beta.

Any particular asset also may be affected by idiosyncratic risk or market risk that is specific to the asset in question. To see the impact of systematic risk on the return on any asset j, we can rewrite the CAPM relation without using expected values:

$$R_j - R_f = \beta_j[R_m - R_f] + \varepsilon_j \qquad (8.10)$$

where ε_j is a term that reflects the idiosyncratic risk of the asset. Equation 8.10 essentially says that the actual return on asset j is equal to the risk-free rate plus the asset's beta times the actual excess return on the market plus a random shock that reflects risk specific to asset j. If the expected value of ε_j is zero, Equation 8.10 becomes the CAPM equation in expected value terms. If R_j is the actual return on some well-diversified portfolio j rather than a single asset, the assumption that $E(\varepsilon_j) = 0$ is equivalent to presuming that the diversification effects of the portfolio cause all idiosyncratic risks to net out.

We can express the total risk of the portfolio (using variance as our measure of risk) in terms of its systematic and idiosyncratic components:

$$\mathrm{Var}(R_j) = \beta_j^2 \mathrm{Var}(R_m) + \mathrm{Var}(\varepsilon_j) + 2\beta_j \mathrm{Cov}(R_m, \varepsilon_j) \tag{8.11}$$

By definition, the idiosyncratic disturbance term is uncorrelated with returns on the market portfolio—otherwise, it would not be a truly idiosyncratic risk. This means that the last term in the previous equation is equal to zero, and we can express total risk as just the sum of the systematic and idiosyncratic risk:[8]

$$\mathrm{Var}(R_j) = \beta_j^2 \mathrm{Var}(R_m) + \mathrm{Var}(\varepsilon_j) \tag{8.12}$$

Multifactor Asset Pricing Models

The CAPM has been sharply criticized as an unrealistic representation of systematic risk. Specifically, significant academic work has shown that the excess return on the market is not the only factor that significantly affects all asset returns.[9] Other systematic risk factors known to affect all stock returns, for example, include leverage, market capitalization, dividend yields, and the ratio of book to market equity.

Numerous alternatives to the CAPM have been proposed that presume excess returns on any asset are a function of multiple systematic risk factors. The particular factors differ depending on the particular model in question, but the basic form of the relation is usually the same:[10]

$$R_j - R_F = \delta_1 \gamma_1 + \delta_2 \gamma_2 + \cdots + \delta_k \gamma_k + \varepsilon_j \tag{8.13}$$

where γ_1 is the first systematic risk factor and δ_1 is the price of the first risk factor in asset j. In other words, δ_1 measures the sensitivity of returns on asset or portfolio j to changes in the first systematic risk factor and so on for the other risk factors through k. The number of risk factors, k, can be small or large depending on the particular model, all of which collectively reflect the systematic risk of asset j's returns. Like the CAPM, the term ε_j reflects the idiosyncratic risk of asset or portfolio j—in other words, the risk that is specific to asset or portfolio j.

Identifying systematic risk factors can be difficult, and the systematic risk factors usually need to have a few important characteristics. For one thing, the systematic risk factors should be mutually exclusive and uncorrelated with each other—that is, $\text{Cov}(\gamma_m \gamma_{m+1}) = 0$ for all m. In addition, the idiosyncratic risk term should be uncorrelated with all the systematic risk factors—that is, $\text{Cov}(\gamma_m \varepsilon_j) = 0$ for all m. Finally, the systematic risk factors should exhaustively span all of the possible sources of systematic risk impacting asset prices. Some factors that fall into these categories are macroeconomic, such as *real consumption growth*. Other factors cannot be identified directly, so *factor-mimicking portfolios*—portfolios whose returns are perfectly correlated with the underlying risk factor—must be chosen as substitutes.

Under the previous assumptions about the idiosyncratic risk term and systematic risk factors, the total risk of asset or portfolio j can be decomposed using variance as the measure of risk:

$$\text{Var}(R_j) = \delta_1^2 \text{Var}(\gamma_1) + \delta_2^2 \text{Var}(\gamma_2) + \cdots + \delta_k^2 \text{Var}(\gamma_k) + \text{Var}(\varepsilon_j)$$

MEASURES OF RISK FOR ALLOCATING CAPITAL INTO ASSET CLASSES

Perhaps the most important application of the measures of risk discussed in this section is facilitating ex ante decisions about how to allocate capital into asset classes on a risk-adjusted basis. The asset allocation decision first requires a plan sponsor or portfolio manager to identify the markets, as opposed to specific securities, in which to invest. Individual securities sharing common financial characteristics are grouped into those broader asset classes. Asset classes for potential investment are then selected based on several criteria: the ability to monitor performance, liquidity, and redundancy, and the ability to estimate risk, legal limitations, and diversification advantages. Once the asset classes have been identified, the weight of each asset class in the investment portfolio must be determined.

Mean-Variance Optimization

Nobel laureate Harry Markowitz first described the goal of portfolio theory as the process of identifying an *efficient set of portfolios*. An efficient portfolio is a portfolio for which no greater expected return can be found without a corresponding increase in risk. Alternatively, efficient portfolios are those for which no greater certainty of returns can be achieved without a decrease in expected return. Once this efficient set of portfolios is identified at the asset class level, the investment manager chooses an actual allocation on that frontier that best conforms to the desired risk/return targets of the investors in the fund.[12]

The set of efficient portfolios is commonly called the *efficient frontier*. A typical set of such efficient portfolios is depicted in Figure 8.2. This plot associates the expected return on a portfolio with a given level of risk or, conversely, the risk of a portfolio with a given expected portfolio return.

The concave line depicted in the Figure 8.2 is the efficient frontier formed by tracing the boundary of all portfolios that are combinations of selected asset classes. Points inside the frontier are inefficient because less return for the risk is achieved. Points outside the line, by contrast, are more desirable, but are not obtainable (that is, infeasible). Portfolio 1 is the minimum risk portfolio and offers the least risk of any combination of asset classes, whereas Portfolio 3 is the maximum return/maximum risk portfolio. Although Portfolio 3 corresponds to 100 percent investment in the asset class with the greatest return, Portfolio 1, by contrast, usually will not be

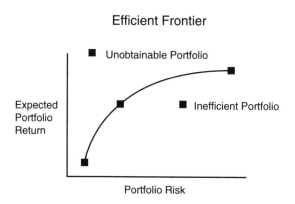

FIGURE 8.2 Efficient frontier.

composed only of the least risky asset class owing to the risk-reducing effects of diversification across asset classes with different risks. For moderate return and risk, portfolios away from the endpoints, such as Portfolio 2, typically are chosen. Such portfolios usually consist of investments in many asset classes, thereby taking significant advantage of diversification effects.

The most common type of efficient frontier is the one popularized by Markowitz, which treats portfolio variance as a sufficient measure of risk. This frontier is called the *mean-variance-efficient frontier,* and portfolios on that frontier are called, not surprisingly, *mean-variance-efficient portfolios.* Figure 8.2 is an example of a mean-variance-efficient frontier when the x-axis indicating the portfolio risk is measured with standard deviation of the historical returns on each asset class.

Given a potential set of asset classes, the efficient frontier can be identified by *portfolio optimization.* Portfolio optimization involves a mathematical procedure called *quadratic programming* in which two objectives are considered: to maximize return and minimize risk. Portfolios on the mean-variance-efficient frontier are found by searching for the portfolio with the least variance given some minimum return. Repetition of this procedure for many return levels generates the efficient frontier.

One of the critical inputs into the portfolio optimization problem clearly is portfolio risk, which is measured as the variance or standard deviation of returns in a mean-variance portfolio optimization problem. The actual variance used as a measure for the risk of asset classes is the historical sample variance for each asset class over some sample period. The sample period is usually as historically long as possible (for example, 25+ years). Importantly, the historical variance of asset class returns is based solely on returns to the asset class itself and is not based on any actively managed portfolio involving that asset class.

Mean-Downside Risk Portfolio Optimization

If the underlying distributions of asset and portfolio returns are not normally distributed, the asset class weights produced in solving the previous problem will not necessarily put the investor on the efficient frontier. Thus, minimizing variance for a given level of return will yield portfolio weights that do not compensate the investor for the risks of the portfolio with which the investor is concerned. To do that, we need to rely on a measure of downside risk as a proxy for total risk rather than just variance.

Once we have determined such a measure of downside risk, which considers all the higher-order moments with which we are concerned (such as the BTR), the problem becomes analogous to the simple mean-variance Markowitz model. The goal is to find a feasible portfolio that minimizes downside risk for some specified level of return.[13] Because higher-order moments are considered, no assumptions are being made about normally distributed returns or symmetric asset returns. The risk measure chosen (for example, the BTR or BTP) and the calculation of this measure is what distinguishes this type of model from the standard mean-variance Markowitz model.

Unfortunately, the mathematical technique used to solve the mean-variance portfolio optimization problem is not applicable in this case. The objective function—minimize downside risk—is nonlinear, and nonlinear optimization problems are a science unto themselves. Optimality in such models, in fact, is very difficult to determine.[14]

Finally, recognize that generating the efficient frontier with portfolio optimization techniques does not tell the plan manager the best portfolio actually to hold. The efficient frontier is a set of many portfolios, and a single optimal portfolio for the plan is not immediately obvious. The ultimate portfolio actually chosen should be the portfolio on the efficient frontier that best approximates the risk/return preferences of the residual claimants and/or sponsor of the fund.

MEASURES OF RISK-ADJUSTED PERFORMANCE

In addition to serving as the foundation for the allocation of capital into asset classes on a risk-adjusted basis, the measures of risk discussed earlier also provide the foundation for the measurement of performance. Specifically, when a portfolio manager's performance is evaluated, some measure of risk must be used to characterize and quantify the risk-adjusted returns of that manager—that is, how much risk was taken to generate some level of returns.

Performance evaluation is inherently backward-looking and ex post in nature. All measures of risk-adjusted performance are based on managers' past actual performance. True, inferences are sometimes drawn about how managers may perform in the future based on how they have performed in the past. But at its core, performance measurement relies solely on returns that have actually been realized in the past.

One important aspect of performance measurement involves the choice of an appropriate time series of historical return data—namely, the frequency and sample period. Reporting time periods are established by the Association for Investment Management and Research (AIMR) guidelines and other internal reporting instructions. To the extent that the choice of a time period over which to evaluate historical performance is left to the evaluator, there are no hard and fast rules except to choose a period that is long enough to yield good statistical estimates (at least 3 years of monthly data or at least 30 observations) and that corresponds with any strategic directives the manager has been given. For example, a manager mandating to maximize the long-run value would suggest a longer evaluation time horizon, whereas a manager scalping initial public offerings (IPOs) might have a shorter sample data period for performance analysis purposes.

Measures of performance fall into two major categories, corresponding to the two perspectives on risk. Namely, risk-adjusted performance can be evaluated by examining either returns relative to various measures of total risk or returns relative to systematic and/or idiosyncratic risk. We discuss the major measures of performance in each of these categories in the next section.[15]

Total Risk Measures of Performance

Recall that total risk is a measure of the risk of a portfolio owing to systematic risk, idiosyncratic risk, or both. From the standpoint of the manager, both of these risks are important. Both affect compensation, peer evaluation, and other qualitative assessments of performance. But from the standpoint of the investors in the portfolio, what is of concern is how the risk of the portfolio impacts the investor's total invested wealth at risk. For example, an investor with all of his or her wealth invested in the portfolio being evaluated cares about both the systematic and idiosyncratic risk of the portfolio—any risk is relevant. However, an investor who has placed money into numerous different investment vehicles that are reasonably well diversified may care less about total portfolio risk and more about the portfolio's systematic risk. In the latter case, after all, idiosyncratic risk may be significant in a specific portfolio, but will have been almost completely diversified away by the investor.

Therefore, measures of risk-adjusted performance based on total risk are most appropriate when investors in the portfolio being evaluated have most of their wealth invested in the portfolio in question or when the portfolio in question is sufficiently diversified that it exhibits virtually no idiosyncratic risk on its own.

Return to Risk Ratio   The Return to Risk Ratio is the ratio of average historical returns to the standard deviation of that manager's returns:[16]

$$\frac{\overline{R}_j}{\sigma_j}$$

(8.15)

where an overbar represents the sample average of the return on portfolio j and where σ_j is the standard deviation of portfolio j's returns over the chosen sample period. This is perhaps the simplest measure of return per unit of risk, where risk is defined as the standard deviation of actual returns. The Return to Risk Ratio thus quantifies the return per unit of total risk, where portfolio risk is presumed to be reflected entirely in the sample variance of the actual returns examined.

Sharpe Ratio The Sharpe Ratio is quite similar to the Return to Risk Ratio and reveals a manager's excess returns per unit of risk, where risk is again defined as the historical standard deviation of returns. Specifically, the Sharpe Ratio is the ratio of the manager's average historical return minus the average Treasury bill (that is, risk-free) rate to the standard deviation of historical manager returns:[17]

$$\frac{\overline{R_j - \bar{R}_F}}{\sigma_j} \tag{8.16}$$

This measure can be viewed as the risk-adjusted return of assets acquired hypothetically assuming that Treasuries were used to finance the acquisition —in other words, the bang for the Treasury buck per unit of portfolio variability. Alternatively, by focusing on the cut performance of the actual manager vis-à-vis Treasury bills, the measure can be viewed as the benefit to holding risky assets relative to the opportunity cost of not holding riskless Treasuries.

Sharpe Ratios provide a way to compare and rank portfolios on a risk-adjusted basis, with higher Sharpe Ratios being more desirable. The Sharpe Ratio of a particular portfolio can be compared to the Sharpe Ratios of other benchmark portfolios or peer groups for risk-adjusted, comparative performance analysis. Thus, Sharpe Ratios can be used either to evaluate performance relative to the performance of other funds or indexes or to evaluate the return/risk profile of a manager in isolation as excess return per unit of risk.

Like the Return to Risk Ratio, the Sharpe Ratio is a performance measure based on the total risk of the portfolio. Variance, moreover, is presumed to be the only relevant summary statistic for capturing total risk. Therefore, the Sharpe Ratio makes two important implicit assumptions. First, because the measure is based on total risk, and thus aggregates systematic and idiosyncratic risk, this measure of performance is most appropriate when an investor has all or most of his or her wealth in the portfolio being evaluated. In other words, the Sharpe Ratio does not take into consideration that the investor may be holding other portfolios that result in the diversification of idiosyncratic risk across portfolios. Second, because standard deviation is used as a proxy for risk, the Sharpe Ratio assumes that the assets in the portfolio have return distributions that can be completely characterized by mean and variance. For portfolios including assets whose returns are not well described by a symmetric distribution, the Sharpe Ratio will reveal only part of the risk/return picture.

Tracking Error Tracking error is defined as the standard deviation of excess returns (that is, the portfolio return less the returns on the relevant benchmark or index portfolio). The resulting statistic reveals the total risk of the portfolio in question, controlling for common factors influencing both the actual portfolio and the benchmark. In other words, the tracking error of a portfolio reveals the total risk in excess of the risk of the benchmark.

Consider the Sharpe Ratios for the portfolios j and m. The total risk of the two portfolios, which serves as the denominator for each Sharpe Ratio, is defined using the standard deviation of returns over some sample period —σ_j and σ_m. Now suppose one wishes to compare the total risk of portfolio j in excess of portfolio m. In this case, total risk is the tracking error of portfolio j with respect to portfolio m. Using variance instead of standard deviation, the tracking error can be defined by the following equation:

$$\sigma_{j-m}{}^2 = \text{Var}(R_j - R_m) = \text{Var}(R_m) - 2\text{Cov}(R_f R_m)$$

(8.17)

Note that tracking error takes into consideration the total risk of each portfolio and the co-movements between returns in the two portfolios.

Although Sharpe Ratios can be compared across managers and portfolios to gain insight into relative risk-adjusted performance, a simple comparison does not take into consideration the common factors that might be influencing both portfolios. We do not mean factors in the sense of asset pricing models, but are referring to anything that could cause two portfolio managers to have performance driven by similar decisions. Regardless what those factors are, it is important to take them into consideration. To see why, suppose one wanted to measure the risk of portfolio j relative to portfolio m and incorrectly attempted to do that by subtracting the denominator of the Sharpe Ratio for m from the denominator of the Sharpe Ratio for j. The result would simply be a subtraction of the two standard deviations, which would not take into consideration the covariance in the two portfolios.

Modified Sharpe Ratio The Modified Sharpe Ratio is a measure of excess portfolio returns to risk where both excess returns and risk are defined relative to a benchmark portfolio. Specifically, the Modified Sharpe Ratio measures the average portfolio returns less the average benchmark portfolio returns per unit of tracking error:

$$\frac{\overline{R}_j - \overline{R}_m}{\sigma_{j-m}}$$

(8.18)

This measure of risk offers a reasonably complete picture of the average benchmark-relative returns per unit of benchmark-relative total risk. It can be interpreted as the reward per unit of risk of investing in the actual portfolio rather than in the benchmark. Indeed, the traditional Sharpe Ratio is actually a special case of the Modified Sharpe Ratio where the benchmark portfolio is just a Treasury bill portfolio.

The Modified Sharpe Ratio can be extremely useful in comparing the performance of alternative investment portfolios. Unlike a simple comparison of two actual Sharpe Ratios, the Modified Sharpe Ratio takes into consideration the common factors that may be influencing risk and return in both portfolios. Like the Sharpe Ratio, however, the Modified Sharpe Ratio is a total risk performance measure. Because total risk includes both systematic and idiosyncratic risk, the Modified Sharpe Ratio may be less appropriate for investors who hold shares in a large number of different, diversified portfolios—that is, for investors whose idiosyncratic risks are largely diversified away. Also, like the Sharpe Ratio, variance remains the sole statistical summary of risk; asymmetric distributions and fat tails are therefore ignored.

It is worth noting the close similarity between the Modified Sharpe Ratio and the statistic commonly used for tests of significance—the *t-statistic*. If the denominator of the Modified Sharpe Ratio, the tracking error, is adjusted for (divided by) sample size, the result is the standard error or the mean:

$$s_{j-m} = \frac{\sigma_{j-m}}{\sqrt{N}}$$

(8.19)

The t-statistic measures excess returns divided by the standard error of the mean:

$$t = \frac{\overline{R}_j - \overline{R}_m}{\dfrac{\sigma_{j-m}}{\sqrt{N}}} = \frac{\overline{R}_j - \overline{R}_m}{s_{j-m}}$$

(8.20)

Although the original Sharpe Ratio can be used for an ex post risk-adjusted performance measure, the t-statistic also can be used as a test of the significance of excess returns earned. Further, it is a source, based on actual ex post historical manager data, for ex ante probabilistic inference of future excess returns.

Sortino Ratio   The Sortino Ratio is the average excess manager return per unit of downside risk—specifically, the BTR or downside semistandard deviation for a given return target T:

$$\frac{\overline{R}_j - \overline{R}_F}{BTR_j}$$

(8.21)

As with the Sharpe Ratio, higher Sortino Ratios indicate more favorable risk/return relations, and the Sortino Ratio of a particular fund is most useful when compared to Sortino Ratios of comparable funds or benchmarks.

The Sortino Ratio is essentially the same as the traditional Sharpe Ratio with one important difference—total risk is defined as downside risk rather than portfolio variance. For this reason, the Sortino Ratio is more attractive than the Sharpe Ratio when measuring the performance of portfolios whose returns are asymmetric. Unlike the Sharpe and Modified Sharpe Ratios, the Sortino Ratio is still a measure of total risk and thus is still inappropriate for investors whose total holdings are diversified and reflect no real idiosyncratic risks.

Measures of Idiosyncratic and Systematic Performance

In the case of investors in a portfolio with only a small fraction of their retirement assets or wealth invested in that portfolio, measures of risk based on either systematic or idiosyncratic risk may be of more interest than measures of total risk. For example, if a pension beneficiary invests in privately managed funds outside of his or her pension account in such a manner that his or her total investment portfolio is reasonably well diversified, he or she may prefer to evaluate alternative investments based on the return per unit of systematic risk rather than total risk. Several such performance measures are available—as well as measures based on idiosyncratic risk.

The particular means by which performance (returns) is adjusted for risk depends, of course, on the specific assumptions made about how risk is defined. Specifically, an asset pricing model must be assumed to hold in order to separate risk into its systematic and idiosyncratic components. Despite its lack of realism, the most common model used for such purposes is the CAPM. In addition, several performance measures based on multifactor risk also are available.

Jensen's Alpha One performance measure implied by the CAPM is *Jensen's alpha*, which measures the average excess return on a portfolio relative to the excess return predicted by the CAPM. To estimate this measure of performance, we need to run the following linear regression:

$$(R_p - R_f) = \alpha + \beta_p[R_m - R_f] + \varepsilon_p \tag{8.22}$$

where R_p is the time series of returns on the portfolio and where β_p is the covariance of portfolio returns and market returns divided by the variance of market returns.

If the CAPM holds, the estimated regression intercept should equal zero. We assume, moreover, that idiosyncratic risk is diversified away so that $E(\varepsilon_p) = 0$. As a result, the CAPM implies that the excess return on the portfolio exactly compensates investors for the systematic risk of the portfolio.

The estimated intercept indicates any positive excess returns above and beyond returns that are commensurate with the systematic risk of the position. In other words, Jensen's α measures the manager-specific returns in excess of those returns that are no more than a compensation for the systematic risk of the portfolio. A positive α indicates a value added by the portfolio manager, and negative α indicates that active management is penalizing investors in the fund.

However, if the CAPM is not the appropriate asset pricing model, Jensen's α can be a very biased measure of risk. Consider, for example, a portfolio of small-cap equities. One reason the CAPM may not be the best asset pricing model is that firm size is known to explain expected excess returns beyond those predicted by the CAPM relation. Specifically, small-cap firms tend to be riskier and have higher expected returns than large-cap firms. Consequently, the Jensen's α for a small-cap portfolio might be positive, suggesting at face value that returns to active management are positive. In reality, however, the positive estimate of α might simply reflect the greater systematic risk of the portfolio due to its small-cap concentration that is not reflected in the CAPM.

Treynor Ratio The Treynor Ratio is another measure of performance that assumes that the CAPM is the relevant means by which risk can be decomposed into systematic and idiosyncratic components. The Treynor Ratio is the analog of the Sharpe Ratio when only the price of systematic risk in the portfolio (the β of the portfolio) is deemed relevant to the investor. Specifically, the Treynor Ratio measures average excess returns over the chosen sample period relative to the portfolio's CAPM beta:

$$\frac{\overline{R}_j - \overline{R}_m}{\beta_j}$$

(8.23)

This summary measure of risk-adjusted performance yields an estimate of average excess returns per unit of systematic risk for portfolio j.

Appraisal Ratio   The Appraisal Ratio is the third CAPM-based performance measure. The Appraisal Ratio is defined as α/σ_ϵ, where α is Jensen's α and Σ_ϵ is the standard deviation of the residuals from the CAPM regression. The former is an estimate of the average excess return on a portfolio over and above the excess return that exactly compensates investors for the systematic risk of the portfolio, and the latter is a proxy for the idiosyncratic risk of the portfolio. The Appraisal Ratio thus reveals the average value added by managers (above the systematic risk-based excess return) per unit of idiosyncratic risk.

MARKET RISK MEASUREMENT FOR RISK MANAGEMENT PURPOSES

We have reviewed the various means by which risk can be defined conceptually. We have also examined the application of those risk measures to the ex ante allocation of capital into asset classes and the ex post analysis of risk-adjusted performance. In this section, we consider how the general measures of risk can be used to generate ex ante assessments of risk for the purpose of risk management and control.

Risk management is the process by which an organization tries to ensure that the risks to which it is exposed are those risks to which it thinks it is and needs to be exposed. In investment management, risk management therefore requires the investment manager to make an ongoing determination that the risks actually taken are commensurate with the risk/return target desired by investors. Performance evaluation plays a significant role in that process by enabling the plan to evaluate whether or not the risks that managers are taking are being commensurately reflected in realized returns. At the same time, market risk measurement can also be used for the purpose of risk control. Risk management and control is an ex ante process by which the plan tries to prevent excessive risks from being taken regardless of how they might impact returns. In other words, ex ante risk management tries to prevent large, unexpected losses arising from extremely risky investments by evaluating only the potential risk of those investments.

Fundamentally, market risk measures used for risk management and control trace to the same concepts of risk in probability and statistics on which performance measures rely. The critical distinction is that performance measures are based on the actual performance of a specific portfolio or manager, whereas market risk measures for risk management and control are based on the risk inherent to the instruments themselves. Whereas manager-specific data is used to estimate risk for performance evaluation purposes, instrument-specific data is used to estimate risk for monitoring and control purposes. The distinction will become clearer in the following section, where various risk measures and their relation to more traditional measures of investment risk are discussed.

Value at Risk (VaR)

Value at Risk (VaR) is a summary statistic that quantifies the exposure of a portfolio to market risk. Measuring risk using VaR allows the plan to make statements like the following: "We do not expect losses to exceed $1 million in more than 1 out of the next 20 months." VaR has a well-earned reputation as a useful summary measure of risk. It is comprehensive, enabling market risk to be examined at the instrument, fund, and aggregate portfolio levels. VaR also is consistent, facilitating the comparison of risk measures across different asset classes and securities. Because it summarizes market risk as a potential dollar loss, VaR is also an intelligible measure of risk that can easily be reported to plan managers and trustees.

In the context of the risk measures outlined in the section "Building Block Definitions of Risk" VaR also can be viewed as a way of summarizing a probability distribution or a sample distribution from which probabilistic inferences are drawn. Recall, for example, that variance is a way of summarizing a distribution of returns by describing how much dispersion those returns exhibit around the mean. Typically, VaR is used to summarize the point in the return distribution below which lies a certain amount of probability. VaR that is estimated at the 5 percent confidence level, for example, is a measure of the level below which returns are not expected to fall more than 5 percent of the time.

Distinctions Between VaR and Measures of Risk for Performance One of the main distinctions between VaR and measures of risk used for performance evaluation is that the latter uses actual portfolio returns data, whereas the former does not. VaR begins with the instruments in a portfolio at a particular time and then builds up to the estimate of risk from which ex ante inferences may be drawn. In other words, the statistics used to summarize risk are not particularly different in performance evaluation and VaR estimation; what differs is the probability or sampling distribution for which those statistics are calculated.

To measure performance, we simply looked at the distribution of historical portfolio returns and then chose a statistic like the mean or variance to summarize return and risk. To estimate the VaR of a portfolio, possible future values of that portfolio must be generated over a specific period of time called the *risk horizon*. The risk horizon is the interval over which the plan is concerned with changes in portfolio value (for example, monthly). The resulting distribution of possible portfolio changes is called the *VaR distribution*, which represents what the portfolio *might do* rather than what the portfolio *has done*. Once the VaR distribution is created for a chosen risk horizon, the VaR itself is just a number on the curve—that is, the change in the value of the portfolio leaving the specified amount of probability in the left-hand tail.

Creating a VaR distribution for a particular portfolio and a given risk horizon can be viewed as a two-step process. In the first step, the price or return distributions for each individual security or asset in the portfolio are generated. The instruments used as the basis for the portfolio VaR calculation are whatever instruments are in the portfolio at the time of the risk measurement. (This is quite distinct from performance measurement, which, focusing on portfolio-level returns, considers all instruments held in the portfolio over a specific period of time in the past.) The resulting VaR distributions for each instrument represent possible value changes in all the component assets over the risk horizon. Mathematically, for an asset whose per-period (for example, monthly) return distribution is known to be $f(R)$, the VaR at the x percent confidence level can be defined with the following equation:

$$0.05 = \int_{-\infty}^{Var} f(R)dR$$

(8.24)

Next, the individual distributions somehow must be aggregated into a portfolio distribution using the appropriate measures of correlation. The resulting portfolio distribution then serves as the basis for the VaR summary measure.

An important assumption in almost all VaR calculations is that the portfolio whose risk is being evaluated does not change over the risk horizon.

This assumption of no turnover was not a major issue when VaR first arrived on the scene at derivative dealers. They were focused on 1- or 2-day—sometimes *intraday*—risk horizons and thus found VaR both easy to implement and relatively realistic. However, when it comes to generalizing VaR to a longer time horizon that is of more interest to institutional investors, the assumption of no portfolio changes becomes problematic. What does it mean, after all, to evaluate the 1-year VaR of a portfolio using only the portfolio's contents today if the turnover in the portfolio is 20 to 30 percent per day?

Methods for Calculating VaR   Methods for generating both the individual asset risk distributions and the portfolio risk distribution range from the simplistic to the indecipherably complex.[18] By far the easiest way to create the VaR distribution used in calculating the VaR statistic is just to assume that distribution is normal. Mean and variance are then sufficient statistics to fully characterize a normal distribution; they are all that is required to make probabilistic inferences about the distribution. For example, 5 percent of the probability in a normal distribution lies 1.65 standard deviations below the mean. So, a 5 percent VaR statistic for a portfolio of normally distributed returns can be computed by multiplying the current value (V) of the portfolio by its mean return minus 1.65 times its standard deviation:

$$VaR = V(\mu - 1.65\sigma) \tag{8.25}$$

The variance used in the previous calculation is a neutral market estimate of the instrument's variance; this variance does not come from an actively managed position. For example, a moving average of the last 60 observed variances in the particular instrument in question may be used as the estimate for volatility.

In the case of two assets, the VaR of the portfolio can be computed in a similar manner using the variances of the two assets' returns. These variance-based risk measures then are combined using the correlation of the two assets' returns. The result is a VaR estimate for the portfolio.

The simplicity of the variance-based approach to VaR calculations lies in the assumption of normality. By assuming that returns on all financial instruments are normally distributed, the risk manager eliminates the need to come up with a VaR distribution using complicated modeling techniques. All that really must be done is to come up with the appropriate variances and correlations.

At the same time, however, by assuming normality, the risk manager has limited the VaR estimate. Normal distributions, as noted earlier, are symmetric. Therefore, any potential for skewness or fat tails in asset returns is totally ignored in the variance-only approach.

In addition to sacrificing the possibility that asset returns might not be normally distributed, the variance-only approach to calculating VaR also relies on the critical assumption that asset returns are totally independent across increments of time. A multiperiod VaR can be calculated only by calculating a single-period VaR from the available data and then extrapolating the multiday risk estimate. For example, suppose variances and correlations are available for historical returns measured at the daily frequency. To get from a 1-day VaR to a T-day VaR—where T is the risk horizon of interest —the variance-only approach requires that the 1-day VaR be multiplied by the square root of T.

For return variances and correlations measured at the monthly frequency or lower, this assumption might not be terribly implausible. For daily variances and correlations, however, serial independence is a very strong and usually an unrealistic assumption in most markets. The problem is less severe for short risk horizons, of course. So, using a 1-day VaR as the basis for a 5-day VaR might be acceptable, whereas a 1-day VaR extrapolated into a 1-year VaR would be highly problematic in most markets.

Despite the simplicity of most variance-based VaR measurement methods, many practitioners prefer to avoid the restrictive assumptions underlying that approach—that is, symmetric return distributions that are independent and stable over time. To avoid these assumptions, a risk manager must actually generate a full distribution of possible future portfolio values—a distribution that is neither necessarily normal nor symmetric.

Historical simulation is perhaps the easiest alternative to variance-based VaR. This approach generates VaR distributions merely by rearranging historical data—in other words, resampling time series data on the relevant asset prices or returns. This can be about as easy computationally as variance-based VaR, and it does not presuppose that everything in the world is normally distributed. Nevertheless, the approach is highly dependent on the availability of potentially massive amounts of historical data. In addition, the VaR resulting from a historical simulation is totally sample dependent.

More advanced approaches to VaR calculation usually involve some type of forward-looking simulation model, such as Monte Carlo. Implementing simulation methods typically is computationally intensive, expensive, and heavily dependent on personnel resources. For that reason, simulation has remained largely limited to active trading firms and institutional investors. Nevertheless, simulation does enable users to depart from normality assumptions about underlying asset returns without forcing them to rely on a single historical data sample. Simulation also eliminates the need to assume independence in returns over time—as a result, VaR calculations are no longer restricted to 1-day estimates that must be extrapolated over the total risk horizon.

Relations Between VaR and Measures of Risk Used for Performance Evaluation   As noted, the principal distinction between a market risk measurement used for risk management like VaR and risk measures used to calculate performance are the underlying distributions used to calculate the relevant summary statistics about risk. To see this, just suppose for a moment that we are working with the same probability distribution and that distribution is known.

With the same portfolio distribution used as the basis for calculating risk statistics, the close correspondence between risk measures used for performance evaluation and risk measures used for risk management and control becomes obvious. For example, assume that the common return distribution is a normal distribution. In that case, we can divide the average excess portfolio returns by the 5 percent variance-based VaR (expressed as a return) and multiply the result by 1.65 to get the Sharpe Ratio:

$$\left(\frac{\overline{R}_p - \overline{R}_f}{VaR - R_p} \right) 1.65 = \left(\frac{\overline{R}_p - \overline{R}_f}{1.65\sigma_p} \right) 1.65 = \left(\frac{\overline{R}_p - \overline{R}_f}{\sigma_p} \right) \quad (8.26)$$

It should not be surprising that these two statistics are so closely related—variance-based VaR estimates and the Information Ratio are also related. In the Sharpe Ratio, standard deviation is the only measure of risk. In the VaR calculated when returns are normally distributed, 1.65 times the standard deviation subtracted from the mean is the only measure of risk. When both calculations are based on the same standard deviation, the fundamental result is the same. In short, we may be summarizing the information contained in the returns distribution differently using the Sharpe Ratio and VaR, but the information itself is the same because the distribution is the same.

It should be clear that unless the previous VaR statistic and Sharpe Ratio are calculated using exactly the same variance, the correspondence between the two statistics will break down. This should be the case. As noted, the variance used for the Sharpe Ratio is the variance of actual historical portfolio returns, whereas the variance used for the VaR calculation is a function of the variances and covariances of the instruments in the portfolio as of the date of the calculation and based not on actual performance, but rather on neutral market data.

Benchmark-Relative VaR   VaR can be calculated in an absolute sense for a specific portfolio or for a given portfolio relative to some index portfolio or benchmark. In an absolute VaR, only the distribution of actual portfolio returns is used to calculate the VaR statistic. In a benchmark-relative VaR, the distribution summarized with the VaR statistic is the distribution of the difference between returns on the target portfolio and returns on the benchmark. The resulting VaR statistic then measures the loss associated with the chosen confidence level and risk horizon relative to the benchmark loss. In other words, absolute VaR summarizes the absolute loss that is not expected to occur more than some percentage—say, 5 percent—of the time. A 5 percent benchmark-relative VaR, by contrast, summarizes the potential for a loss below the loss expected with the same probability on the benchmark portfolio. For example, suppose the monthly benchmark-relative VaR on an equity portfolio benchmarked to the S&P 500 is $1 million at the 5 percent confidence level. This means that with a 5 percent probability, the equity portfolio in question will underperform the S&P 500 by more than $1 million.

Downside Risk Measures

As an alternative to VaR, some institutions summarize their risk for risk management and control purposes using downside risk measures rather than variance-based measures that assume symmetry in the underlying distribution. BTP and BTR were discussed as statistical measures of risk, and those statistics can be used directly for risk management and control purposes. In other words, if a pension plan's sole objective is to avoid a shortfall of assets below a liability target of, say, 5 percent, the BTP and/or BTR calculated with a target of $T = 5$ percent could serve as the basis for risk-control decisions.

As in the case of VaR, the primary distinction between applications of downside risk measures for performance evaluation and for risk control is the underlying return distribution being summarized by the statistic. When actual portfolio returns are the basis for the calculation, BTR can serve as the basis for risk-adjusted performance evaluation through the Sortino Ratio. When the downside semivariances of the instruments held in a portfolio on any given day are used to estimate future possible returns, the BTR summary measure reveals different information entirely.

Reasons for Measuring Market Risk Ex Ante

In order for VaR or other measures of ex ante market risk to make sense, the investment policy and asset allocation decision must first be accepted as *sacrosanct*. VaR should compliment rather than compete with the primary investment management goals of the investment plan. It is a tool for helping the plan determine whether the risks to which it is exposed are those risks to which the plan thinks it is and wants/needs to be exposed. VaR will never tell the plan how much risk to take. It will only tell the plan manager how much risk is being taken.

Taking the investment policy as a given, a plan manager can apply VaR in at least four ways to the operation of his or her funds.[19] First, one of the primary benefits of VaR is that it facilitates the consistent and regular monitoring of market risk. The plan can calculate and monitor VaR on a variety of different levels. When calculated and monitored at the portfolio level, the risks taken by individual asset managers—whether they are internal traders and portfolio managers or external account managers—can be evaluated on an ongoing basis. Market risk can be tracked and monitored at the aggregate fund level, as well as by asset class, by issuer/counterparty, and the like.

Second, VaR can benefit the plan by helping to reduce any unnecessary transactional scrutiny by directors and trustees. In this way, VaR can actually help give portfolio managers more autonomy than they might otherwise have without a formalized, VaR-based risk management process.

A third application of VaR involves measuring and monitoring market risk using a formal system of predefined risk targets or thresholds. In essence, risk thresholds take ad hoc risk monitoring one step further and systematize the process by which VaR levels are evaluated and discussed for portfolios or managers—or in some cases, for the whole investment fund. A system of risk thresholds is tantamount to setting up a tripwire around an investment field, where the field is characterized by a fund's investment policy and risk tolerance. This tripwire is defined in terms of the maximum tolerable VaR allocated to a manager or portfolio and then is monitored by regularly (for example, weekly) comparing actual VaRs to these predefined targets. Investment managers are permitted to leave the field when they want, but the tripwire signals senior managers that they have done so. When a tripwire is hit (a VaR threshold is breached), an *exception report* is generated, and discussions and explanations are required.

The hallmark of a well-functioning risk target system is not that targets are never breached or that all executions are rectified through liquidating or hedging current holdings. Rather, the primary benefit of a risk target system is the formalization of a process by which exceptions are discussed, addressed, and analyzed. Therefore, risk thresholds are a useful means by which asset managers can systematically monitor and control their market risks without attenuating the autonomy of their portfolio managers. Because the primary purpose of risk limits is to systematize discussions about actual market risk exposures relative to defined risk tolerances, huge investments in VaR calculation systems, moreover, typically are not required. Even an imprecise measure of VaR will usually accomplish the desired result of formalizing the risk-monitoring process.

A more extreme version of risk targets and risk thresholds is a system of rigid risk limits. This application of VaR is also known as a *risk budget.* In a risk budget, the fund's total VaR is calculated and then allocated to asset classes and specific portfolios in terms of absolute and benchmark-relative VaR as well as Shortfall at Risk (SaR). Managers are then required to remain within their allocated risk budget along these risk dimensions. So, whereas risk targets resemble a tripwire around a field that managers must account ex post for crossing, a true risk budget acts as an electric fence around the field that managers simply cannot cross ex ante.

A total risk budget defined across all portfolios can create numerous problems for many institutional investors. First, risk budgeting relies at some level on the absolute VaR of a fund and its portfolios. To the extent that the measurement methodology is imperfect, the risk budget will be wrong. If the VaR measurement methodology is more biased for some asset classes or security types than others, some managers could be penalized or rewarded simply because of flaws in the measurement methodology. In the extreme, relatively riskier funds could be given a risk budget that is too high, whereas relatively safer funds could be allocated too little VaR.

Second, risk budgeting defined across both asset classes and portfolios can contradict and call into question the fund's asset allocation decision. This can be especially problematic if a board of trustees must approve changes in the asset allocation unless hitting a risk limit in the risk budget triggers the change. Because many institutional investors allocate capital into asset classes annually using traditional mean-variance asset allocation and portfolio optimization techniques, a VaR budget for asset classes and portfolios, where VaR is measured using a variance-based approach, would have to be enforced annually. If the risk budget is enforced more frequently than annually, the risk budget will call into question the asset allocation simply because volatility changes in the markets on a regular basis. Variance-induced changes in VaR, therefore, prompt a shift in the asset allocation through the risk budget. Even though the practical consequence is a change in the asset allocation itself, the actual trigger is the risk budget, so the board may never be consulted.

To avoid this problem, risk budgeting should be limited to rebalancing funds between portfolios within the same asset class. Even then, asset managers contemplating a risk budget will need to allocate a considerable sum of money for the VaR calculation system to ensure that the calculation method is not biased against particular managers or financial instruments.

Relation to Asset Allocation

Although risk measures used for performance evaluation purposes are clearly ex post measures of market risk, risk measures used for both asset allocation and risk-management purposes are both ex ante. The question naturally arises as to how the two are different.

Conceptually, the ex ante measurement of risk for asset allocation and risk management are not different at all. Both rely on the same basic building block definitions of risk, and both use tactics-neutral data about financial instruments rather than specific managers. Nevertheless, the applications are different in several important ways.

One distinction between the measurement of risk for asset allocation and risk management is the specific asset for which risk is being measured. Asset allocation focuses on risk measurement exclusively at the level of asset classes, whereas most applications of VaR or BTR involve portfolio-specific and often security-specific information. Returns on asset classes are usually sufficient to solve the asset allocation problem, whereas that is rarely adequate to engage in the monitoring of risk for risk-control purposes (for example, catching leveraged derivatives).

Another distinction lies in the frequency with which the evaluations are undertaken. Asset allocation and rebalancing are often extremely time consuming and costly. Large pension plans typically have an annual asset allocation with quarterly or monthly rebalancing horizons. When risk is measured to monitor trading activities, the time horizon is often much shorter, thus necessitating a different means by which risk is measured.

Finally, risk is defined solely as variance in most asset allocation problems because of the prevalence of the Markowitz mean-variance portfolio optimization paradigm. In principle, an efficient frontier can be generated based on other definitions of risk, such as BTR, but such exercises are significantly more cumbersome and resource intensive. Measures like VaR and BTR can, however, be calculated for risk control and monitoring purposes without the optimization. These measures, however, need not be variance based. Risk measurement for risk-management purposes thus provides the plan with additional insights about downside risks that may not be adequately captured in a variance statistic.

Because of the similarities between ex ante risk measures for asset allocation and risk management, variance-based VaR measures in particular can actually result in serious problems when the asset allocation is also undertaken using mean-variance optimization. If both measures of risk are based on the exact same variance, both the asset allocation and VaR will reveal equivalent information. But if the variance is different for the VaR because the frequency of VaR measurement is higher than the frequency of the asset allocation decision, the variance will change with market movements and could lead to rebalances in the asset allocation. On the one hand, this may be based on new, better information than the original asset allocation. On the other hand, that is what rebalancing targets are for, and frequent rebalancing triggered by VaR (or risk budgets) could become extraordinarily impractical and costly.

CONCLUSIONS

We have attempted to demonstrate how various measures of risk are related and can be used in different ways to measure risk for performance evaluation and for risk management and control. The various economic and statistical means by which risk itself is measured in finance do not really differ based on the application. However, the data and assumptions used in those applications do strongly influence the result.

In general, any measure of risk that is based on historical returns on an actively managed portfolio is appropriate for performance evaluation, but not risk measurement for risk control. Historical returns on an actual actively managed portfolio are ex post measures of risk and may have no bearing on the risk of a position held from today through tomorrow. True, the measures of risk used for risk management and control purposes are also based on historical data, which lies at the core of any statistical inference problem. However, that data, unlike data for performance evaluation, is tactics neutral. It should not and cannot depend on tactical management decisions, but rather should be confined to neutral market data about the risk inherent in instruments themselves.

The investment management process can be viewed as a cycle in which asset allocation leads to performance evaluation, performance evaluation leads to risk management, and risk management leads to asset allocation. When capital is first allocated into asset classes, ex ante measures of risk are required. Similarly, measuring risk ex ante for risk-control purposes facilitates the security selection process. Measuring risk ex post, in turn, helps determine how effective the other types of risk measures were based on actual data. Perhaps the best way to distinguish between measures of risk used for performance evaluation and those used for risk-control decisions, therefore, is to follow this rule: When evaluating performance, measure the risk of the manager based on his or her actual past performance; when evaluating risk going forward, measure the risk of the instruments currently held based on their actual past performance, regardless of who was trading them.

Note: The authors are grateful to Brian Heimsoth, Geoff Ihle, Andrea Neves, Kamaryn Tanner, and especially Pat Lipton for their helpful comments and their extensive work with us on this subject. The standard disclaimer applies, however, and we alone are responsible for any remaining errors or omissions. The views expressed herein are the views of the authors alone and do not necessarily represent the views of either the State of Wisconsin Investment Board or of CP Risk Management LLC and its clients.

NOTES

[1]We focus on monthly returns for simplicity. In reality, any frequency can be used.

[2]Returns can be computed either arithmetically or using continuous compounding. We use the former because it enables us to consider explicitly any dividend payments.

[3]See Christopher Culp, Kamaryn Tanner, and Ron Mensink, "Risk, Returns, and Retirement," *Risk* (October 1987). For a more detailed discussion, see Kamaryn T. Tanner, "An Asymmetric Distribution Model for Portfolio Optimization," manuscript, Graduate School of Business, The University of Chicago (1997).

[4]Rarely are any of these statistics adequate in isolation. They usually must be considered together, as we will explain in more detail later.

[5]We drop the subscript notation *j* for simplicity, noting that all statistics still refer to any asset or portfolio *j*.

[6]The sum is often divided by N instead of $N+1$, but for large samples, the results change little.

[7]The most common means by which risk factors affect asset returns is through a relation that is presumed to be linear. Although this need not be the case, we confine our discussion to linear factor models. For a more general discussion, see John Cochrane, "Asset Pricing," manuscript (1999).

[8]Readers may recognize the CAPM expression using actual returns as a type of linear regression. In a typical Ordinary Least Squares regression, we assume that $Cov(R_j, \varepsilon_j) = 0$. But this is a statistical assumption; whether it is actually true is an empirical matter.

[9]See, for example, Eugene F. Fama and Kenneth R. French, "Common Risk Factors in the Returns on Stocks and Bonds," *Journal of Financial Economics* (February 1993).

[10]This particular representation is linear. For a more general discussion, see Cochrane, op. cit.

[11]See the reproduction in Harry Markowitz, *Portfolio Selection* (London: Blackwell, 1991).

[12]Attempting to ascertain the true risk/return preferences of investors is admittedly difficult, but nevertheless plays an important part in the investment management process.

[13]See Tanner, op. cit.

[14]See Tanner, op. cit.

[15]To keep this survey simple, we do not provide citations for the performance measures discussed. Most of these measures and their original sources can be found in any investments textbook. See, for example, Zvi Bodie, Alex Kane, and Alan J. Marcus, *Investments* (Chicago: Irwin Professional Publishing, 1993). A more advanced discussion and more recent literature survey can be found in Mark Grinblatt and Sheridan Titman, "Performance Evaluation," in *Handbooks in Operations Research & Management Science*, vol. 9, R. Jarrow et al., eds. (Amsterdam: Elsevier Science, 1995).

[16]This is also sometimes called the *Information Ratio*. Many practitioners also refer to the Modified Sharpe Ratio, which is discussed later, as the Information Ratio. To avoid any confusion, we do not use the term Information Ratio to describe any performance measures in this document.

[17]Strictly speaking, the ratio should be the average excess historical returns divided by the standard deviation of the *difference* between actual portfolio returns and the Treasury bill rate. In doing the actual calculation, most people simply calculate the standard deviation of portfolio returns as the denominator. If the risk-free rate is truly risk free, the variance of the risk-free rate is zero and the variance of the actual portfolio return *less* the risk-free rate should equal the variance of the actual return. Sometimes people actually do calculate the standard deviation of the residual because the Treasury bill rate does exhibit some positive variability.

[18]Brief summaries of these methods are provided in Christopher L. Culp, Merton H. Miller, and Andrea M.P. Neves, "Value at Risk: Uses and Abuses," *Journal of Applied Corporate Finance* (Winter 1998), and Christopher L. Culp, Ron Mensink, and Andrea M.P. Neves, "Value at Risk for Asset Managers," *Derivatives Quarterly* (Winter 1998).

[19]See Christopher L. Culp and Ron Mensink, "Use and Misuse of a Risk Management Tool," *Pensions & Investments* (August 1998).

CHAPTER 9

Model Risk

Emanuel Derman*

Complex financial models have empowered market participants to make increasingly rational investment decisions based on causal relationships between factors affecting securities prices. Models have also contributed to increased aggregate market efficiency. But Emanuel Derman asserts that increased reliance on models also induces significant levels of risk, due to their assumptive nature. This chapter is a amalgam of two papers written by Derman, "Model Risk" and "The Great Pretender."

Securities markets in the past 20 years have seen the emergence of an astonishingly theoretical approach to valuation, market making, and arbitrage in complex market sectors. Many securities firms now base their bid and offer prices for complex securities on detailed analytic or computer models built by scientists.[1] Most of this theory centers on *derivatives*, instruments whose value stems from their contractually defined relation to more elementary securities or market parameters. In this generalized sense, derivatives encompass many products: Index futures and options are derivatives on the underlying index, collateralized mortgage obligations (CMOs) are derivatives on interest and prepayment rates, and we can even regard bonds as derivatives on interest rates. There are many more examples from convertible bonds to credit derivatives.

Theoretical models abound. In the fixed-income world, the theoretical approach was probably sparked by the shock to bond portfolio values as interest rates jumped in the late 1970s. Duration, convexity, and other

This article is adapted from material owned by Goldman Sachs & Co., 2001 and is included with their permission. Copyright © 2001 by Goldman Sachs, Inc. All rights reserved.

*I am grateful to Alex Bergier, Barbara Dunn, Didi Hu, and Iraj Kani for their comments.

theoretical risk and sensitivity measures grew in both sophistication and popularity. You can now attend 2-day courses in fitting yield curves and extracting zero-coupon rates. The increased interest-rate volatility also triggered the development of caps, floors, swaps, and swaptions, whose valuation and trading were all heavily model driven. In the equity world, program trading of the mismatch between actual futures prices and their theoretical fair value was made possible by rapid electronic computation and trading.

Equity and fixed-income option trading and structuring grew in part because of the confidence that developed in using the Black-Scholes model and its extensions. The growth in model building and model adoption has also depended on the rapid acceleration in computing power. Computing and modeling have played a sort of leapfrog: More power allowed for fancier models, which then ran too slowly, and so in turn required even more power. Advanced users now think of hedging exotic equity index options with standard options, so that one person's derivative has become another person's underlyer.[2]

This reliance on models to handle risk carries its own risks. In this report, we analyze the assumptions made in using models to value securities, and list the consequent risks.

There are at least three different meanings implied by the word *model* in finance:

- **A fundamental model.** A system of postulates and data, together with a means of drawing dynamical inferences from them
- **A phenomenological model.** A description or analogy to help visualize something that cannot be directly observed
- **A statistical model.** A regression or best-fit between different data sets

Most common financial models fall predominantly into one of these categories.

Fundamental models cover models like the Black-Scholes theory in which a set of postulates about the evolution of stock prices, data about dividend yield and volatility, and a theory of dynamical hedging together allow the derivation of a differential equation for calculating options values. These are models that attempt to build a fundamental description of some instrument or phenomenon.

Phenomenological models are less fundamental and more expedient, but may be equally useful. For example, some simple bond option models treat the yield of the underlying bond as being normally distributed. This is a useful picture with a plausible feel to it. But it's only a toy, good in a limited range, and not as deep or insightful a description as the Black-Scholes model. The first two classes of models embody some sort of cause and effect. The last class, statistical models, relies on correlation rather than causation. Users of these models probably hope that the correlation is a consequence of some dynamics whose detailed modeling they are avoiding or postponing. An example is a mortgage prepayment model that regresses prepayment rates against various long- and short-term interest rates and mortgage lifetimes. Modelers imagine homeowners performing certain cost-benefit analyses in deciding whether and when to prepay. Strictly, statistical models describe tendencies rather than dynamics. But knowing tendencies, if they really exist and persist, can be valuable.

SOME FACTS ABOUT MODELS

Models Assume Cause and Effect

When you build a valuation model of any type, you are implicitly assuming that the objects of your concern are causally related to each other and that the relationship is stable, at least for the time that you intend to apply the model.

Financial Models' Variables May Be People's Opinions

In the physical sciences where quantitative modeling originated, the variables in models are universal quantities like time, position, and mass that (presumptively) have an existence even when human beings are absent. In contrast, in the financial world, you are dealing with variables that clearly represent human expectations. Even the simplest statement "more risk, more return" refers to *expected* risk and return, not realized quantities. These are hidden variables: They cannot be directly observed except perhaps by surveying market participants or by implying their values insofar as they impact other measurable quantities by way of a theory or model. Thus, models that use concepts like return or volatility are in most cases assuming a causal and stable connection between the values of these hidden (often unarticulated) variables and security values. You can start to see how many links there are in the chain from model to usage.

Models Translate Opinions into Values

Model users don't just switch on a model and trade according to its results. Having a valuation model doesn't absolve the model user from thinking about the value of a security. Instead, it makes the security value a dependent variable, and requires the user to think about and estimate the values of other independent variables that are easier to grasp and quantify. Mostly, a security valuation model is a way of translating one's thoughts and intuitions about these other variables into a dollar value for the security. For example, the Black-Scholes options valuation model asks a user for an estimate of future volatility and then translates that estimate into a fair option value. Variations in volatility are much smoother and less dramatic than variations in option value. In this way, good models make it easier to extrapolate security values known under a limited range of market conditions to more distant regimes.

Uncertainty Is Fundamental

The overwhelming unknown in financial models is certainty. In the physical sciences, the mathematics of statistics and distributions and, finally, the calculus of stochastic processes made their appearance late in the drama. In the financial world, they are the first actors on stage. Everyone expects to predict the position of a man-made satellite, let alone Newton's falling apple, with high precision. No one expects to predict the value of a stock in the future with much precision at all.

Models Need Domain Knowledge

The financial domain is a nitty-gritty world filled with stocks that trade only at certain times with discrete ticks. Usable models exist for some particular sector with particular trading rules, settlement conventions, and other practicalities. Models and modelers need intimate knowledge of the domain they are working in. Financial modeling is as much about content as it is about technical skills.

Financial Models Are Software

Financial models most often end up being implemented as computer programs because they need to do many simple things rapidly and repeatedly, they need to draw on large amounts of stored information, or no simple analytic solution to the mathematics is available so numerical techniques are required. In addition, much of the gain from using models comes from applying them to portfolios of securities. The handling of portfolios on a computer requires the construction of databases, user interfaces, and price feeds. So, both the model itself and the mechanism for employing it involve building software.

A Model Is Only a Model . . .

The real world is often an inchoate swirl of actions, occurrences, facts, and figures. There are more things than we've even thought of naming or categorizing. So, even the finest model is only a model of the phenomena, not the real thing. A model is just a toy, though occasionally a very good one, in which case people call it a theory. A good scientific toy can't do everything and shouldn't even try to be totally realistic. It should represent as naturally as possible the most essential variables of the system and the relationships between them, and allow the investigation of cause and effect. A good toy doesn't reproduce every feature of the real object; instead, it illustrates for its intended audience the qualities of the original object most important to them. A child's toy train makes noises and flashes lights; an adult's might contain a working miniature steam engine. Similarly, good models should aim to do only a few important things well.

CONSTRUCTING MODELS

You can understand the things that go wrong with models if you understand how they are developed. Model building is as much art and apprenticeship as it is engineering and science. Nevertheless, it's possible to delineate some of the procedures involved in constructing a financial valuation model:

- Understand the securities, the markets, and the way market participants think about valuation and risk factors.
- Isolate the most important variables that participants use to analyze value and risk.
- Decide which of these variables are susceptible to mathematical modeling.
- Separate the dependent variables from the independent variables. Also decide which are directly measurable and which are more in the nature of human expectations, and therefore only indirectly measurable.
- For some variables, the uncertainty in their future value has little effect on security values,[3] and they can be treated as known to a good approximation. For other variables, uncertainty is critical. Specify the variables that can be treated as deterministic and those that must be regarded as stochastic.
- Develop a qualitative picture that represents how the independent variables affect the dependent ones.
- Think about how to get the market values of independent observable variables and how to deduce the implied values of indirectly measurable ones.
- Formulate the picture mathematically. Decide what stochastic process best describes the evolution of the independent stochastic variables.
- Consider the difficulties of solving the model and then perhaps simplify it to make the solution as easy as possible. But only reluctantly give up content for the sake of an easy or elegant analytical solution.

- Develop a scheme for an analytic or numerical solution.
- Program the model.
- Test it.
- Embed it in the software and human environment.

THE TYPES OF MODEL RISK

Inapplicability of Modeling

The most fundamental part of risks is that modeling is just not applicable. For example, it's possible that forecasting stock price movements is more like forecasting political occurrences than like projecting spacecraft trajectories. Psychology and gamesmanship are more relevant than mathematics. There's always a temptation to think that complex mathematics has an applicability of its own, but you need a vision of how things work and interconnect before you use mathematics to represent it. You need the analogy or picture first; mathematics is largely the language you represent it in. In terms of risk control, you're worse off thinking you have a model and relying on it than simply realizing there isn't one.

Incorrect Model

At some level, all models are ultimately incorrect. But even without being a perfectionist, the following are some of the ways in which model development can go wrong:

- You may not have taken into account all the factors that affect valuation. For example, you may have assumed a one-factor model of interest rates. This is probably a reasonable approximation for valuing Treasury bonds, but much less reasonable for valuing options on the slope of the yield curve.
- You may have incorrectly assumed that certain stochastic variables can be approximated as deterministic.
- You may have assumed incorrect dynamics for a factor. For example, you might have modeled bond *prices* as normally distributed for the sake of analytic simplicity. In practice, bond *yields* are more likely to be lognormal. This discrepancy is worse for short maturities, but may be forgivable for long maturities.

- You may have made incorrect assumptions about relationships. For example, you may have ignored the correlation between corporate credit spreads and corporate stock prices in valuing convertible bonds. Is this correlation important for the particular property of convertible bonds you are interested in extracting from your model?
- The model you developed may be inappropriate under current market conditions, or some of its assumptions may have become invalid. For example, interest rate volatility is relatively unimportant in currency option pricing at low interest rate volatilities, but may become critical during exchange rate crises.
- A model may be correct in an idealized world (with no trading costs, for example), but incorrect or approximate when realities (like market frictions) are taken into account.
- A model may be correct in principle, but the market may disagree in the short run. This is really another way of saying the model is limited in the sense that it didn't take other short-term factors into account (including market sentiment), that can influence price.
- A model may be correct, but the data driving it (rates, volatilities, correlations, spreads, and so on) may be badly estimated.
- A model may be reasonable, but the world itself may be unstable. A good model today may be inappropriate tomorrow. For example, the sentiment about interest rates may be linked to gold prices one year and to oil prices the next.

Correct Model, Incorrect Solution

You can make a technical mistake in finding the analytic solution to a model. This can happen through subtlety or carelessness. There are some well-known published errors or misunderstandings in the case of some complex derivatives, leading to so-called model arbitrage. It takes careful testing to ensure that an analytic solution behaves consistently for all reasonable market parameters.

Correct Model, Inappropriate Use

There are always implicit assumptions behind a model and its solution method. But human beings have limited foresight and a great imagination, so that, inevitably, a model will be used in ways its creator never intended. This is especially true in trading environments, where not enough time can be spent on making interfaces fail-safe, but it's also a matter of principle: You just cannot foresee everything. So, even a correct model, correctly solved, can lead to problems. The more complex the model, the greater this possibility.

As an example, most Monte Carlo valuation models require the choice of a number of simulation paths and steps. Speed requires few simulations, whereas accuracy demands many. Different securities require different simulation parameters to get a reasonable answer. A user who values a high-variance security with the same parameters as a low-variance security can get inaccurate and even biased results.

The only practical defense is to have informed and patient users who clearly comprehend both the model and method of the solution and, even more important, understand what can go wrong. In the previous example, one should start by valuing the security with a variety of simulation parameters, and perhaps more than one solution method, to examine the accuracy and convergence of the results.[4]

You may have errors in the numerical solution to a correctly formulated problem, or there may simply be natural limits to the accuracy of some approximation scheme. Finite difference solution methods can be unstable, inaccurate, or converge slowly. Only careful and knowledgeable testing can help here.

Many of the worst risks center on implementation. These days, models are sophisticated programs that are thousands of lines long with rich data structures that are used to perform detailed computation. Models undergo revisions by people who were not the original authors. Equally important in making them useful, models need user interfaces, position databases, trade entry screens, and electronic price feeds.

Programming mistakes in any of these areas can lead to widespread and hard-to-detect errors. You can make errors in logic, rounding, or counting the days between dates or the coupons to maturity to name only a few possibilities. In addition, there are occasional hardware flaws, such as the widely publicized Pentium floating point error.

Similarly, as programmers strive for greater execution speed, the model is at risk from the natural tension between clarity of style and code optimization.

Many models need the future value of some volatility or correlation. This value is often based on historical data. But history may not provide a good estimate of future value, and historical values may be unstable and vary strongly with the sampling period.

AVOIDING MODEL RISK

Regard Models as Interdisciplinary Endeavors

There is no magic strategy for avoiding risk, but the following general guidelines based on experience in our group at Goldman Sachs may be helpful.

Models are generally not back-of-the-envelope formulas handed over to coders to turn into executable instructions. Modeling is multidisciplinary: It touches on the practicality of doing business, financial theory, mathematical modeling and computer science, computer implementation, and the construction of user interfaces. Models end up as computational computer programs embedded in human and machine interfaces that are themselves computer programs. The risks lie in the knowledge of the business, the applicability of the financial model, the mathematics and numerical analysis used to solve it, the computer science used to implement and present it, and in the transmission of information and knowledge accurately from one part of the model, in the larger sense of the word, to the next. It helps to be knowledgeable in all of these areas in order to notice an error and then diagnose it.

But, in many firms, model users are traders, salespeople, or capital market personnel who may be physically and organizationally removed from the model creators. Furthermore, the model implementors are programmers who are often similarly separated from the model theorists. To avoid risk, it's important to have modelers, programmers, and users who all work closely together, understand each other's domains well enough to know what constitutes a warning symptom, and have a good strategy for testing a model and its limits. Too much specialization is harmful. In our group, the modelers themselves write production code for insertion into risk-management systems. Programmers and modelers work in closely knit teams around a particular product or business area. Informed model users are particularly invaluable. Because of the large role of computing, we also try to accentuate the importance of software engineering as a discipline.

Test Complex Models in Simple Cases First

Test models against simple known solutions. If you can solve a model in some simple case, by constructing a tree diagram or solving some equation, compare your computer solution to the simple solution and make sure they're identical.

Test the Model's Boundaries

Often, a new model overlaps on older and simpler models. In that case, test the boundaries. If it's an option model, make sure that when the option is deep in the money it behaves like a forward. For a convertible bond model, guarantee that it behaves like a straight bond when it's deep out of the money. Too many complex models go wrong because complexity obscured the error in the simple part of the model. One of the most avoidable mistakes I saw was a convertible bond model that innovatively priced many of the options features embedded in convertible bonds, but sometimes counted the number of coupons to expiration incorrectly.

Don't Ignore Small Discrepancies

If there are any small discrepancies noticed by users or programmers, don't ignore them. Track down their origin. Small disagreements often serve as warnings of potentially large disagreements and errors under other scenarios.

Provide a Good User Interface

Thorough testing is easier with a flexible and friendly interface. We spend much time building interfaces that allow a what-if analysis and graphical display of the results of a model under many different scenarios. Even after many years of use, some errors only become apparent when you notice kinks in a graphical display of the model's results.

Diffuse the Model Slowly Outwards

It is impossible to avoid errors during model development, especially when they are created under trading floor duress. Therefore, in addition to being careful, it's important to have an orderly procedure for disseminating the use of a model. So, after the model is built, the developer tests it extensively. Thereafter, other developers play with it too. Next, traders who depend on the model for pricing and hedging use it. Finally, it's released to salespeople. After a suitably long period during which most wrinkles are ironed out, it's given to appropriate clients. This slow diffusion helps eliminate many risks, slowly but steadily.

Pride of Ownership

One of the best defenses against modeling error is to ensure that both models and systems are built by people who like doing it and who take pride in their work.

The following is a speculation about the imperfect science of financial modeling. When I started working on Wall Street, I simply assumed it made good sense to apply the techniques of physics and applied mathematics to financial modeling. Differential calculus, partial differential equations, Fourier series, Monte Carlo calculation, and stochastic calculus—all these tools for describing continuous motion—seemed also unquestionably useful for describing the movements of markets and stocks, yield curves, and volatilities. In particle physics, the field from which I came, these methods and the axioms they were applied to had triumphed. There, people with a penchant for overly cute names dreamed of grand unified theories (GUTs) and even theories of everything (TOEs).

It was Einstein who brought to fruition this mental approach to discovering the laws of the universe, transforming into a methodology the almost unbelievable insights that lay behind Newton's mechanics and Maxwell's electromagnetics. Einstein's method wasn't based on observation or empiricism; he simply tried to perceive and then enunciate the very principles that dictated the way things should work. His theories were almost metatheories—rules about the allowed forms that, once adopted, would almost strip the theorist of any subsequent choice. In a speech on the principles of research given in honor of Max Planck, the discoverer of the quantum, in 1918, Einstein said, "There is no logical path to these laws; only intuition, resting on sympathetic understanding of experience, can reach them." In this way, he discovered special and general relativity, as well as many aspects of the quantum nature of matter. (If you want to get an entertaining feel for the persistent struggle for vision behind Einstein's work, take a look at Dennis Overbye's recent biography, *Einstein in Love*, [New York: Viking Press, 2000].)

Looking at the motion of yield curves in the mid-1980s, I at first saw no reason why financial theorists shouldn't shoot for their TOE too. Why shouldn't there be one model that described all interest rate motions, producing one set of rational market prices for all interest-rate-sensitive instruments? If you'd asked me in 1986 what yield-curve theories would look like in 2000, I would have imagined everyone using one theory for valuing all instruments from bond options through caps and swaptions to mortgages. Despite my naive idealism, I nevertheless knew that you shouldn't expect the sort of accuracy in finance that you obtain in rocketry or hydrodynamics, let alone in the atomic physics of electromagnetic radiation.

I wasn't alone in expecting the financial world to be deeply amenable to theory. Recently, I met again, for the first time in 13 years, someone who was an analyst with an undergraduate degree at Goldman Sachs in 1985 and is now a professor of finance. He told me that he chose to study for a Ph.D. in finance because he expected it to become the physics of the late twentieth century. Fifteen years on, I say without regret that things aren't the way I had expected. There is no unified theory. Interest rate trading desks are pragmatic and typically use a variety of models—one for bond options, perhaps another for caps, one for swaptions, and often a totally different one for the Bermudan variety. Of course, the desks try to calibrate all their models consistently, but there's no really grand attempt at comprehensiveness.

Some of this willingness to compromise stems from the need for computational speed, but even with infinitely fast computers, I doubt that there would be an ultimate model on the horizon. So-called market models derive simple valuation formulas for complex derivatives by the trickery of conveniently choosing as a currency unit whatever traded instrument makes the payoff for each complex derivative look simple. This makes any single complex product easy to value, but veils the complexity of the relationship between different products. Using all these models at once is a bit like living in Manhattan and telling someone about a forthcoming trip: "It's a $40 cab ride to Kennedy, then a 6-hour flight to L.A., and finally a 100-mile drive to Palm Springs." You've used three different distance metrics—dollars, hours, and miles—but it's not hard to relate them to each other if you know geography. The geography of currency volatilities, however, is less simple.

So why is it that the techniques of physics and applied mathematics hardly ever give you more than the most approximate version of the truth about financial values?

In the end, there may be no absolute truth about financial values. In my experience, most finance practitioners raised in the tradition of the physical sciences don't expect too much from financial theory. It's not that physics is better; rather, finance seems to be harder. Paul Wilmott, in his textbook *Derivatives*, (New York: John Wiley and Sons, 1998), writes that "every financial axiom I've ever seen is demonstrably wrong—The real question is *how* wrong is the theory and how useful is it regardless of its validity. Everything you read in any theoretical finance book, including this one, you must take with a generous pinch of salt." I couldn't agree more. In fact, the very title of Wilmott's latest book, *Wilmott on Derivatives*, aptly illustrates his point. The "Wilmott" in *Wilmott on Derivatives* lends a touch of authority to the exposition of the subject, but in so doing, it implies a deficiency of authority in the subject matter itself. Imagine a 1918 textbook called *Einstein on Gravitation*. Unlike finance, the theory of gravitation gets its weight from the ineluctability of its internal arguments and its accounting for previously inexplicable subtleties, and needs no Einstein to lend it gravitas.

So why do the methods of hard science work less well in finance? One possible answer is that, in physics, once you know the dynamics, the parameter values are universal. No one disagrees significantly about the value of the gravitational constant or the mass of the earth you must use to calculate a satellite trajectory. Ignoring quantum mechanics, your accuracy is limited in practice by how well you know these values and, of course, how well you've taken account of all other known influences. But in finance, to calculate the fair value of a stock, the parameters you need are the *expected* dividends; to calculate the value of an option, you need the *expected* volatility. Science uses theory to move from the known to unknown. Finance uses theory to move from one expectation to another.

When you propose a model or theory, you're saying "Let's pretend . . . " and then you see what happens as you work out the consequences. But what are you pretending about? When you propose a model of the physical world, you're pretending you can guess the structure God created. It sounds a plausible thing to do; every physicist believes he or she has a small chance of guessing right, otherwise he or she wouldn't be in the field. But when you propose a financial model, you're pretending you can guess another person's mind. When you try out a simple yield-curve model, you're saying, "Let's pretend that people care only about future short rates and that they think they're distributed lognormally." As you say that to yourself, if you're honest, your heart sinks. You know immediately that there is no chance you are truly right. To pretend you can figure out God's intention doesn't sound preposterous. To pretend you can figure out a person's does. Perhaps it's because God doesn't pretend, so when you tackle nature, you're the only one doing the pretending. When you tackle people, you're pretending you can figure out another pretender.

I find myself relying on a critical difference between people and nature as an explanation of the inadequacies of financial theory. But aren't people part of nature too? Erwin Schrodinger, the unconventional father of the wave equation in quantum mechanics, wrote a short summary of his personal views on determinism and free will in the epilogue to *What Is Life?* (Cambridge: Cambridge University Press, 1992), his influential lectures on the physicochemical basis of living matter. "My body functions as a pure mechanism according the Laws of Nature," he wrote. "Yet I know, by incontrovertible direct experience, that I am directing its motions, of which I foresee the effects, that may be fateful and all-important, in which case I feel and take full responsibility for them." The only way he could reconcile these two apparently contradictory experiences—his deep belief in the susceptibility of nature to human theorizing and his equally firm sense the individual autonomy that must lie beneath any attempt to theorize—was to infer that "every conscious mind that has ever said or felt 'I' . . . is the person, if any, who controls the 'motion of the atoms' according to the Laws of Nature." Schrodinger was following a long line of earlier German philosophers who thought that all the various worldly voices referring to themselves in conversation as "I" were not really referring to independent I's, but to the same universal I—God or nature. It's a comforting notion. But it still doesn't explain why, if all the I's add up to God, it's so much harder to predict the world of I's than the world of God.

NOTES

[1] Or ex-scientists, depending on your opinion about what they do.

[2] This is not as unprecedented as it sounds. Money itself is a derivative that gets its value from its convertibility into more consumable assets.

[3] For example, in valuing stock options, the future uncertainty in interest rates is largely unimportant, because option value varies smoothly with rate so the uncertainty averages out. There is consequently no need to know the volatility of interest rates. This is not the case with bond options, whose pay-offs vary sharply and nonlinearly with interest rates.

[4] The following verbatim quote from someone building a model conveys a sense of the conflict involved in releasing it to users: "It's always a dilemma to release a [model] . . . If I do not release it, and tell people to contact me to price . . . options . . . people think I am holding back. When I tell people they should be very careful in choosing methods and parameters, they always say, 'I know, I know' and get a little impatient. I guess one just has to put some trust in those people who use them."

REFERENCES

Derman, Emanuel, Piotr Karasinski, and Jeffrey S. Wecker. "Understanding Guaranteed Exchange-Rate Contracts in Foreign Stock Investments." (June 1990).
Derman, Emanuel, Alex Bergier, and Iraj Kani. "Valuing Index Options When Markets Can Jump." (July 1991).
Derman, Emanuel. "Valuing and Hedging Outperformance Options." (January 1992).
Derman, Emanuel and Iraj Kani. "The Ins and Outs of Barrier Options." (June 1993).
————. "The Volatility Smile and Its Implied Tree." (January 1994).
Derman, Emanuel, Deniz Ergener, and Iraj Kani. "Static Options Replication." (May 1994).
Derman, Emanuel, Deniz Ergerer, Iraj Kani, and Indrajit Bardhan. "Enhanced Numerical Methods for Options with Barriers." (May 1995).
Derman, Emanuel, Iraj Kani, and Joseph Z. Zou. "The Local Volatility Surface: Unlocking the Information in Index Option Prices." (December 1995).

CHAPTER 10

Technology and the Capital Markets

Ben Warwick

This chapter discusses the behaviorally based risks associated with identifying pricing anomalies, such as curve fitting, anchoring, and other cognitive illusions. It also examines the problems inherent in trading market inefficiencies. The author then explains his belief that Value at Risk (VaR) is vastly inferior to multifactor attribution analysis in measuring the risk of an investment portfolio.

There can be few fields of human endeavor in which history counts for so little as in the world of finance.—John Kenneth Galbraith

The business of U.S. oil production was changed single-handedly by a one-armed mechanic from Southern Texas named Patillo Higgins. The year was 1889, and Higgins became interested in a hill that rose above the flat coastal plain near Beaumont after taking his Baptist Sunday school class there for a picnic. Higgins had discovered half a dozen small bubbling springs and lit the gas that escaped from them. The children were quite amused; Higgins was intrigued. The hill was called Spindletop, and Higgins became convinced that an abundance of cheap oil lay beneath it.[1]

Higgins commenced drilling in 1893. He had no success at this first attempt. He also failed to find oil in later efforts in 1895 and 1896. Although Higgins had promised his partners that they would become rich, they began to lose faith in the project. Higgins became jokingly referred to as "the Millionaire."

Reprinted from *Searching for Alpha: The Quest for Exceptional Investment Performance* (New York: John Wiley & Sons, 2000), 145–158. Copyright © 2000 by John Wiley & Sons. All rights reserved.

In spite of his difficulties, Higgins never lost faith in his vision. He eventually convinced a mining engineer named Anthony Lucas, who had considerable experience prospecting in salt domes like Spindletop, of the potential of the region. Lucas felt that the area could yield a well with a production of 50 barrels per day. They hired Guffy and Galey, the most famous and successful wildcatting team of that era, and commenced operations in the fall of 1900. On January 10, 1901, while attempting to free their drill from a rock formation, the famous Lucas Gusher blew. Oil sprayed over a hundred feet above the derrick for 9 days until the well was capped. The actual production of the well was an astounding 80,000 barrels per day. It was the beginning of the Texas oil boom.

Higgins' experience is similar in many ways to that of Richard Olsen, who assembled a team of physicists and statisticians to study tick-by-tick data from financial markets. Conventional wisdom held that trading information of that detail was useless noise. But in the last few years, economic orthodoxy has embraced Olsen's view. "Academics as well as traders recognize that potentially lucrative information is embedded in the seemingly chaotic movements of prices from moment to moment," according to a 1997 article in *Business Week*.[2] Market microstructure is now one of the most active research areas in finance.

But like oil reserves, which naturally decline as oil fields are drained, market inefficiencies dry up as more traders enter the fray. Just one year after Higgins' discovery, there were 285 active wells operating at Spindletop. Similarly, there are more active investment management firms than ever before. Participants in both of these businesses have realized that with increased competition, developing a strategic advantage is of paramount importance.

Both the oil industry and the investment management business have embraced technology to develop an edge in the marketplace. Computer power has roughly doubled every 18 months—a prediction made in 1974 by Intel founder Gordon Moore that has been amazingly accurate. Instead of relying on gut instinct like Mr. Higgins, petroleum conglomerates are now using three-dimensional seismic imaging and microbial soil analysis to determine where hidden caches of oil may lie. The high cost of these new tools and the steadily declining amount of oil left to be found have made the oil business quite competitive. As a result, only the most highly capitalized firms have been able to maintain exploration facilities.

David Shaw, a former computer science professor turned investment manager, stated that when his firm was founded in the early 1980s, there were a number of easily identifiable market inefficiencies that could be exploited. The profits earned from this trading could be used to subsidize the costly research required to find more esoteric market eccentricities.

According to Shaw, increased competition has caused many strategies that used to work to disappear. He has stated that his firm has spent hundreds of millions of dollars in research.[3] There is no question that technology plays an important role in investment management, but an over-reliance on computers in the development of a sustainable advantage can introduce several problems.

The first is the danger of *curvefitting*. Computers may unleash new investment opportunities, but sometimes they foster the illusion that a false methodology has merit. If enough trading rules are considered over time, some rules are bound by pure luck to produce superior performance even if they do not genuinely possess predictive power over asset returns. For instance, David Leinweber, managing director of First Quadrant Associates L.P., sifted through a U.N. database and found that the single best predictor of the S&P 500 stock index was butter production in Bangladesh.[4] But most of the time, distinguishing between a statistical anomaly and a tradable inefficiency is not as easy as the previous example would indicate.

To make matters worse, many psychologists believe that the human brain has a strong tendency to make errors in judgment. One of the most persistent areas of illusion is a tendency toward overconfidence. Many studies have shown that when asked questions that require considerable reasoning to solve, the level of accuracy increases with the respondent's intelligence. But the degree of confidence in the validity of those answers increases to a much greater degree. Overconfidence is at its greatest in our own area of expertise—just when it can do the most damage. Cognitive illusions, according to researchers Amos Tversky and Daniel Kahneman, are "neither rational nor capricious."[5]

Another frequently encountered perceptual flaw is known as *anchoring*. A classic experiment consists of asking a subject to state the percentage of African nations in the United Nations. Before asking the question, the researcher turns a wheel of fortune in full view of the subject, stopping it on some number between 1 and 100. The researcher frequently tells the subject that the number of the wheel has absolutely no relation to the question, but invariably the number has a strong effect on the answer given by the respondent. If the number 12 comes up, for example, the answer is likely to be smaller than if the wheel stops on 90.[6] The subjects unconsciously anchored their responses to the randomly selected number.

Propagandists frequently use anchoring in altering societal opinion. During the Gulf War, the Bush Administration followed bulletins of allied air attacks with extremely low estimates of civilian Iraqi casualties (their announcement varied from 2 to 10 deaths per incident). Their intent was to prevent public opinion from swaying away from President Bush's imperative against Saddam Hussein. Pentagon officials were betting that even the most skeptical observers would anchor their mental adjustments close to the original estimate.[7] Only after hostilities ended did the real figures surface (actual numbers were in the tens of thousands), but by then public opinion was of little consequence.

Anchoring and curvefitting often go hand in hand. Because securities price changes have a tendency to exhibit more extreme outliers than one would expect, traditional statistical techniques are often not usable in market analysis. The remaining nonparametric statistical tools are much more inferential in nature—meaning that the results must be interpreted. If the results of such a study are in conflict with the analyst's first impressions, he or she may struggle to overcome his or her original hypothesis. The analyst may (either consciously or unconsciously) incorporate as many constraints in his or her research as possible to prove his or her first impression. In this case, anchoring is given full backing by pride and self-satisfaction.

An over-reliance on technology also fosters a mistaken belief that a commitment to employing the most powerful computers will give an individual a distinct advantage over his or her competitors. In reality, such a commitment will only reduce the possibility that one is not left behind by the competition. The profits associated with money management are high enough that an investment firm's search for a performance edge is rarely constrained by a lack of technology. As a result, nearly all investment managers have proportionately large research and development budgets. And when a number of these firms begin to operate in the same markets with similar strategies, the degree of market efficiency can rise dramatically.

Andrew Lo and A. Craig MacKinley put a unique spin on this issue in their book *A Non-Random Walk Down Wall Street*. When they began examining stock price changes in 1985, they were shocked to find a substantial degree of autocorrelative behavior—evidence that previous price changes could have been used to forecast changes in the next period. Their findings were sufficiently overwhelming to refute the Random Walk Hypothesis, which states that asset price changes are totally unpredictable.

The most important insight from their work occurred when they repeated the study 11 years later, using prices from 1986 to 1996. This newer data conformed more closely with the random walk model than the original sample period. Upon further investigation, they learned that over the past decade several investment firms—most notably Morgan Stanley and D.E. Shaw—were engaged in a type of stock trading specifically designed to take advantage of the kinds of patterns uncovered in their earlier study. Known at the time as *pairs trading*—and now referred to as *statistical arbitrage*—these strategies fared quite well until recently; they are now regarded as a very competitive and thin-margin business because of the proliferation of hedge funds engaged in this type of market activity.[8]

Lo and MacKinley believe that the profits earned by the early statistical arbitrageurs can be viewed as economic rents that accrued via their innovation, creativity, and risk tolerance. Now that others have begun to reverse-engineer and mimic their methodologies, profit margins are declining. Therefore, neither the evidence against the random walk, nor the more recent trend toward the random walk, are inconsistent with the practical version of the Efficient Market Hypothesis (EMH).[9] In short, market inefficiencies are not always market opportunities.

Due to the growing sophistication of market participants and increasing efficiency of markets, the investment management business has become a game in which success is measured by a painfully small margin of 1 to 2 percent per year. A combination of frustration and bafflement has led many money managers to place a higher priority on the numerous approaches to risk management than on the urgent search for maximum return. Many seem to be thinking, "Maybe I can't score a higher return than the competition, but perhaps I can make the same return with lower risk."

Value at Risk (VaR) is Wall Street's latest salvo in the attempt to quantify risk. Simply defined, VaR is an estimate of maximum potential loss to be expected over a chosen timeframe. Its primary appeal is its ease of interpretation as a summary measure of risk, as well as its consistent treatment of risk across different financial instruments and asset classes. By describing risk using a possible percentage loss (that is, "returns in the next month should not exceed 5 percent with 95 percent confidence"), VaR facilitates direct comparisons of risk across different portfolios. But most importantly, the methodology boils risk down to one simple number that can be quickly calculated and easily digested by senior management.

Financial innovation often precedes a problem that has caused firms to lose substantial amounts of capital. VaR is no exception to this rule. The early 1990s were rife with one derivatives trading scandal after another. Daiwa Bank, NatWest, and Metallgesellschaft were but a few of the many financial companies, banks, and brokerages that were rocketed by losses. But none were as big, or as shocking, as the losses experienced by Barings Bank, the veritable 233-year-old institution that proudly counted Queen Elizabeth as a client.

The incident occurred in the bank's Singapore office. The trader responsible for supervising the bank's Japanese stock-index arbitrage operation, Nick Leeson, apparently grew tired of the strategy's muted returns and began making massive directional bets in the Nikkei stock index futures market. A working-class barrow boy who grew up in a rundown public housing project in London, Leeson stood to make a huge bonus if his bets were successful.

Unbeknownst to his superiors, Leeson was running a shell game, secretly hiding losses in a special ledger that he also controlled because Barings, in a cost-cutting move, allowed him to act as both trader and back-office settlement manager. Leeson kept up the charade for more than 2 years while earning over \$1 million annually in wages and bonuses.[10] Ultimately, the trading losses exceeded the capitalization of the company, and the oldest Bank in London was purchased for £1 by Dutch ING Bank.

The Barings incident points to clear failures in the supervision of the company's activities by its senior management. Apparently, few of the bank's managers questioned the huge reported profits that were the result of a relatively low-risk arbitrage strategy. Simple common sense might have suggested that the reported results from Singapore were implausible. Yet the bank continued pledging collateral for the operation until its demise.

Ironically, if Barings would have implemented a VaR system, it might not have prevented the collapse of the bank. Since VaR only monitors market risk, it cannot adequately reflect the risks associated with a liquidity crisis or with unsupervised personnel. The inability to capture many qualitative factors and exogenous risk variables points to the need to combine VaR with checks and balances, procedures, policies, controls, limits, and reserves.[11]

One of the positive attributes of VaR is its effect on bank compensation plans. The use of VaR has encouraged banks to evaluate their proprietary traders not only by the profit they make, but also by the risk that they are exposed to. Before VaR, it was a common practice among banks to remunerate traders simply by their contribution to the banks' earnings, with no regard to potential losses. These traders might rationally believe that it is better for them to take extremely large risks to make a larger bonus, if the downside to such a gamble is merely the loss of employment. For employers, it introduces a problem that is referred to as a *moral hazard*. Another example of a moral hazard is a driver who disregards a stoplight, knowing that if he or she crashes, the insurance company will buy him or her a new vehicle.

Despite its misgivings, VaR is rapidly gaining acceptance in many large corporations. Indeed, if financial institutions are required to disclose their VaR risk profiles, regulators can more effectively calculate the capital adequacy an organization must hold in order to prevent default. VaR also enables firms to determine which businesses offer the greatest expected returns at the least level of risk. Considering the increasing acceptance of the VaR methodology, it is easy to understand why fiduciaries have tried to adopt the technology to the world of investment management. Unfortunately, the goals of risk management in banking and investing are quite different.

The first and foremost goal of risk management in banks is to avoid catastrophic losses. Banks must strive to give the appearance of being conservatively managed and insulated from financial shocks so that they can protect the bank's capital position and its core business, which is serving as a source of credit and liquidity in all market conditions.[12] Most banks operate their risk management units autonomously, which separates it from the various profit centers that it monitors.

In contrast to bankers, investment managers are charged with the responsibility of delivering performance above a stated benchmark. Further, alpha generation should be earned by taking reasonable risks, so that client accounts are not exposed to unnecessary peril during periods of market turmoil. It is not enough for investment managers to avoid large losses. They must constantly monitor the rate at which risk is taken and profits are accrued, even during normal market conditions. For this reason, the risk management function within an investment firm is usually fully integrated into the research and portfolio construction departments.

Bank risk managers are focused on the type of catastrophic risk that will compromise their asset base enough to force the bank out of business. There is little pressure on banks to increase their return on assets, which average slightly over 1 percent, because fees and commission income has become an increasingly large percentage of their revenues. Risk managers in the banking world are encouraged to use conservative risk estimates that are upwardly biased. The Bank of International Settlements, which formed a set of regulatory guidelines for banks in the Group of Ten countries, recommends multiplying potential market risks by a factor of three. Many banks follow this guideline. A risk manager in a bank will not get fired for overestimating risk.

For investment management, there is a serious cost to the overestimation of risk. If the risk level is incremented upwards to be conservative, the ability for the manager to generate alpha is handicapped. By artificially constraining the amount of risk inherent in a portfolio, the threat of consistent underperformance is introduced.[13]

Investment managers who are considering utilizing a VaR system (or have been asked by a large client to do so) should pay attention to the method's sensitivity to changes in the variables used. Most of these variables are calculated using assumptions about the correlation between markets, the distribution of returns, and the amount of historical data used. A recent study examined 8 common VaR methodologies and found that the results varied by more than 14 times for the same portfolio.[14]

A valuable perspective on the issue of risk management for alpha managers can be gained by considering the objectives of their investors. Over the years, most sophisticated investors have realized that asset allocation is the most critical factor in determining portfolio performance. Studies have shown that this decision accounts for as much as 90 percent of the return of a portfolio. Most of the time, large investors have determined their asset mix (say, 60 percent stocks and 40 percent bonds) before they consider the less important decision of which individual investment managers will be used to capture these returns.

By settling on an appropriate asset allocation, investors have accepted the risk associated with their chosen benchmarks. What investors are demanding, and what the active managers should be trying to deliver, is a superior risk-adjusted return above their given benchmark. So, for the investment manager, the biggest risk is either achieving returns inferior to their benchmark or exposing the client to extraneous risk in the attempt to deliver benchmark returns.

Although neither of these issues is directly addressed by VaR, the tools needed to compare the risk and return attributes of an investment manager's portfolio relative to a benchmark have existed for over 50 years. Called *factor analysis*, the technique attempts to uncover common sources of variability in return data. Factor models have been used to predict portfolio behavior and, in conjunction with other types of analysis, to construct customized portfolios with certain desired characteristics, such as the ability to track the performance of an index.

For example, suppose that an investor was interested in understanding the performance difference between an actively managed mutual fund and the S&P 500 index. The investor has no information about the portfolio construction of either investment. Armed solely with the historical performance of the two investments and a database of economic data, the market sector sensitivities of the two portfolios can be compared.

Figure 10.1 shows that the actively managed portfolio has a larger exposure to financial, utility, and transportation stocks. In contrast, the S&P 500 index is weighted more in the technology, healthcare, and consumer products sectors. These sector-weighting differences account for more than 96 percent of the difference between the advisor's return and that of the index.

Factor analysis can be quite useful in determining the biases of investment managers. In this example, the actively managed portfolio is concentrated more on value stocks than growth stocks. This bias can either be conscious (the manager feels that value stocks will outperform) or unconscious (past experiences in the markets might be influencing his or her stock selection). Regardless of intent, the increased sensitivity that biased portfolios frequently exhibit to changes in the business cycle or increased inflationary pressures often becomes apparent only after the fact. Unless these exposures are realized and controlled, the possibility of an investment manager underperforming his or her benchmark during a difficult period is substantial.

In many respects, the history of American whale hunting closely parallels the development of the investment management business. The first organized whaling in the American colonies began in New York in 1640. Using

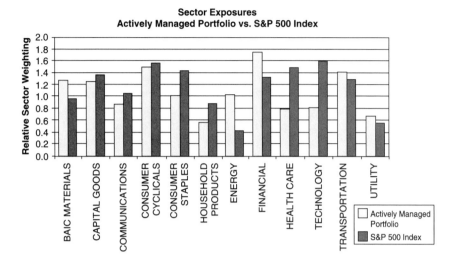

Source: *Journal of Portfolio Management* (November/December 1989): 9.

FIGURE 10.1　Sector exposures of actively managed portfolio versus S&P 500 index.

small rowboats, colonial whalemen speared the beasts in the shallow beaches of the Northeast and extracted whale oil by boiling the blubber in large cast-iron kettles called *trypots*.

As the number of whales near the shore inevitably declined, the colonists were forced to stalk their prey in deeper waters. Larger and more expensive boats had to be designed, and voyages ultimately lasted up to 2 years. Eventually, the whalemen were forced to go as far away as the Arctic Ocean for whales.

The decline of the whaling industry was almost exclusively a result of limited supply. Whales became so rare that the costs of finding them exceeded the revenues derived from selling whale oil and baleen. The last American whaling ships finally ceased operation in 1938.[15]

Does the business of alpha generation share the same fate as that of whaling? Will market inefficiencies become so difficult to find that research costs exceed revenues? Will alpha generation, like whaling, cease to be a viable business because of the lack of quarry?

Obviously, alpha generation has become more difficult with the passage of time. There is little doubt that investment skills have improved over the years, especially in the period since Harry Markowitz's seminal paper on risk and return. Yet when well-known investment consultant Peter Berstein studied the return of portfolio managers from 1970 to present, he found that alpha generation over time has dissipated dramatically. There are two possible reasons for this observation. The first (and most obvious) explanation is that market efficiency has increased significantly over the time period studied to the extent that is nearly impossible to generate excess return (see Figure 10.2).

The second and subtler rationale has to do with manager motivation. With the growing popularity of indexing, active managers have grown increasingly sensitive to tracking *error risk* (the risk of not achieving results comparable to a benchmark). The passion that institutional clients have with benchmarking has made large tracking errors extremely perilous for managers.[16] Thus, even if a manager was able to construct an optimized portfolio—one that had the best return at a given level of risk—he or she may not implement it if the characteristics of the portfolio differed significantly from his or her benchmark. If this hypothesis is true, then with managers having no incentive to maximize returns, alpha generation over a benchmark like the S&P 500 would fall over time even among the best managers.[17]

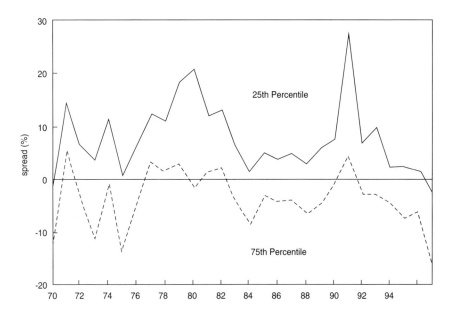

FIGURE 10.2 Vanishing edge.

In reality, both explanations hold some merit. If alpha generation is indeed getting more difficult, there are a number of steps investment managers can do to increase their likelihood of success. One of the most critical is to hold fast to a rigorous, defined method of hypothesis testing.

Science is based on two phenomena that every scientist agrees are true —externality and corroboration. Externality is the perception that knowledge exists that has not been discovered. It describes the motivation of the scientific endeavor—to add to the body of understanding about natural systems. Corroboration is the tendency of our perceptions to reflect our preconceived notions about the world. What we assume to be true appears to be true. The scientific method is designed to foil corroboration so that a researcher can see the world as it truly is—not merely how it appears to be.

A simplified version of the scientific method begins with simple market observation. A hypothesis is then formulated to explain what is causing the observation. The hypothesis must then be tested and the statistical significance of the results must be determined. If the results of the study are not conclusive, the hypothesis needs to be revised, the experiment was carried out incorrectly, or the analysis of the results was in error.

When applied to the social sciences like finance, the scientific method is path dependent. It is not enough to generate statistically pleasing results. If enough tests are performed, the odds favor that some false anomalies will be uncovered. For this reason, only those market inefficiencies that can be logically explained should be considered valid.

Although oil production and renewable resource are not words that often appear together, something mysterious seems to be occurring in the oil fields off the coast of Louisiana. During production at Eugene Island 330, a large discovery in 1973 peaked to 15,000 barrels per day, and in 1989 had slowed to less than 4,000 barrels per day.

But suddenly—some would say almost inexplicably—Eugene Island's fortunes reversed. The field is now producing 13,000 barrels per day, and probable reserves have skyrocketed from 60 million barrels to over 400 million barrels. This puzzling phenomenon has led some scientists to a radical theory—that Eugene Island is rapidly refilling itself, perhaps from some continuous source miles below the earth's surface. This may indicate that oil may not be the limited resource it was assumed to be.[18]

Like all natural systems, the capital markets have a tendency to act in an unpredictable fashion. As long as occasionally irrational people are around to program computers, it is unlikely that technological advances will result in perfectly efficient markets. And as long as market anomalies exist, there will be smart people around to exploit them.

NOTES

[1]Daniel Yergin, *The Prize* (New York: Simon and Schuster, 1991), 82.

[2]Peter Coy, "Mining Profits from Microdata," *Business Week* (December 1, 1997).

[3]James Picerno, "Alarming Efficiency," *Institutional Investor* (May 6, 1999): 43–48.

[4]Ibid.

[5]Massimo Pitatelli-Palmarino, *Inevitable Illusions: How Mistakes of Reason Rule Our Minds* (New York: John Wiley & Sons, 1994).

[6]Ibid.

[7]Ibid.

[8]Picerno, "Alarming Efficiency," *Institutional Investor* (May 6, 1999): 43–48.

[9]Andrew Lo and A. Craig MacKinley, *A Non-Random Walk Down Wall Street* (Princeton, NJ: Princeton University Press, 1999), 186.

[10]"Billion Dollar Man," *Asia Week* (December 29, 1995): 17.

[11]Christopher Culp, Ron Mensink, and Andrea Neves, "Value at Risk for Asset Managers," *Derivatives Weekly* (1999).

[12]Bluford Putnam, "Risk Management for Banks and Funds Is Not the Same Game," *Global Investor* (September 1998).

[13]Bluford Putnam, "An Investment Paradigm for the New Millennium," *Global Investor* (November 1997).

[14]Tanya Beder, "VaR: Seductive But Dangerous," *Financial Analysts Journal* (September 10, 1995): 12–24.

[15]New Bedford Whaling Museum, The History of Whaling Web Site, (www.whalingmuseum.org), 1999.

[16]Peter Bernstein, "Where, Oh Where Are the .400 Hitters of Yesteryear?" *Financial Analysts Journal* (November 2, 1998): 6–14.

[17]Ibid.

[18]Christopher Cooper, "It's No Crude Joke: This Oil Field Grows Even as It's Tapped," *Wall Street Journal* (November 12, 1999): A1.

CHAPTER 11

Horizon Problems and Extreme Events in Financial Risk Management

Peter F. Christoffersen, Francis X. Diebold, and Til Schuermann

Central to the ongoing development of practical financial risk management methods is recognition of the fact that asset return volatility is often forecastable. Although there is no single horizon relevant for financial risk management, most would agree that in many situations the relevant horizon is quite long, certainly longer than a few days. This fact creates some tension because although short-horizon asset return volatility is clearly highly forecastable, much less is known about long-horizon volatility forecastability.

INTRODUCTION

There is no one magic relevant horizon for risk management. Instead, the relevant horizon will generally vary by asset class (such as equity versus bonds), industry (such as banking versus insurance), position in the firm (such as trading desk versus CFO), and motivation (such as private versus regulatory), among other things, and thought must be given to the relevant horizon on an application-by-application basis. But one thing is clear: In many risk management situations, the relevant horizons are long—certainly longer than just a few days—an insight incorporated, for example, in Bankers Trust's RAROC system, for which the horizon is 1 year.

Simultaneously, it is well known that short-horizon asset return volatility fluctuates and is highly forecastable, a phenomenon that is very much at

Prepared for *Federal Reserve Bank of New York Economic Policy Review* (1998).

the center of modem risk management paradigms. Much less is known, however, about the forecastability of long-horizon volatility, and the speed and pattern with which forecastability decays as the horizon lengthens. A key question arises: Is volatility forecastability important for long-horizon risk management, or is a traditional constant-volatility assumption adequate?

In this chapter we address this question, exploring the interface between long-horizon financial risk management and long-horizon volatility forecastability, and, in particular, whether long-horizon volatility is forecastable enough such that volatility models are useful for long-horizon risk management. We report on recent relevant work by Diebold, Hickman, Inoue, and Schuermann (1998), Christoffersen and Diebold (1997), and Diebold, Schuermann, and Stroughair (1998).

To assess long-horizon volatility forecastability, it is necessary to have a measure of long-horizon volatility, which can be obtained in a number of ways. We proceed in the section "Obtaining Long-Horizon Volatilities from Short-Horizon Volatilities: Scaling and Formal Aggregation by considering two ways of converting short-horizon volatility into long-horizon volatility: scaling and formal model-based aggregation. The defects of those procedures lead us to take a different approach in the section "Model-Free Assessment of Volatility Forecastability at Different Horizons, where we estimate volatility forecastability directly at the horizons of interest, without making assumptions about the nature of the volatility process, and arrive at a surprising conclusion: Volatility forecastability seems to decline quickly with horizon and seems to have largely vanished beyond horizons of 10 or 15 trading days.

If volatility forecastability is not important for risk management beyond horizons of 10 or 15 trading days, then what is important? The really big movements such as the U.S. crash of 1987 are still poorly understood, and ultimately the really big movements are the most important for risk management. This suggests the desirability of directly modeling the extreme tails of return densities, a task potentially facilitated by recent advances in extreme value theory. We explore that idea in "Forecasting Extreme Events" and conclude in "Concluding Remarks."

OBTAINING LONG-HORIZON VOLATILITIES FROM SHORT-HORIZON VOLATILITIES: SCALING AND FORMAL AGGREGATION[1]

Operationally, risk is often assessed at a short horizon, such as 1 day, and then converted to other horizons, such as 10 or 30 days, by scaling by the square root of horizon, as in Smithson and Minton (1996a, b) or J.P. Morgan (1996). For example, to obtain a 10-day volatility, we multiply the 1-day volatility by $\sqrt{10}$. Moreover, the horizon conversion is often significantly longer than 10 days. Many banks, for example, link trading volatility measurement to internal capital allocation and risk-adjusted performance measurement schemes, which rely on annual volatility estimates. The temptation is to scale 1-day volatility by $\sqrt{252}$. It turns out, however, that scaling is both inappropriate and misleading.

Scaling Works in Independent, Identically Distributed (iid) Environments

In this section, we describe the restrictive environment in which scaling is appropriate.

Let v_t be a log price at time t, and suppose that changes in the log price are independently and identically distributed:

$$v_t = v_{t-1} + \varepsilon_t \qquad \varepsilon_t \overset{\text{iid}}{\sim} (0, \sigma^2)$$

Then the 1-day return is

$$v_t - v_{t-1} = \varepsilon_t$$

with standard deviation σ. Similarly, the h-day return is

$$v_t - v_{t-h} = \sum_{i=0}^{h-1} \varepsilon_{t-i}$$

with variance $h\sigma^2$ and standard deviation $\sqrt{h}\sigma$. Hence, we arrive at the $\sqrt{h}$ rule: To convert a 1-day standard deviation to an h-day standard deviation, simply scale by $\sqrt{h}$. For some applications, a percentile of the distribution of h-day returns may be desired; percentiles also scale by $\sqrt{h}$ if log changes are not only iid, but also normally distributed.

Scaling Fails in non-iid Environments

The scaling rule relies on 1-day returns being iid, but high-frequency financial asset returns are distinctly not iid. Even if high-frequency portfolio returns are conditional-mean independent (which has been the subject of intense debate in the efficient markets literature), they are certainly not conditional-variance independent, as evidenced by hundreds of recent papers documenting strong volatility persistence in financial asset returns.[2]

To highlight the failure of scaling in non-iid environments and the nature of the associated erroneous long-horizon volatility estimates, we will use a simple GARCH(1,1) process for 1-day returns:

$$y_t = \sigma_t \varepsilon_t$$

$$\sigma_t^2 = \omega + \alpha y_{t-1}^2 + \beta \sigma_{t-1}^2$$

$$\varepsilon_t \sim \text{NID}(0,1),$$

$t = 1, \ldots, T$. We impose the usual regularity and covariance stationarity conditions, $0 < \omega < \infty$, $\alpha \geq 0$, $\beta \geq 0$, and $\alpha + \beta < 1$. The key feature of the GARCH(1, 1) process is that it allows for time-varying conditional volatility, which occurs when α and/or β is nonzero. The model has been fit to hundreds of financial series and has been tremendously successful empirically—hence its popularity. We hasten to add, however, that our general thesis—that scaling fails in the non-iid environments associated with high-frequency asset returns—does not depend in any way on a GARCH(1,1) structure. Rather, we focus on the GARCH(1,1) case because it has been studied the most intensely, yielding a wealth of results that enable us to illustrate the failure of scaling both analytically and by simulation.

Drost and Nijman (1993) study the temporal aggregation of GARCH processes.[3] Suppose we begin with a sample path of a 1-day return series, $\{y_{(1)t}\}_{t=1}^{T}$, which follows the previous GARCH(1,1) process.[4] Then Drost and Nijman show that, under regularity conditions, the corresponding sample path of h-day returns, $\{y_{(h)t}\}_{t=1}^{T/h}$, similarly follows a GARCH (1,1) process with

$$\sigma_{(h)t}^2 = \omega_{(h)} + \beta_{(h)} \sigma_{(h)t-1}^2 + \alpha_{(h)} y_{(h)t-1}^2$$

where

$$\omega_{(h)} = h\omega \frac{1 - (\beta + \alpha)^h}{1 - (\beta + \alpha)}$$

$$\alpha_{(h)} = (\beta + \alpha)^h - \beta_{(h)},$$

and $|\beta_{(h)}| < 1$ is the solution of the quadratic equation,

$$\frac{\beta_{(h)}}{1 + \beta_{(h)}^2} = \frac{a(\beta + \alpha)^h - b}{a(1 + (\beta + \alpha)^{2h}) - 2b},$$

where

$$a = h(1 - \beta)^2 + 2h(h - 1)\frac{(1 - \beta - \alpha)^2(1 - \beta^2 - 2\beta\alpha)}{(\kappa - 1)(1 - (\beta + \alpha)^2)}$$

$$+ 4\frac{(h - 1 - h(\beta + \alpha) + (\beta + \alpha)^h)(\alpha - \beta\alpha(\beta + \alpha))}{1 - (\beta + \alpha)^2}$$

$$b = (\alpha - \beta\alpha(\beta + \alpha))\frac{1 - (\beta + \alpha)^{2h}}{1 - (\beta + \alpha)^2},$$

and κ is the kurtosis of y_t. The Drost-Nijman formula is neither pretty nor intuitive, but it is important because it is the key to correctly converting a 1-day volatility to an h-day volatility. It is painfully obvious, moreover, that the $\sqrt{h}$ scaling formula does not look at all like the Drost-Nijman formula.

Despite the fact that the scaling formula is incorrect, it would still be very useful if it were an accurate approximation to the Drost-Nijman formula because of its simplicity and intuitive appeal. Unfortunately, this is not the case. As $h \to \infty$, the Drost-Nijman results, which build on those of Diebold (1988), reveal that $\alpha_{(h)} \to 0$ and $\beta_{(h)} \to 0$, which is to say that temporal aggregation produces the gradual disappearance of volatility fluctuations. Scaling, in contrast, *magnifies* volatility fluctuations.

A Worked Example

Let us examine the failure of scaling by $\sqrt{h}$ in a specific example. We parameterize the GARCH(1,1) process to be realistic for daily returns by setting $\alpha = 0.10$ and $\beta = 0.85$, which are typical of the parameter values obtained for estimated GARCH(1,1) processes. The choice of ω is arbitrary; we set $\omega = 1$.

The GARCH(1,1) process governs 1-day volatility; now let us examine 90-day volatility. In Figure 11.1, we show 90-day volatilities computed in two different ways. We obtain the first (incorrect) 90-day volatility by scaling the 1-day volatility, σ_t, by $\sqrt{90}$. We obtain the second (correct) 90-day volatility by applying the Drost-Nijman formula.

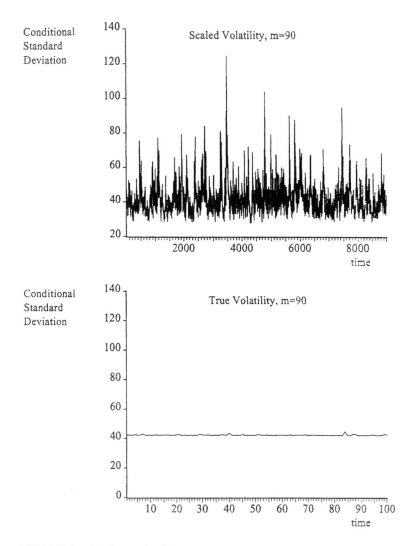

FIGURE 11.1 90-day volatility.

It is clear that although scaling by $\sqrt{h}$ produces volatilities that are correct on average, it magnifies the volatility fluctuations when they should in fact be damped. That is, scaling produces erroneous conclusions of large fluctuations in the conditional variance of long-horizon returns when in fact the opposite is true. Moreover, we cannot claim that the scaled volatility estimates are conservative in any sense; rather, they are sometimes too high and sometimes too low.

Formal Aggregation Has Problems of Its Own

One might infer from the preceding discussion that formal aggregation is the key to converting short-horizon volatility estimates into good long-horizon volatility estimates that can be used to assess volatility forecastability. In general, such is not the case; formal aggregation has at least two problems of its own. First, temporal aggregation formulas are presently available only for restrictive classes of models; the literature has progressed little since Drost and Nijman. Second, the aggregation formulas assume the truth of the fitted model when in fact the fitted model is simply an approximation, and the best approximation to h-day volatility dynamics is not likely to be what one gets by aggregating the best approximation (let alone a mediocre approximation) to 1-day dynamics.

MODEL-FREE ASSESSMENT OF VOLATILITY FORECASTABILITY AT DIFFERENT HORIZONS[5]

The model-dependent problems of scaling and aggregating daily volatility measures motivate the model-free investigation of volatility forecastability in this section. If the true process is GARCH(1,1) we know that volatility is forecastable at all horizons, although forecastability will decrease with horizon in accordance with the Drost-Nijman formula. But GARCH is only an approximation, and in this section we proceed to develop procedures that allow for the assessment of volatility forecastability across horizons with no assumptions made on the underlying volatility model.

The Basic Idea

Our model-free methods build on the methods for evaluation of interval forecasts developed by Christoffersen (1998). Interval forecasting is very much at the heart of modern financial risk management. The industry-standard Value at Risk (VaR) measure is effectively the boundary of a one-sided interval forecast, and just as the adequacy of a VaR forecast depends crucially on getting the volatility dynamics right, the same is true for interval forecasts more generally.

Suppose that we observe a sample path $\{y^t\}_{t=1}^T$ of the asset return series y_t and a corresponding sequence of one-step-ahead interval forecasts, such as $\{(L_{t|t-1}(p), U_{t|t-1}(p))\}_{t=1}^T$, where $L_{t|t-1}(p)$ and $U_{t|t-1}(p)$ denote the lower and upper limits of the interval forecast for time t made at time $t - 1$ with desired coverage probability p. We can think of $L_{t|t-1}(p)$ as a VaR measure and $U_{t|t-1}(p)$ as a measure of potential upside. The interval forecasts are subscripted by t as they will vary through time in general. In volatile times a good interval forecast should be wide, and in tranquil times it should be narrow, keeping the coverage probability p fixed.

Now let us formalize matters slightly. Define the *hit sequence*, I_t, as

$$I_t = \begin{cases} 1, \text{ if } y_t \epsilon [L_{t|t-1}(p), U_{t|t-1}(p)] \\ 0, \text{ otherwise,} \end{cases}$$

for $t = 1, 2, \ldots, T$. We will say that a sequence of interval forecasts has correct *unconditional coverage* if $E[I_t] = p$ for all t, which is the standard notion of *correct coverage*.

Correct unconditional coverage is appropriately viewed as a necessary condition for the adequacy of an interval forecast. It is not sufficient, however. In particular, in the presence of conditional heteroskedasticity, or data-dependent noise, and other higher-order dynamics, it is important to check for the adequacy of conditional coverage, which is a stronger concept. We will say that a sequence of interval forecasts has correct conditional coverage with respect to an information set Ω_{t-1} if $E[I_t(\Omega_{t-1}] = p$ for all t. The key result is that if $\Omega_{t-1} = \{I_{t-1}, I_{t-2}, \ldots, I_1\}$, then correct conditional coverage is equivalent to $\{I_t\} \overset{\text{iid}}{\sim} \text{Bernoulli}(p)$, which can readily be tested.

Consider now the case where no volatility dynamics are present. The optimal interval forecast is then constant, and given by $\{(L(p), U(p))\}$, $t = 1, \ldots, T$. In that case, testing for correct conditional coverage will reveal no evidence of dependence in the hit sequence, and it is exactly the independence part of the iid Bernoulli(p) criterion that is designed to pick up volatility dynamics. If, on the other hand, volatility dynamics *are* present but ignored by a forecaster who erroneously uses the constant $\{L(p), U(p)\}$ forecast, then a test for dependence in the hit sequence will reject the constant interval as an appropriate forecast. The ones and zeros in the hit sequence will tend to appear in time-dependent clusters corresponding to tranquil and volatile times.

It is evident that the interval forecast evaluation framework can be turned into a framework for assessing volatility forecastability: If a naive, constant interval forecast produces a dependent hit sequence, then volatility dynamics are present.

Measuring and Testing Dependence in the Hit Sequence

Now that we have established the close correspondence between the presence of volatility dynamics and dependence in the hit sequence from a constant interval forecast, it is time to discuss the measurement and testing of this dependence. We discuss two approaches.

First, consider a runs test, which is based on counting the number of strings, or *runs*, of consecutive zeros and ones in the hit sequence. If too few runs are observed (for example, 0000011111), the sequence exhibits positive correlation. Under the null hypothesis of independence, the exact finite sample distribution of the number of runs in the sequence has been tabulated by David (1947), and the corresponding test has been shown by Lehmann (1986) to be uniformly most powerful against a first-order Markov alternative.

We complement the runs test by a second measure, which has the benefit of being constrained to the interval $[-1,1]$ and thus easily comparable across horizons and sequences. Let the hit sequence be first-order Markov with an arbitrary transition probability matrix. Then dependence is fully captured by the nontrivial eigenvalue, which is simply $S \equiv \pi_{11} - \pi_{01}$, where π_{ij} is the probability of a j following an i in the hit sequence. S is a natural persistence measure and has been studied by Shorrocks (1978) and Sommers and Conlisk (1979). Note that under independence, $\pi_{11} = \pi_{01}$, so $S = 0$, and conversely, under strong positive persistence, π_{11} will be much larger than π_{01}, so S will be large.

An Example: The Dow Jones Composite Stock Index

We now put the volatility testing framework to use in an application to the Dow Jones Composite Stock Index, which comprises 65 major stocks (30 industrials, 20 transportations, and 15 utilities) on the New York Stock Exchange. The data start on January 1,1974 and continue through April 2, 1998, resulting in 6,327 daily observations.

We examine asset return volatility forecastability as a function of the horizon over which the returns are calculated. We begin with daily returns and then aggregate to obtain nonoverlapping h-day returns, $h = 1, 2, 3, \ldots$, 20. We set $\{L(p), U(p)\}$ equal to ± 2 standard deviations and then compute the hit sequences. Because the standard deviation varies across horizons, we let the interval vary correspondingly. Notice that p might vary across horizons, but that such variation is irrelevant. We are interested only in dependence of the hit sequence, not its mean.

At each horizon we measure volatility forecastability using the p of the runs test, that is, the probability of obtaining a sample that is less likely to conform to the null hypothesis of independence than the sample at hand. If the p is less than 5 percent, we reject the null of independence at that particular horizon. The top panel of Figure 11.2 shows the p across horizons of 1 through 20 trading days. Notice that despite the jaggedness of the line, a distinct pattern emerges. At short horizons of up to 1 week, the p is very low and thus there is clear evidence of volatility forecastability. At medium horizons of 2 to 3 weeks, the p jumps up and down, making reliable infer-

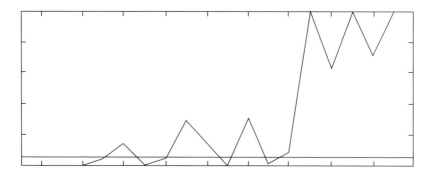

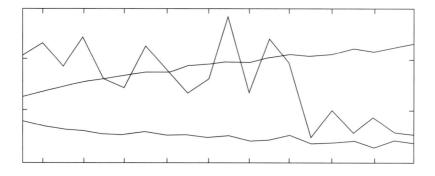

Notes: The hit sequence is defined relative to a constant ± 2 standard deviation interval at each horizon. The top panel shows the P-value for a runs test of the hypothesis that the hit sequence is independent. The horizontal line corresponds to a 5 percent significance level. The bottom panel shows the nontrivial eigenvalue from a first-order Markov process fit to the hit sequence. The 95 percent confidence interval is computed by simulation.

FIGURE 11.2 Volatility persistence across the horizons in the Dow Jones Composite Index.

ence difficult. At longer horizons of greater than 3 weeks, we find no evidence of volatility forecastability.

We also check the nontrivial eigenvalue. In order to obtain a reliable finite-sample measure of statistical significance at each horizon, we use a simulation-based resampling procedure to compute the 95 percent confidence interval under the null hypothesis of no dependence in the hit sequence (that is, the eigenvalue is zero). In the bottom panel of Figure 11.2, we plot the eigenvalue at each horizon along with its 95 percent confidence interval. The qualitative pattern that emerges for the eigenvalue is the same as for the runs test: Volatility persistence is clearly present at horizons less than 1 week, probably present at horizons between 2 and 3 weeks, and probably not present at horizons beyond 3 weeks.

Multicountry Analysis of Equity, Foreign Exchange, and Bond Markets

Christoffersen and Diebold (1997) assess volatility forecastability as a function of horizon for many more assets and countries. In particular, they analyze stock, foreign exchange, and bond returns for the United States, United Kingdom, Germany, and Japan, and they obtain results very similar to those presented previously for the Dow Jones Composite Index of U.S. equities.

For all returns, the finite-sample p values of the runs tests of independence tend to rise with the aggregation level, although the specifics differ somewhat depending on the particular return examined. As a rough rule of thumb, we summarize the results saying that for aggregation levels of less than 10 trading days, we tend to reject independence, which is to say that return volatility is significantly forecastable, and the converse is true for aggregation levels greater than 10 days.

The estimated transition matrix eigenvalues tell the same story. At very short horizons, typically from 1 to 10 trading days, the eigenvalues are significantly positive, but they decrease quickly, and approximately monotonically, with the aggregation level. By the time one reaches 10-day returns —and often substantially before—the estimated eigenvalues are small and statistically insignificant, indicating that volatility forecastability has vanished.

FORECASTING EXTREME EVENTS[6]

The quick decay of volatility forecastability as the forecast horizon lengthens suggests that if the risk management horizon is more than 10 or 15 trading days, less energy should be devoted to modeling and forecasting volatility and more energy should be devoted to modeling directly the extreme tails of return densities, a task potentially facilitated by recent advances in extreme value theory (EVT).[7] The theory typically requires independent and identically distributed observations, an assumption that appears reasonable for horizons of more than 10 or 15 trading days.

Let us elaborate. Financial risk management is intimately concerned with tail quantiles (such as the value of the return, y, such that $P[Y > y] = .05$) and tail probabilities (such as $P[Y > y]$, for a large value y). Extreme quantiles and probabilities are of particular interest because the ability to assess them accurately translates into the ability to manage extreme financial risks effectively, such as those associated with currency crises, stock market crashes, and large bond defaults.

Unfortunately, traditional parametric statistical and econometric methods, typically based on the estimation of entire densities, may be ill suited to the assessment of extreme quantiles and event probabilities. Traditional parametric methods implicitly strive to produce a good fit in regions where most of the data fall, potentially at the expense of good fit in the tails, where, by definition, few observations fall. Seemingly sophisticated nonparametric methods of density estimation, such as kernel smoothing, are also known to perform poorly in the tails.

It is common, moreover, to require estimates of quantiles and probabilities not only *near* the boundary of the range of observed data, but also *beyond* the boundary. The task of estimating such quantiles and probabilities would seem to be hopeless. A key idea, however, emerges from EVT: One can estimate extreme quantiles and probabilities by fitting a model to the empirical survival function of a set of data using only the extreme event data rather than all the data, thereby fitting the tail, and only the tail.[8] The approach has a number of attractive features, including the following:

- The estimation method is tailored to the object of interest, the tail of the distribution, rather than the center of the distribution.
- An arguably reasonable functional form for the tail can be formulated from a priori considerations.

The upshot is that the methods of EVT offer hope for progress toward the elusive goal of reliable estimates of extreme quantiles and probabilities.

Let us briefly introduce the basic framework. EVT methods of tail estimation rely heavily on a power law assumption, which is to say that the tail of the survival function is assumed to be a power law times a slowly varying function:

$$p(Y > y) = k(y)\, y^{-\alpha},$$

where the tail index, α, is a parameter to be estimated. That family includes, for example, α-stable laws with $\alpha < 2$ (but not the Gaussian case, $\alpha = 2$).

Under the power law assumption, we can base an estimator of "a" directly on the extreme values. The most popular, by far, is due to Hill (1975). It proceeds by ordering the observations with $y_{(1)}$ (the largest), $y_{(2)}$ (the second largest), and so on, and forming an estimator based on the difference between the average of the m largest log returns and the m-th largest log return:

$$\hat{\alpha} = \left(\left(\frac{1}{m} \sum_{i=1}^{m} \ln(y_{(i)}) \right) - \ln(y_{(m)}) \right)^{-1}.$$

It is a simple matter to convert an estimate of α into estimates of the desired quantiles and probabilities. The Hill estimator has been used in empirical financial settings, ranging from early work by Koedijk, Schafgans, and de Vries (1990) to more recent work by Danielsson and de Vries (1997). It also has good theoretical properties; it can be shown, for example, that it is consistent and asymptotically normal, assuming the data are iid and that m grows at a suitable rate with sample size.

But beware: If tail estimation via EVT offers opportunities, it is also fraught with pitfalls, as is any attempt to estimate low-frequency features of data from short historical samples. This has been recognized in other fields, such as the empirical finance literature on long-run mean reversion in asset returns (see Campbell, Lo, and MacKinley [1997], Chapter 2). The problem as relevant to the present context—applications of EVT in financial risk management—is that for performing statistical inference on objects such as a once-every-hundred-years quantile, the relevant measure of sample size is likely better approximated by the number of nonoverlapping hundred-year intervals in the dataset than by the actual number of data points. From that perspective, our data samples are terribly small relative to the demands placed on them by EVT.

Thus, we believe that best-practice applications of EVT to financial risk management will benefit from an awareness of its limitations as well as its strengths. When the smoke clears, the contribution of EVT remains basic and useful. It helps us to draw smooth curves through the extreme tails of empirical survival functions in a way that is consistent with powerful theory. Our point is simply that we shouldn't ask more of the theory than it can deliver.

CONCLUDING REMARKS

If volatility is forecastable at the horizons of interest, then volatility forecasts are relevant for risk management. But our results indicate that if the horizon of interest is more than 10 or 15 trading days, depending on the asset class, then volatility is not forecastable. Our results question the assumptions embedded in popular risk management paradigms, which effectively assume much greater volatility forecastability at long horizons than appears consistent with the data, and suggest that for improving long-horizon risk management attention is better focused elsewhere. One such area is the modeling of extreme events, the probabilistic nature of which remains poorly understood and for which recent developments in extreme value theory hold promise.

We thank Beverly Hirtle for her insightful and constructive comments, but we alone are responsible for any remaining errors. The views in this chapter are those of the authors and do not necessarily reflect those of the International Monetary Fund.

NOTES

[1]This section draws on Diebold, Hickman, Inoue, and Schuermann (1997, 1998).

[2]See, for example, the surveys of volatility modeling in financial markets by Bollerslev, Chou, and Kroner (1992) and Diebold and Lopez (1995).

[3]More precisely, they define and study the temporal aggregation of *weak* GARCH processes, a formal definition of which is beyond the scope of this chapter. Technically inclined readers should read "weak GARCH" whenever they encounter the word *GARCH* in this chapter.

[4]Note the new and more cumbersome, but necessary, notation, the subscript in which keeps track of the aggregation level.

[5]This section draws on Christoffersen and Diebold (1997).

[6]This section draws on Diebold, Schuermann, and Stroughair (1998).

[7]See the recent book by Embrechts, Kliippelberg, and Mikosch (1997) as well as the papers introduced by Paul-Choudhury (1998).

[8]The survival function is simply one minus the cumulative density function, $1-F(y)$. Note, in particular, that because $F(y)$ approaches 1 as y grows, the survival function approaches 0.

REFERENCES

Andersen, T. and T. Bollerslev. "Answering the Critics: Yes, ARCH Models Do Provide Good Volatility Forecasts." *International Economic Review*, in press, (1998).

Bollerslev, T., R.Y Chou, and K.F. Kroner. "ARCH Modeling in Finance: A Review of the Theory and Empirical Evidence." *Journal of Econometrics* 52 (1992): 5–59.

Campbell, J.Y., A.W. Lo, and A.C. MacKinley. *The Econometrics of Financial Markets* (Princeton: Princeton University Press, 1997).

Christoffersen, P.F. "Evaluating Interval Forecasts." *International Economic Review*, in press, (1998).

Christoffersen, P.F. and F.X. Diebold. "How Relevant Is Volatility Forecasting for Financial Risk Management?" Wharton Financial Institutions Center, Working Paper 97–45, http://fic.wharton.upenn.edu/fic/ (1997).

Danielsson, J. and C.G. de Vries. "Tail Index and Quantile Estimation with Very High Frequency Data." *Journal of Empirical Finance* 4 (1997): 241–257.

David, F.N. "A Power Function for Tests of Randomness in a Sequence of Alternatives." *Biometrika* 34 (1947): 335–339.

Diebold, F.X. *Empirical Modeling of Exchange Rate Dynamics* (New York: Springer-Verlag, 1988).

Diebold, F.X., A. Hickman, A. Inoue, and T. Schuermann. "Converting 1-Day Volatility to h-Day Volatility: Scaling by $\sqrt{h}$ Is Worse Than You Think." Wharton Financial Institutions Center, Working Paper 97–34, http://fic.wharton.upenn.edu/fic/ (1997).

———. "Scale Models." *Risk* 11 (1998): 104–107 (condensed version of Diebold, Hickman, Inoue, and Schuermann, 1997.)

Diebold, F.X. and J. Lopez. "Modeling Volatility Dynamics," in Kevin Hoover, ed. *Macroeconometrics: Developments, Tensions and Prospects* (Boston: Kluwer Academic Press, 1995), 427–472.

Diebold, F.X., T. Schuermann, and J. Stroughair. "Pitfalls and Opportunities in the Use of Extreme Value Theory in Risk Management," in P. Refenes, ed. *Computational Finance* (Boston: Kluwer Academic Press, 1998). Also in Wharton Financial Institutions Center, Working Paper 98–10, http://fic.wharton.upenn.edu/fic/ (1998).

Drost, F.C. and T.E. Nijman. "Temporal Aggregation of GARCH Processes." *Econometrics* 61 (1993): 909–927.

Embrechts, P., C. Kliippelberg, and T. Mikosch. *Modeling Extremal Events* (New York: Springer-Verlag, 1997).

Hill, B.M. "A Simple General Approach to Inference about the Tail of a Distribution." *Annals of Statistics* 3 (1975): 1,163–1,174.

J.P. Morgan. "RiskMetrics Technical Document." 4th edition, New York (1975).

Koedijk, K.G, M.A. Schafgans, and C.G. de Vries. "The Tail Index of Exchange Rate Returns." *Journal of International Economics* 29 (1990): 93–108.

Lehmann, E. L. *Testing Statistical Hypotheses*, 2nd edition, (New York: John Wiley & Sons, 1986).

Paul-Choudhury, S. "Beyond Basle." *Risk* 11(Introduction to a symposium on new methods of assessing capital adequacy. *Risk* 11 [1998]: 90–107).

Shorrocks, A.F. "The Measurement of Mobility." *Econometrica* 46 (1978): 1,013–1,024.

Smithson, C. and L. Minton. "Value at Risk." *Risk* 9 (January 1996a).

———. "Value at Risk (2)." *Risk* 9 (February 1996b).

Sommers, P.M. and J. Conlisk. "Eigenvalue Immobility Measures for Markov Chains." *Journal of Mathematical Sociology* 6 (1979): 253–276.

The Investment Manager's Viewpoint

A Behavioral Framework
for Time Diversification

Kenneth Fisher and Meir Statman

Does the risk of stocks decline with one's investment horizon? This is clearly not the case, but according to the authors, many investors are led by financial product marketers to believe that this is true. This chapter argues that market participants who reach the end of their planned time horizon with paper losses often avoid the relation of the losses and pain of regret by concluding that their true time horizon is a bit longer than they actually planned.

Does time diversification reduce risk? Is the Mona Lisa beautiful? Risk, like beauty, is in the eye of the beholder. We can find the meaning of beauty by examining what viewers find beautiful. And we can find the meaning of risk by examining what investors find risky. Investors find that time diversification reduces risk. What does it teach us about risk?

The purpose of this chapter is to learn about risk from time diversification. Along the way, we learn about the goals of investors, the way they make decisions, the concepts of losses and regret, the use of investment benchmarks, and the design of securities.

The time diversification argument, as Kritzman (1994) writes, is that the risk of stocks declines as the time horizon increases. If so, a large allocation to stocks is suitable for a young person saving for retirement but not for an old person who is already retired. Kritzman goes on to argue, based on the work of Samuelson (1963, 1969), that proponents of time diversification frame the problem incorrectly. According to Samuelson's framing, the risk of stocks does not decline with the investment horizon.

Investors must be very slow to learn that they should frame the problem as Samuelson does. The belief that time diversification reduces risk is as strong as ever. Consider the discussion in the *Stocks, Bonds, Bills, and Inflation Yearbook* by Ibbotson Associates (1997). Ibbotson Associates presents tables of returns for periods of 1, 5, 10, 15, and 20 rolling years. Returns on Large Company Stocks were negative in 20 out of the 71 years from 1926 through 1996. But they were negative in only 2 of 62 overlapping 10-year periods. Ibbotson Associates write that the data are useful for examining the behavior of returns for holding periods similar to those actually experienced by investors and show the effects of time diversification. Holding assets for long periods of time has the effect of lowering the risk of experiencing a loss in asset value.

Why do investors persist in the belief that time diversification reduces risk if, as Samuelson argues, that belief is wrong? One explanation is that time diversification reduces risk if returns are mean reverting. Another is that although time diversification does not reduce risk, it still makes sense for young people to hold a higher proportion of stocks in their portfolios because young people have much of their wealth in human capital, capital that is not counted in investable portfolios. However, Bodie (1995) shows that the first explanation is false and that the second does not apply to a broad class of people who face substantial human-capital risk early in their careers. For such people, the optimal policy is the opposite of the one usually recommended. They should begin with low proportions of stocks in their portfolios and increase these proportions as they age.

Irrationality is last on Kritzman's list of possible explanations for the persistence of the belief that time diversification reduces risk. "Irrationality does not mean that you are a bad person," he writes, "it simply implies that you behave inconsistently." But inconsistent is the poorest possible description of the belief in the risk-reduction benefits of time diversification. Indeed, the belief is consistent, widespread, and resistant to learning.

The time diversification debate is now taking place in the fancy world of options. Bodie (1995) used the language of options to argue that time diversification does not reduce risk. Merrill and Thorley (1996) used the same language to argue that it does. (See Cohen [1996], de Fontenay [1996], Gould [1996], Sirera [1996], and the response by Bodie [1996].)

The language of options seems to have served only to obscure the issue of time diversification. This is too bad because options are indeed at the heart of time diversification. But these are simple options, not fancy ones.

Specifically, time diversification reduces risk because losses, especially realized losses, are at the heart of risk and time diversification involves an option to avoid the realization of losses. The option to avoid the realization of losses has two dimensions: time and benchmarks.

Time enhances the value of the option to avoid the realization of losses. Investors who can wait 10 years have a higher probability of avoiding the realization of losses than investors who can wait only 3 months. Benchmarks also enhance the value of the option. Positions that register losses when the S&P 500 index serves as the benchmark might register gains when inflation serves as the benchmark.

RISK AND CHOICES

We care about risk because risk affects choices. Lopes (1987) identifies two major goals that affect choices: security and potential. Security relates to downside protection, a desire to avoid being poor, whereas potential relates to upside potential, the desire to be rich. Some people are primarily motivated by downside protection and some by upside potential. Still, the two goals exist in some strength in all people. But how high is upside and how low is downside? Upside and downside, like rich and poor, are defined only relative to aspiration levels. For some people, the aspiration level for rich is $100 million. For others, $100,000 will do.

The idea that choices are affected by goals and that goals are defined by aspirations, or benchmarks, is longstanding. Goals and benchmarks are central in Roy's (1952) *safety-first* framework. Investors in that framework, as modified by Telser (1955), begin the process of choice among alternative portfolios by setting maximum probabilities for losses relative to a benchmark. The objective of an investor in the safety-first framework is to maximize the upside potential of a portfolio while keeping the probability of the downside, relative to the benchmark, below some critical level. The safety-first framework has evolved into the *shortfall-risk* or *downside-risk* framework. (See Leibowitz and Langetieg [1989] and Harlow [1991].)

Sheffin and Statman (1997) build on Lopes' work and that of Kahneman and Tversky (1979) in their behavioral portfolio theory. Investors in behavioral theory have the twin goals of downside protection and upside potential, and they have benchmarks for the goals. The goals and benchmarks guide investors as they choose securities and construct portfolios. Fisher and Statman (1997) examine the link between behavioral portfolio theory and portfolio advice by mutual fund companies.

UPSIDE POTENTIAL, DOWNSIDE PROTECTION, PAPER LOSSES, AND REALIZED LOSSES

Time diversification is usually discussed in the context of stocks, but insights are clearer in the context of bonds. This is because bonds highlight the twin goals of upside potential and downside protection. U.S. Treasury zero coupon bonds, and even 20-year bonds, are described by many as risk free. How can zero coupon bonds be risk free when their prices go up and down everyday? The answer is that 20-year zero-coupon bonds are risk free for investors who have a time option—the option to wait 20 years. Investors who can wait 20 years know that they will not be forced to register a loss relative to their benchmark by turning a paper loss into a realized loss. The next section is how O'Connell (1996) describes the time option.

Suppose you want at least $100,000 when you retire 20 years from now. You can buy 100 20-year Treasury strips, each with a face value of $1,000. Your cost is about $25,000, including a broker's markup of some $675. Your yield would be about 7. If rates drop this year, with new strips yielding 6.5 percent, you could sell yours, pocketing a 21 percent gain.

Of course, if interest rates rocket higher, with new strips yielding 8, you would lose 7 percent if you sold. And if you held the strips until they matured or until rates fell again, you would be guaranteed to gain. Stocks offer no such assurance. People who buy zeros and hold them can rest assured they'll get a set return.

The distinction between paper losses and realized losses is central to the time option and time diversification. As O'Connell notes, zero coupon bonds might bring paper losses at any time before maturity and these paper losses would turn into realized losses for investors who cannot wait until maturity. However, for investors who have the time option, zero coupon bonds offer, as O'Connell writes, "a safety net with the bounce of a trampoline."

Stocks do not offer the safety net of bonds, although some wish they did. For example, de Fontenay (1996) argues, "A positive rate of return in the long run is near certainty . . . There is no reason to expect a negative return on the broadest possible stock index . . . " But, as Bodie (1996) points out in his response, "Near certainty is not the same as complete certainty." There is a positive probability that losses on stocks would have to be realized even if stocks are held for a very long, but finite, time.

FRAMING OF LOSSES

The distinction between paper losses and realized losses illustrates the importance of framing. Paper losses and realized losses are identical in substance (in the absence of tax and transaction cost considerations). But the two are different in frames, and frames matter. For example, many investors prefer individual bonds over bond mutual funds. This preference illustrates not only the distinction that investors make between paper losses and realized losses, but it also shows the effect of framing. In particular, individual bonds are perceived by many as risk free, whereas bond mutual funds, funds that are different from individual bonds only in frame, are perceived as risky.

A bond ladder is a portfolio composed of individual bonds with a range of maturities, where each maturity is a rung in the ladder. For example, a $100,000 ladder might include $10,000 in bonds maturing in 1 year, $10,000 in bonds maturing in 2 years, and so on until the last $10,000 in bonds maturing in 10 years. Imagine, for simplicity, that all bonds are U.S. Treasury zero coupon bonds. The advantage of a ladder portfolio, according to its proponents, is that the portfolio is risk free. The portfolio is risk free because investors do not have to realize a loss, relative to the initial yield maturity when they redeem each bond at maturity. But if the ladder portfolio is perceived as risk free, how is it that a portfolio with the same substance is perceived as risky?

The substance of the ladder portfolio is identical to the substance of a mutual fund portfolio that contains the ladder bonds. Both portfolios are bond portfolios with durations of 5.5 years. To focus on time diversification, assume that there are no taxes or transaction costs and assume that both the ladder portfolio and the mutual fund portfolio are replenished when bonds are redeemed so that duration remains at 5.5 years.

The ladder portfolio and the mutual fund portfolio are identical in substance, but the difference in frames is crucial. A ladder portfolio guarantees investors a way to avoid the realization of losses if they wait until maturity. A mutual fund portfolio does not provide such guarantee since a mutual fund has no maturity date. The fact that typical investors perceive the risk of mutual funds as higher than the risk of the individual bonds that make up that fund teaches us that framing matters and risk has to do with having to realize losses. The following is how Quinn (1996) expresses the view that the risk of individual bonds is lower than the risk of a bond mutual fund.

Bond prices can be volatile . . . In the past, that has sometimes shocked inexperienced investors, who grabbed what was left of their money and ran. They might not have done so had they owned individual bonds. If you can hold to maturity, it's safer than any bond fund can be.

Ladder portfolios are perceived as risk free because individual bonds are framed separately from the overall portfolio. Investors frame the 5-year bonds, which they redeem at maturity, in isolation from the 10-year bonds, which might carry unrealized losses. However, such isolation is impossible in mutual fund portfolios. Mutual fund portfolios are perceived as risky because the 5-and 10-year bonds are bundled together in the overall portfolio. Mutual fund investors cannot be assured of avoiding the realization of losses even if they hold the fund for a very long time.

Mutual fund companies are well aware of the many investors who shun bond mutual funds in favor of individual bonds. So they design mutual funds that contain the feature the investors crave—a promise that they would not have to realize losses if they hold until maturity. Fidelity Investments offer Fidelity Target Timeline Funds. "The Target Timeline Funds," notes the brochure, "provide you with some of the advantages of a professionally managed fund, along with those of a single bond. Not only can you select a maturity date of 1999, 2001, or 2003, but the fund will seek to provide a predictable rate of return." Protected Equity Notes (PENs) provide another example of security design.

PENs are securities that combine features of stocks and bonds. Merrill Lynch sold shares of MITTS, its version of PENs, in January 1992 for $10 each. It promised to pay, in August 1997, the original $10 plus 115 percent of the percentage increase in the S&P 500 over the period. The original $10 would be paid even if the S&P 500 were lower in August 1997 than in January 1992. James Glassman (1997) writes about MITTS under the heading, "A Risk Free (no kidding) Bet on the Stock Markets."

Framing returns in a long-term horizon is crucial to the appeal of time diversification. Consider again the Ibbotson Associates analysis of returns on Large Company Stocks over the period from 1926 through 1996. Framed in a 1-year horizon, returns were negative in 20 out of 71 years, but framed in a 10-year horizon, the same returns were negative in only two of 62 overlapping 10-year periods. The difference in framing leads to a difference in choice. The effect of one such framing, described by Kahneman and Lovallo (1993) as *narrow framing*, plays a part in time diversification. Benartzi and Thaler (1996) link it to *myopic loss aversion*.

Subjects in the Benartzi and Thaler's experiment were told that they could choose between two funds: Fund A and Fund B. Unknown to the subjects, the returns of Fund A were New York Stock Exchange (NYSE) index stock returns and the returns of Fund B were 5-year bond returns, both from the 66-year period from 1926 to 1993. In the 1-year version of the experiment, subjects were shown the distribution of 1-year rates of returns. In the 30-year version of the experiment, subjects were shown the distribution of 30-year rates of returns. The effect of framing on choice is striking. The median allocation to stocks of subjects who saw 1-year returns was 40 percent, whereas the median allocation to stocks of subjects who saw 30-year returns was 90 percent.

TIME, BENCHMARKS, AND LOSSES

PENs are risk free when held to maturity and when the benchmark is the purchase price. They are risk free in the sense that there is a zero probability that a loss relative to the purchase price would be realized if redeemed at maturity. Of course, PENs are not risk free if the benchmark is the return on Treasury bills. Indeed, the popularity of PENs teaches us that the purchase price is a very salient benchmark for investors. As Glassman writes, "What investors love is getting their principal back."

The benchmark implied by advocates of bond ladders is the initial yield maturity. Zero coupon bonds are risk free if held to maturity and the benchmark is the initial yield. But the initial yield is not the only possible benchmark for gains and losses. Note that the initial yield is a nominal yield, not a real one. A 7 percent nominal yield provides a 2 percent real gain when inflation turns out to be 5 percent, but it provides a 3 percent real loss when inflation turns out to be 10 percent. When the benchmark is the real yield, a zero-coupon bond is no longer risk free, even if held to maturity. The common benchmark for stocks in the time diversification debate is the return on a risk-free asset, such as Treasury bills. For example, Thorley (1995) estimates that the probability that stocks would register a loss relative to the risk-free benchmark is 30.9 percent when the time horizon is 1 year. That probability declines to 1.3 percent when the horizon is 20 years and to 0.1 percent when the horizon is 40 years. The use of a risk-free asset as the benchmark is central to the application of the Black-Scholes option pricing model in the time diversification debate. Bodie (1995) used the Black-Scholes model to argue that time diversification does not reduce risk, whereas Merrill and Thorley (1996) used the model to argue that it does. However, the Black-Scholes model tells us little about the risk-reduction benefits of time diversification. As Dempsey et al. (1996) note, one insight from the Black-Scholes model is that, under the model's assumptions, there is no stock portfolio that has both a zero probability of falling below the risk-free rate and a positive probability of exceeding the risk-free rate.

The risk-free rate is neither the only benchmark for gains and losses on stocks nor the most salient. A zero return is an alternative, perhaps more salient, benchmark. Zero is the benchmark implied in the Ibbottson Associates analysis discussed earlier. They note the number of periods where stock returns exceeded zero, not the number of periods where stock returns exceeded the risk-free rate.

The choice of benchmarks is crucial for framing outcomes as gains or losses. But which benchmarks do people choose? Shafir, Diamond, and Tversky (1997) note that people tend to adopt benchmarks that are salient and simple. So, for example, people generally frame salary raises in nominal terms, with zero as the benchmark, rather than in real terms, with the rate of inflation as the benchmark. Framing in nominal terms leads to the well-known money illusion where a 15 percent increase in salary when inflation is at 12 percent is perceived as better than a 4 percent increase when inflation is at zero. The tendency to evaluate the returns of zero coupon bonds in nominal rather than real terms is another example of the money illusion.

Shafir, Diamond, and Tversky note that benchmarks are sometimes combined. In these cases, assessments of gains and losses are induced by the various benchmarks, each weighted by its own salience. The model of Chow (1995) provides an example of a combination of benchmarks in an investment context. Chow describes investors who combine a stock index as one benchmark with zero as the other. For instance, a money manager might be expected to beat the S&P 500 while also registering a positive return. Similarly, Leibowitz and Langetieg (1989) describe pension plan sponsors who combine two benchmarks: the risk-free rate and the return necessary to avoid a reportable deficit. The last example illustrates the role of benchmarks as aspiration levels. Pension plan sponsors aspire to achieve a return that is necessary to avoid a reportable deficit because a reportable deficit will get them in trouble. Benchmarks and time horizons are well defined in the example of Chow and that of Leibowitz and Langetieg. But benchmarks and time horizons are not always well defined, creating contention between plan sponsors and money managers.

Plan sponsors argue that money managers are lagging the benchmark. "No," answer money managers. "The benchmark you use is wrong. We are ahead to the right benchmark!" Sometimes contention is over the time horizon. Money managers argue that the horizon used for evaluation use is wrong; they claim, "assess my performance over a full market cycle, not 1 or 3 years."

TIME, BENCHMARKS, AND CHOICES

Kahneman and Tversky (1979) find that most people choose a sure $1,000 gain over a 50-50 gamble for a $2,000 gain or zero. This choice is interpreted as consistent with risk aversion since the expected gain from the gamble is identical to the sure $1,000 gain, but the gamble has higher variance. However, Kahneman and Tversky also find that most people choose a 50-50 gamble for a $2,000 loss or zero over a sure $1,000 loss. The two alternatives have identical expected payoffs, but this time most people choose the one with the higher variance. Are people risk seeking?

Interpretation of choices focuses on the role of benchmarks in framing outcomes as gains or losses. People are averse to losses. They prefer a gamble with a 50 percent chance for a $2,000 loss over a sure $1,000 loss since the same gamble also gives them a 50 percent chance to break even. The effect of aversion to losses and the role of benchmarks in defining losses are evident in many real-life choices. Consider the choices of farmers.

Kunreuther and Wright (1979) find that the poorest farmers devote as large a proportion of their land to cash crops, such as cotton, as the richest farmers. Cash crops are destined for sale in the marketplace and the variance in their prices is higher than the variance in the prices of food crops such as rice, lentils, and peanuts that can be consumed by farmers and their families. So why do poor farmers choose to grow cash crops? The answer is rooted in the benchmark, the amount needed for survival. When land is insufficient for survival on food crops, the probability of survival is higher if farmers grow cash crops than if they grow food crops. Cash crops might seem riskier than food crops when variance serves as a measure of risk. But cash crops are less risky in the sense that they provide a higher probability of survival. Similarly, many investors choose high-variance stocks over low-variance Treasury bills in an attempt to maximize the probability of survival in retirement.

If the benchmark for gains and losses is a large amount of money needed for retirement and current wealth is low, the probability of falling short of the benchmark might be higher with Treasury bills than with stocks. If so, the risk of Treasury bills is higher than the risk of stocks. Gerald Perritt, editor of *Mutual Fund Letter* is quoted by Clements (1997) as saying, "If you are investing in your retirement account for the next 40 years, you don't care about volatility. If you are trying to save enough for retirement, Treasury bills are probably riskier than stocks."

OPTIONS ON TIME AND BENCHMARKS

The probability that losses would have to be realized underlies the perception that time diversification reduces risk. That probability is determined by two factors: the time horizon and benchmark. The probabilities that losses would have to be realized with stocks and zero coupon bonds are presented in Figure 12.1. Stocks are risky when the time horizon is 10 years and the yield to maturity on 10-year zero coupon bonds serve as the benchmark since there is a positive probability that losses relative to that benchmark would have to be realized. But 10-year zero coupon bonds are not risky when the time horizon is 10 years and the bonds' initial yield maturity serves as the benchmark.

Investment	Benchmark	Time Horizon			
		1 Year	5 Year	10 Year	Forever
10 year zero-coupon bonds	Initial yield to maturity on a 10-year zero-coupon bond	positive	positive	zero	Not Applicable
	Zero return	positive	positive	zero	Not Applicable
Stocks	Initial yield to maturity on a zero-coupon bonds of a maturity equal to the time horizon	30.9%	13.2%	5.7%	zero
	Zero return	positive	positive	positive	zero

Source: The 30.9%, 13.2% and 5.7% figures are from Thorley (1995).

FIGURE 12.1   Time horizons, benchmarks, and the probability of losses.

Time diversification is discussed in a setting where time horizons and benchmarks are set before investment choices are made and neither time horizons nor benchmarks are changed later. In this setting, causality goes from time and benchmarks to investment outcomes. In practice, however, investors often exercise the option to modify both time horizons and benchmarks. Moreover, causality goes from investment outcomes to time horizon and benchmarks.

March (1988) notes that aspirations change in response to experience. So, for example, investors who initially aspired to beat inflation now aspire to beat the S&P 500 index. Similarly, investors who initially set their time horizon to 20 years might change that horizon to 3 or 30 years. Some changes in benchmarks and time horizons are adaptations to external factors such as changes in family needs. But other changes are internal. A few years of extraordinary S&P 500 returns lead some investors to shift their benchmark from the rate of inflation to the return on the S&P 500. Similarly, a few years of negative S&P 500 returns lead some investors to shift their time horizon from 3 to 10 years. Many of the internally driven changes in benchmarks and time horizons are responses to the emotions of regret and pride.

REGRET, PRIDE, AND OPTIONS ON TIME AND BENCHMARKS

Consider a man who plans to buy a $100,000 house in 10 years. He has the $67,556 now. Would he invest the money in stocks or Treasury bills? He thinks, using the assumptions in Thorley (1995), that the expected annual return on stocks is 12 percent and the expected annual return on Treasury bills is 4 percent. So he expects his money to grow to $209,819 if he invests in stocks and to $100,000 if he invests in Treasury bills. He also finds that there is a 5.7 percent probability that stocks would trail Treasury bills over the 10-year horizon. Imagine that he chose to invest in stocks, that 10 years have passed, and that he finds that he was not a lucky man. The value of the stock portfolio is only $95,000.

The investor suffers a hit to the pocketbook. The house he can buy now is not as big as it would have been had he chosen Treasury bills. But the investor suffers another hit, a hit to his self-evaluation. This is the hit of regret. Regret is the emotional pain that we feel when we find out, after the fact, that we would have been better off had we made a different choice. Regret kicks in most forcefully when a loss is realized since realization extinguishes all hope that a paper loss would vanish.

The emotional counterpart to regret is pride, the joy that kicks in most forcefully when a gain is realized. An investor who bought stocks 10 years ago and now has $300,000, three times the $100,000 benchmark, has more than a big house. He feels pride for choosing stocks over Treasury bills 10 years ago.

Pride accompanies positive feedback and regret accompanies negative feedback. Both positive and negative feedback are crucial to learning and people who have a motivation to succeed expose themselves to both by setting benchmarks that are at least moderately difficult to achieve. Consider the ring toss.

Lopes (1987) describes a game originally used by McClelland (1958) in his studies of achievement motivation. Subjects throw rings onto a peg from a distance that they choose. They can choose to stand so close to the peg that success is virtually guaranteed, or they can choose to stand so far that success is virtually impossible. McClelland found that people who have a high motivation to succeed choose intermediate distances from the peg, balancing the probability of failure and regret with the probability of success and pride.

Motivated investors, like motivated ring tossers, choose benchmarks that are difficult but not impossible to achieve. Still, negative feedback is painful and, as Taylor and Brown (1988) note, people distort negative feedback and the pain of regret that it brings. As a consequence, normal human thought is associated with overly positive self-evaluations. One strategy for blunting the pain of regret and enhancing the joy of pride involves shirking responsibility for bad outcomes and claiming responsibility for good outcomes. This is the sentiment in the stockbrokers' lament: When the stock goes up, the customer says, "I bought the stock," but when the stock goes down, the customer says, "My broker sold me the stock."

Another strategy for blunting the pain of regret involves an exercise of the benchmark option or time option. People who set their benchmark at a $100,000 house and find out 10 years later that they are $5,000 short might exercise the benchmark option, the option to switch to a $95,000 house benchmark. This is the sour-grapes method of blunting regret. Alternatively, they might exercise the time option, the option to extend their time horizon by another year or two in the hope of reaching $100,000 by then. This method of blunting regret is captured in the quip, "A long-term investment is a short-term speculation that did not work out." Sellers of houses often talk about their losses as losses of *liquidity*, not money.

Some investors have time options that extend without limits. McGough and Siconolfi (1997) describe investors in the Steadman mutual funds who continue to hold onto shares bought 40 years ago. The shares register paper losses after all these years and the losses are likely to deepen since the Steadman funds have expense ratios of 25 percent per year. Still, says the investor, he "never wanted to sell it at a loss." If his time option extends without limit, he is likely to get his wish.

CONCLUSION

Time diversification is about the link between risk and time. As Lopes (1987) wrote, "Uncertainty is embedded in time. There is a now in which some things are true, a future in which other things may be true, and a still farther future in which we may reflect on the past. At the point of choice we look forward along this track, and we also anticipate looking back. The temporal element is what gives risk both savor and sting."

Risk is about more than money; it is also about emotions: hope and fear, and pride and regret. Investors hope for gains and they fear losses; they anticipate the pride that accompanies gains and the regret that accompanies losses. Time gives investors control over emotions. Stock investors with 10-year horizons have better hope of realizing gains than investors with 5-year horizons. Stock investors with 10-year horizons also have a better chance at looking back with pride for having chosen stocks over Treasury bills 10 years ago.

Time horizon is perfectly fixed in the time diversification debate, but it is not fixed in real life. In real life, investment outcomes often determine the time horizon. Investors who reach the end of their planned time horizon with paper losses often avoid the realization of the losses and the pain of regret by concluding that their true time horizon is actually a bit longer than they originally planned; their losses are only paper losses.

Financial advisors often use the time diversification argument to persuade investors to invest in stocks. They argue, as de Fontenay does, that "A positive rate of return [from stocks] in the long run is near certainty." Many investors find the time diversification argument persuasive, especially investors with options to extend the time horizon without limit, until they can realize a gain. Financial advisors have a second argument, the dollar-averaging argument, for investors not quite persuaded by the time diversification argument. "Divide your money into equal installments," they say, "and invest one installment each month." The belief that dollar averaging reduces risk is as persistent as the belief that time diversification reduces risk (Statman 1995).

The elements that make dollar cost averaging powerful as a tool for the reduction of risk are identical to those that make time diversification powerful, with one exception. It is the difference between paper losses and realized losses. Time diversification is the answer to investors who fear the regret that comes with realized losses. Dollar cost averaging is the answer to investors who also fear the regret that comes with paper losses. Dollar cost averaging works for investors with long horizons who still dread the regret they would feel if their stocks declined over short horizons.

Investors believe that time diversification reduces risk. Is that belief rational? Van Eaton and Conover (1998) assure us that it is. But we need no such assurance. When models of rationality collide with real-life behavior, it is the models that must give way. Indeed, it is real life that guides us to better models.

REFERENCES

Benartzi, Shlomo and Richard Thaler. "Risk Aversion or Myopia? Choices in Repeated Gambles and Retirement Investments," Working Paper, The Anderson School at UCLA, 1996.

Bodie, Zvi. "On the Risk of Stocks in the Long Run." *Financial Analysts Journal* 51, no. 3 (May/June 1995): 18–22.

———. "Rejoiner: Long Run Risks in Stocks." *Financial Analysts Journal* (March/April 1996): 74–76.

Chow, George. "Portfolio Selection Based on Return, Risk, and Relative Performance." *Financial Analysts Journal* (March/April 1995): 54–60.

Clements, J. "Sometimes the Greatest Danger You Face on Market's Ups and Downs." *Wall Street Journal* (May 27, 1997): C1.

Cohen, George M. "Letter to the Editor: Long Run Risk in Stocks." *Financial Analysts Journal* (March/April 1996): 72–73.

Dempsey, Mike, Robert Hudson, Kevin Littler, and Kevin Keasey. "On the Risk of Stocks in the Long Run: A Resolution to the Debate?" *Financial Analysts Journal* (September/October 1996): 57–62.

de Fontenay, P. "Letter to the Editor: Long Run Risk in Stocks." *Financial Analysts Journal* (March/April 1996): 73.

Fisher, Kenneth L. and Meir Statman. "Investment Advice from Mutual Fund Companies." *The Journal of Portfolio Management* (Fall 1997): 9–25.

Gould, Gordon L. "Letter to the Editor: Long Run Risk in Stocks." *Financial Analysts Journal* (March/April 1996): 73–74.

Glassman, James. "A Risk Free (No Kidding) Bet on the Stock Markets." *Herald Tribune* (August 23–24, 1997).

Harlow, Van. "Asset Allocation a Downside Risk Framework." *Financial Analysts Journal* 47, no. 5 (1991): 28–40.

Ibbotson Associates. *Stocks, Bonds, Bills, and Inflation Yearbook* (Chicago: Ibbotson Associates, 1997), 42.

Kahneman, Daniel and A. Tversky. "Prospect Theory: Analysis of Decision Making Under Risk." *Economettica* (1979): 263.

Kahneman, Daniel and Dan Lovallo. "Timid Choices and Bold Forecasts: A Cognitive Perspective on Risk Taking." *Management Science* 39, no. 1 (January 1993): 17–31.

Kritzman, Mark. "What Practitioners Need to Know about Time Diversification." *Financial Analysts Journal* 50, no. 1 (January/February 1994): 14–18.

Kunreuther, H. and G. Wright. "Safety First, Gambling, and the Subsistence Farmer," edited by J.A. Roumasset, J. M. Boussard, and I. Singh, *Risk, Uncertainty, and Agricultural Development.* (New York: Agricultural Development Council, 1979), 213–230.

Leibowitz, Martin and Terance Langetieg. "Shortfall Risk and the Asset Allocation Decision: A Simulation Analysis of Stock and Bond Risk Profiles." *Journal of Portfolio Management* 16, no. 1 (1989): 61–68.

Lopes, Lola L. "Between Hope and Fear: The Psychology of Risk." *Advances in Experimental Social Psychology* 20 (1987): 255–295.

March, James G. "Bounded Rationality, Ambiguity, and the Engineering of Choice." *Bell Journal of Economics* (1978): 587–608.

———. "Variable Risk Preferences and Adaptive Aspirations." *Journal of Economic Behavior and Organization* (1988): 5–24.

McClelland, D.C. "Risk Taking in Children with High and Low Need for Achievement," edited by J.W. Atkinson, *Motives Infantasy, Action, and Society* (Princeton, NJ: Van Nostrand, 1958), 306–321.

McGough, Robert and Michael Siconolfi. "Buy and Fold: Their Money's Fleeing, But Some Investors Just Keep Hanging On." *Wall Street Journal* (June 18, 1997): Al.

Merrill, Craig and Steven Thorley. "Time Diversification: Perspectives from Option Pricing Theory." *Financial Analysts Journal* 52, no. 3 (May/June 1996): 13–19.

O'Connell, Vanessa. "Zero Coupon Bonds Offer Safety Net with a Bounce." *San Jose Mercury News* (May 29, 1996): Cl, C20.

Quinn, Jane Bryant. "Weighing the Pros and Cons of Buying Bonds vs. Bond Funds." *San Jose Mercury News* (August 5, 1996).

Roy, A.D. "Safety First and the Holdings of Assets." *Econometrica* 20, no. 3 (July 1952): 431–449.

Samuelson, P. "Risk and Uncertainty: A Fallacy of Large Numbers." *Scientia* (April/May 1993).

———. "Lifetime Portfolio Selection by Dynamic Stochastic Programming." *Review of Economics and Statistics* (August 1969).

Sirera, Martin C. "Letter to the Editor: Long Run Risk in Stocks." *Financial Analysts Journal* (March/April 1996): 74.

Shafir, Eldar, Peter Diamond, and Amos Tversky. "Money Illusion." *The Quarterly Journal of Economics* CXII, no. 2 (May 1997): 341–373.

Sheffin, Hersh and Meir Statman. "Behavioral Portfolio Theory," Working Paper, Santa Clara University, November 1997.

Statman, Meir. "Behavioral Framework for Dollar Averaging." *The Journal of Portfolio Management* (Fall 1995): 70–78.

Taylor, Shelley E. and Jonathan D. Brown. "Illusion and Well Being: A Social Psychological Perspective on Mental Health." *Psychological Bulletin* 103, no. 3 (1988): 193–210.

Telser, Lester. "Safety First and Hedging." *Review of Economic Studies* 23, no. 60 (1955–1956): 1–16.

Thorley, Steven R. "The Time Diversification Controversy." *Financial Analysts Journal* 51, no. 3 (May/June 1995): 67–75.

Van Eaton, Douglas, R. and James A. Conover. "Misconceptions about Optimal Equity Allocation and Investment Horizon." *Financial Analysts Journal* (March/April 1998): 52.

CHAPTER 13

Converging Correlations and Market Shocks: Implications for Managing Risk

Louis Llanes

This paper argues that the risk of equity investing has increased, mainly due to the diverging correlations of global equity markets during periods of turmoil. As a result, it is vital to consider a number of risk-reducing strategies, such as tactical asset allocation during periods of rising interest rates, industry-level security selection, and rebalancing.

INTRODUCTION

Investment professionals who are engaged in asset allocation must deal with the impact of a changing world economy. The development of an efficient portfolio is becoming increasingly difficult due to the structural change in correlation over time. The average world equity market has become increasingly correlated with the U.S. stock market especially during periods of higher volatility. The risk of owning stocks may be higher than what would normally be estimated using long-term statistics such as standard deviation. When the U.S. stock market declines, correlations have increased substantially among global equity markets, leaving little room for a diversification cushion. Synchronized downside price movement between the emerging markets and the United States have caused the global equity allocations to behave as if they were one asset class. Important geographical, economic, and financial variables may be the cause of the structural change in correlation.

It is helpful to distinguish unexpected price activity as being structural or temporary. This way of categorizing a market's movement can be used to decide how to rebalance and trade investments given the portfolio's time horizon and objectives. A temporary market shock may give the manager a reason to rebalance the portfolio. A structural market shock may be a reason to readjust the allocation given the potential for a different market environment going in the future. It is also useful to understand the common reasons for a market crisis so that you can look for the unexpected. We examine some of the common traits found before a market crisis.

Portfolio management techniques can be used to help investment professionals improve the risk-adjusted performance of their portfolio in an environment where global equity correlation is rising. A mixture of strategic and tactical portfolio management techniques is helpful in mitigating risk and improving the efficiency of client portfolios. Methods for rebalancing based on changes in volatility and monetary policy can also be utilized when making investment decisions regarding a market shock. A shift in the portfolio mix toward international bonds, commodities, natural resource stocks, and Treasury bills and notes have been observed to lower portfolio risk during a structural decline of the U.S. stock market. Developed international markets, emerging markets, and corporate bonds have historically performed poorly during these same periods. Increasing the opportunity set of investments available to clients is more important in this environment. Portfolio managers who are currently avoiding managed futures may consider adding this asset class.

EVIDENCE OF INCREASING CORRELATION OF GLOBAL EQUITIES

The risk and return of a portfolio are determined by the return, standard deviation, and correlation of the underlying investments. The correlation between investments is a crucial element in determining an efficient portfolio. It is also well known that the correlations among most asset classes are typically unstable. The risk of rising correlation can have a significant impact on the asset mix that is appropriate for a client. Increasing correlation usually raises the overall risk of a portfolio because the assets are moving more closely together. In this scenario, the investments in the portfolio begin to behave similar to each other, which dilutes the benefits of diversification.

World equity markets are showing signs of a structural increase in correlation. A structural change in correlation is considered long term and is

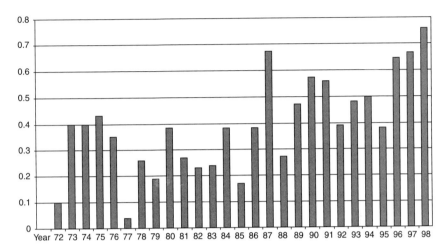

Source: Charles H. Wang. "The Geocultural, Economic, and Financial Reasons for World Equity Market Correlations." Acadian Asset Management, November 1999.

Note: Correlations are estimated using MS C1 monthly returns each year.

FIGURE 13.1   World average correlation.

usually due to permanent changes of the financial structure between the assets. On the other hand, a temporary shift in correlation is short term and is expected to revert to the mean. A graph of the average cross-sectional correlation of example world equity markets is shown in Figure 13.1. During the 26-year period between 1972 and 1998, the average correlation of the countries in the Morgan Stanley Capital International (MSCI) index has increased significantly (Wang 1999). More and more correlations are becoming significantly different from zero. From 1972 to 1979, only 30 percent of the correlation coefficients were significantly different from zero. In contrast, this percentage increased to 90 percent in 1998. Although each individual country has periods when the correlation rises and falls, the underlying structural correlation appears to be rising in developed equity markets.

Market practitioners desire risk reduction the most when the overall level of volatility is rising. Unfortunately, the evidence suggests that global equities move more closely together when the markets are becoming more volatile. Figure 13.2 shows a graph overlaying the correlation between the Europe, Australia, and Far East (EAFE) index and the standard deviation of the S&P 500 index. On a 3-year rolling basis using monthly data, it is

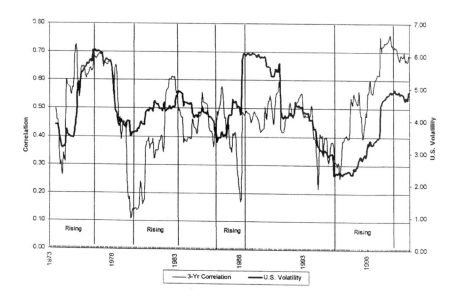

FIGURE 13.2 U.S. volatility versus EAFE correlation from 1971 to 2000.

clear that during the 28-year period between 1973 and 2000, correlation between international and domestic stocks rose when the U.S. stock market became more volatile. It is very possible that the risk tolerance for global equities will decrease when the perceived outlook for stocks in the United States is uncertain.

From 1966 to 2000, the United States experienced 11 pronounced price declines in the stock market. Table 13.1 summarizes declining markets measured by the S&P 500 index. The table lists the beginning and ending months of each decline, the length of time between peaks and troughs, the high and low price level of the S&P 500, and the percent decline. The average bear market during this period lasted 10 ¹/₂ months and dropped 25.19 percent in price. Notice that the length of time between a peak and trough became shorter in recent bear markets. For example, the declines beginning in November of 1980 and January of 1973 lasted 22 months. In contrast, the decline in 1998 lasted 4 months.

During falling stock prices in the United States, investors tend to shift assets toward higher-quality Treasury bonds and avoid international stocks. Table 13.2 is a correlation matrix including rising and falling markets. Table 13.3 is a correlation matrix of asset classes during falling markets alone.

TABLE 13.1 U.S. Stock Market Declines from 1966 to 2000

Beginning Month	Ending Month	# of Months	Market High	Market Low	Percent Decline
3/00	12/00	10	1552.87	1254.07	−19.24%
7/98	10/98	4	1190.58	923.30	−22.45%
1/94	4/94	4	482.85	435.86	−9.73%
7/90	10/90	4	369.78	294.51	−20.36%
8/87	10/87	3	337.88	216.46	−35.94%
10/83	7/84	10	173.10	147.77	−14.63%
11/80	8/82	22	141.96	101.44	−28.54%
9/76	3/78	19	107.83	86.44	−19.84%
1/73	10/74	22	120.24	62.28	−48.20%
11/68	5/70	7	108.37	69.29	−36.06%
1/66	10/66	10	93.95	73.20	−22.09%
	Average	10.5			−25.19%

Source: Blythe Lane Investment
Performance is measured using the S&P 500 Index.

TABLE 13.2 Correlation Matrix Including Rising and Falling Markets

	S&P 500	T-Bond	Corp. Bond	Int'l Bond	EAFE	Emg. Mkt.	GSCI
S&P 500	1.00						
T-Bonds	0.30	1.00					
Corp. Bonds	0.37	0.83	1.00				
Int'l Bonds	0.04	0.38	0.29	1.00			
EAFE	0.50	0.18	0.18	0.56	1.00		
Emg. Mkts.	0.53	−0.07	0.07	0.00	0.50	1.00	
GSCI	−0.04	−0.06	−0.12	0.07	−0.01	0.02	1.00

Source: Blythe Lane Investment Management.

Asset Class	Corr.
S&P 500	1.00
Emg. Mkts.	0.53
EAFE	0.50
Corp. Bonds	0.37
T-Bonds	0.30
Int'l Bond	−0.04
GSCI	0.04

TABLE 13.3 Correlation Matrix of Asset Classes During
a Declining U.S. Stock Market

	S&P 500	T-Bond	Corp. Bond	Int'l Bond	EAFE	Emg. Mkt.	GSCI
S&P 500	1.00						
T-Bonds	0.16	1.00					
Corp. Bonds	0.34	0.85	1.00				
Int'l Bonds	−0.02	0.47	0.34	1.00			
EAFE	0.57	0.08	0.14	0.35	1.00		
Emg. Mkts.	0.87	0.02	0.28	0.37	0.73	1.00	
GSCI	0.01	−0.03	−0.08	0.08	−0.11	−0.05	1.00

Source: Blythe Lane Investment

Asset Class	Corr.
S&P 500	1.00
Emg. Mkts.	0.87
EAFE	0.57
Corp. Bonds	0.34
T-Bond	0.16
GSCI	0.01
Int'l Bond	−0.02

Note that the correlation between emerging markets and developed markets increases as the U.S. stock market falls. For example, the correlation of emerging markets increased from an overall sample correlation of .53 to .87 during falling markets. On the other hand, Treasury bonds have historically had lower correlation during falling markets. The correlation of Treasury bonds decreased from .30 during all market conditions to .16 during a falling stock market.

Investors with a significant allocation in U.S. stocks have historically gained the most benefit from international bonds, commodity-linked investments, and higher-quality treasury securities. An inspection of the rank order of correlations does not reveal significant changes in order during rising or falling markets. The Goldman Sachs Commodity Index (GSCI) and international bonds have changed their order during falling prices but not significantly.

Occasionally, the markets experience unusual downside price action simultaneously. In order to isolate these events, we examined seven different asset classes to quantify their historical normal range of monthly returns. A statistical summary is presented on Table 13.4. The asset classes presented

TABLE 13.4 Bottom 5 Percent of Monthly Returns — Statistical Summary

	12/68– 12/00 S&P 500	12/79– 12/00 T-Bond	12/68– 12/00 Corp. Bond	12/77– 12/00 Int'l Bond	1/70– 12/00 EAFE	12/87– 12/00 Emg. Mkt.	12/69– 12/00 GSCI
Number of Observations	384	252	384	276	371	156	372
Median Monthly Return	1.20	0.80	0.60	0.60	1.10	1.45	0.95
High	16.80	14.40	13.80	11.00	17.90	19.00	25.80
Low	−21.50	−7.50	−8.90	−9.30	−14.40	−28.90	−15.60
90th Percentile	−3.97	−3.10	−2.30	−3.00	−4.80	−7.90	−4.89
95th Percentile	−5.79	−4.20	−3.50	−4.70	−7.15	−10.98	−6.80

Source: Blythe Lane Investment Management

are U.S. stocks, domestic Treasury bonds, corporate bonds, developed international markets, emerging markets, international bonds, and commodity-linked investments. The benchmark used for these asset classes were the S&P 500, Salomon Treasury Index, Salomon Corporate Index, Salomon Nondollar Denominated World Bond Index stated in U.S. dollar terms, MSCI EAFE, International Emerging Market Equity Index, and the Goldman Sachs Commodity Total Return Index. We then classified the lowest 5 percent of returns as being outliers to the downside using a percentile statistical method. For example, from 1968 through 2000, we observed that 95 percent of the monthly returns for the S&P 500 index were greater than −5.79 percent.

It is interesting to note that international equities have historically experienced unusual downside price movement simultaneously with the U.S. stock market. For example, the EAFE index has experienced 19 months with returns less than −7.15 percent. As shown in Tables 13.5 and 13.6, seven of those months occurred in the same month that the S&P 500 experienced returns in the bottom 5 percent. Emerging markets have also experienced this phenomenon; however, conclusions are difficult to make due to the limited amount of data available. From 1987 to 2000, emerging markets experienced 8 months with returns less than −10.98 percent. Two of those months have been synchronized with unusual downside price action in the S&P 500 index.

TABLE 13.5 Simultaneous Declines versus the S&P 500

	# of Declines	Total Declines	% Total
Treasury Bonds	1	14	7.1%
Corporate Bonds	2	21	9.5%
International Bonds	2	15	13.3%
EAFE	7	19	36.8%
Emerging Markets	2	8	25.0%
GSCI	1	20	5.0%

Source: Blythe Lane Investment Management

TABLE 13.6 Month Holding Period Return

Benchmark	90th Percentile	Median	10th Percentile
S&P 500	−6.0	3.1	13.1
T-Bonds	−4.3	2.2	10.0
Corp. Bonds	−3.8	2.0	7.9
Int'l Bonds	−4.8	2.0	11.0
EAFE	−7.8	2.8	15.0
Emg. Markets	−13.8	4.3	22.1
GSCI	−8.4	3.7	14.4

Source: Blythe Lane Investment Management

IMPORTANT DETERMINANTS OF GLOBAL EQUITY CORRELATION

Three main forces including geocultural, economic, and financial factors determine the structural correlation between the price movements of stock markets in different countries (Wang 1999). Geocultural factors include the language spoken and the distance between countries. The culture between countries has a major impact on laws and the level of comfort for conducting trade. Over time, these relationships have actually strengthened. The explanatory power of language and distance has increased from 1972 to 1992. Economic forces also play a major role in determining the comovement of stock prices between two countries. The degree of correlation between the growth in gross domestic product (GDP), the capitalization to GDP ratios, and the amount of bilateral trade all have been found to have a statistically significant relationship to global stock market correlation between countries. In addition, interest rates and the slope of the yield curve also play a key role. These factors are becoming increasingly linked through the integration of Europe.

THE INTEGRATION OF EUROPE

The integration of Europe has been at work for some time now and the impact on correlation is becoming evident. For investors outside the Euro zone, currency and interest-rate risk concentration becomes a concern and has triggered portfolio adjustments. This has led some portfolio managers to reclassify the Euro zone as a single asset class.

The correlation of countries in Europe has increased after the introduction of the Euro (Roulet 1999). A study conducted by MSCI analyzed the correlation of 15 countries in Europe before and after the introduction of the Euro. The pre-Euro period analyzed started in April of 1995 and ended in July of 1997. The after-Euro period began in August 1997 and ended in November of 1999. Most of the post-convergence correlations were far above their preconvergence period. The average correlation between the pre- and postconvergence periods increased from 0.41 to 0.55 (+14.2 percent). The major implication of this study is that the value of country asset allocation may be diminished in Europe.

TYPES OF MARKET SHOCKS

A market shock is defined as a large unexpected price movement. They are most noticeable when an unforeseen news event occurs. These large price moves can provide a feedback loop for information and give valuable information about the sentiment of large providers of liquidity in the marketplace.

There are generally two types of market shocks—structural and temporary (Kaufman 1995). A temporary market shock occurs when the price movement is short term in nature and the preexisting price trend continues. After the dissemination of unexpected information, many traders quickly liquidate positions that are perceived to be risky. After some time has passed and the situation can be analyzed, the information may be deemed irrelevant and the prior price trend continues. An example of a temporary price shock occurred in August 1991 with the news regarding the Gorbachev abduction. The Dow Jones Industrial Average gapped down on August 19, 1991 on strong volume. Two days later the news was disregarded and the Dow moved to a higher level than before the announcement. The key factor to watch when analyzing unexpected events is how the market reacts after the initial shock. Does the prior trend continue? If so, the shock is likely to be temporary. On the other hand, if the price reverses and does not look back, you may have a structural price shock on your hands.

A structural shock will usually continue in the direction of the initial volatile move. The catalyst for a structural shock can happen when economic news is not incorporated in the current price of the market. If the market continues to move in the direction of an initial price shock after enough time has been allowed for information to be analyzed, a trend change may be occurring. This feedback loop can be used when deciding whether to make tactical asset allocation adjustments or to rebalance the strategic allocation.

Common Symptoms of a Structural Market Shock

When a severe market shock occurs, there is usually a large supply-and-demand imbalance due to lack of liquidity (Bookstaber 1999). Although it is very difficult to predict a market shock in advance, we have found it useful keep a list of common symptoms found before a structural market shock occurred in history. The following is our current list:

- Large institutions have a large degree of concentration in a particular asset.
- A relatively small number of investors and institutions are exposed to a market to provide liquidity to the marketplace.
- Investors and/or institutions are using large amounts of leverage compared to the capital employed to finance investment transactions.
- Certain financial transactions remain very popular even though they do not make economic sense or have very little margin of safety incorporated in their pricing.
- A large group of investors begin to have a homogenous tolerance for risk.
- New regulations are implemented that affect the ability of institutions to invest in a certain type of asset.
- The marketplace develops a common expectation about the future prospects of an investment or groups of investments.
- Monetary and/or fiscal policy is changing.

A good example of structural market shock would be the crisis in Thailand in the early 1990s (Warwick 2000). At that time, Thailand was a fast growing country showing much promise. Much of their growth had been due to the currency policy of the country. Thailand had pegged their currency (the baht) to the U.S. dollar. The dollar had been generally weak until 1995. Because the baht was pegged to a declining U.S. dollar, exports were artificially boosted. The market price of their goods became relatively inexpensive in the world market place. Subsequently, the dollar began to rally, causing their products to be expensive. Due to heavy capital flows from the United States into Thailand, many U.S. financial institutions including banks and brokerage firms had significant risk exposure to the creditworthiness of Thai financial institutions. The real-estate bubble was a warning cry to international investment participants because Thai financial institutions would have much less ability to repay their obligations to foreign providers of capital. U.S. investors wanted out of many investments made in Thailand, causing pressure on the baht. In a futile attempt, the government poured resources into supporting the baht. This made matters worse. The large and quick decline of the baht spread to other Asian economies including Malaysia, Hong Kong, South Korea, and Japan. When very large groups of people decide to take the same action in a very short period of time, liquidity is lost and unusual price action is experienced.

PORTFOLIO MANAGEMENT TECHNIQUES USED TO ADDRESS INCREASING CORRELATION

In this article, we will focus our strategy to deal with the potential for increasing correlation in three areas. The first area is a shift away from country allocation toward global industry allocation. The second is rebalancing portfolios based on tactical triggers. The two most important tactical triggers we use are based on volatility and monetary policy. The third area is increasing the asset classes available included in portfolios.

Shift Away from Country Allocation to Industry Allocation

There is evidence that the integration of Europe has led to a need to focus on global industry allocation as opposed to country allocation. Typically, global portfolio managers tend to view the world from a country perspective—that is, they group securities by the country from which they came. However, the integration of Europe is now leading to less country differentiation. The diversification benefits across industries have been more pronounced because their correlation is lower than country correlation (Roulet 1999).

The shift away from the country allocation model calls for an up-to-date, well-defined industry classification. In August 1999, MSCI and S&P introduced their solution to address this issue—the Global Industry Classification Standard (GICS). There are indications that its use will be widely accepted and followed as many providers have begun to use this information in real time beginning in January 2001.

Rebalancing—Benefits for Risk-Adjusted Returns

It is well documented that portfolio rebalancing can significantly improve risk-adjusted performance (Goodsall 1998). Periodically buying and selling investments to reduce exposure to asset classes that have appreciated and increase exposure to those that have fallen is a key element of managing the converging correlation problem that is faced by money managers today. For example, we compared two portfolios—one implements a buy-and-hold strategy and the other rebalances every 12 months. They both start in 1979 with percentages in U.S. Treasury bills, bonds, and stocks, and international stocks, bonds, and commodities. From 1979 to 2000, the portfolio that is rebalanced once a year has better risk-adjusted returns. The lowest monthly return was also reduced from 7.29 to 6.6 percent. Another study done by First Quadrant observed similar results from a U.K. perspective (Goodsall 1998). They found that quarterly rebalancing of an international portfolio increased returns over a drift strategy and lowered the standard deviation as well. Goodsall did not find a period in which a drift strategy beat rebalancing on a risk-adjusted basis.

Volatility Contingent Rebalancing   Trigger-based rebalancing is when a manager rebalances his or her portfolio due to a specific event or condition that would indicate that an asset class may possibly be under or over extended in price. One of the most studied trigger-based rebalancing techniques has been based on asset drift. If the percentage allocated to a specific asset class is far enough away from the strategic portfolio's normal mix, the manager would rebalance the portfolio. There is evidence that this technique can add value. Art Lutschanig of Fidelity Investments (and presently with Manugistics) reported at an AIM conference that after reviewing the empirical studies and based on internal studies, Fidelity uses a 10 to 12 percent contingent trigger for major asset classes (Evensky 1997). There are three major areas to consider when devising a trigger-based rebalance strategy—the volatility of the asset class, the amount committed to each asset class, and correlation between the asset classes. One major pitfall of rebalancing is that it often will underperform a buy-and-hold portfolio. It is more pronounced over time when certain asset classes (typically stocks) perform better than 4 percent a year and are not mean reverting (Lowe 1998).

Unusual volatility can be a key element in identifying opportunities to rebalance. When volatility increases to a level beyond the normal range, it may be a good idea to reevaluate the portfolio to see if there may be a rebalancing opportunity. A graph of the 3-month rolling returns for the S&P 500 is illustrated in Figure 13.3. An upper and lower boundary line is also plotted to indicate when the 3-month return was unusually high or low. During

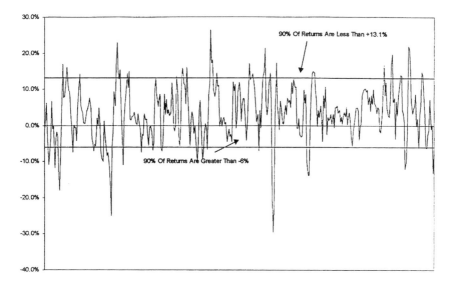

FIGURE 13.3   Rolling 3-month holding period return—S&P 500.

this period, 90 percent of the returns were between +13.1 and −6 percent. When falling outside the range happens, we use that event as an opportunity to see if there are any underlying changes in the fundamentals of the asset class or if this may simply be a temporary price move that should be bought or sold. We generally do not change the strategic allocation based on volatility, but will use it as an opportunity if mean reversion of the return pattern is expected.

Monetary Policy Contingent Rebalancing   Change in monetary policy is often a justification for a shift in the tactical allocation of a portfolio. Changes in the discount rate and the federal fund rate provide significant information about the future direction of the U.S. stock market. The discount rate and federal funds rate can be complimentary to each other because they represent different levels of information. The discount rate is viewed as an indication of the Fed's stance on overall monetary policy. In contrast, the change in the federal funds rate indicates more detailed information because it is more frequently observed and is an operating target that the Fed manipulates.

Monetary policy has a consistent and significant effect on returns and volatility for stocks and bonds. One simple and reliable indicator of U.S.

monetary policy is changes in the discount rate (Jensen 2000). (See Table 13.7.) Not only do changes in monetary policy significantly change the asset allocation outlook, but they also increase the chance that a market shock will occur in stocks. Table 13.8 shows that 85.7 percent of the lowest 5 percent of returns for the S&P 500 occurred when monetary policy has been tight. The implications that monetary policy has on avoiding or reducing exposure to market shocks is fairly clear for the U.S. stock market. The evidence is similar when examining international developed markets and emerging markets with 73.7 and 62.5 percent of the lowest 5 percent of returns occurring during tight U.S. monetary policy.

TABLE 13.7 Global Market Performance by Monetary Policy Period from 1970 to 1998

	Mean Monthly Return		Standard Deviation		
Index	Expansive Period	Restrictive Period	Expansive Period	Restrictive Period	Percent Change
U.S. Stocks	1.9133%	0.7300%	4.6602%	5.1267%	10.0%
EAFE	1.7896%	0.2601%	4.0373%	5.2113%	29.1%

Source: Monetary Conditions and the Performance of Stocks and Bonds (Jensen 2000)

TABLE 13.8 Bottom 5 Percent Declines During U.S. Fed Tightening

	S&P 500	T-Bonds	Corp. Bonds	Int'l Bonds	EAFE	Emg. Mkts.	GSCI
Total # of Declines (Bottom 5%)	21	14	21	15	19	8	20
Total During Fed Tightening	18	9	12	10	14	5	6
% During Fed Tightening	85.7%	64.3%	57.1%	66.7%	73.7%	62.5%	30.0%
Total During U.S. Bear Markets	9.000	5.000	9.000	3.000	11.000	3.000	6.000
% During U.S. Bear Markets	42.9%	35.7%	42.9%	20.0%	57.9%	37.5%	30.0%

Source: Blythe Lane Investment Management
Discount rate information obtained from The Federal Reserve Bank of St. Louis FRED database.

Correlations tend to rise when monetary policy is tight. As noted previously, global stock correlations tend to increase when volatility is rising, and volatility tends to rise when monetary policy is tight. Table 13.7 indicates that U.S. stocks and international stocks have shown increased volatility during periods of tight monetary policy. It is also interesting to note that international stocks historically have a larger increase in volatility than U.S. stocks when the Fed is tight. The standard deviation of monthly returns for U.S. stocks has increased 10 percent on average and 29.1 percent for international stocks.

Tactical Considerations during Tight Monetary Policy

Since most large declines in the U.S. stock market occur when monetary conditions are tight, we have found it useful to examine the performance of various asset classes when the U.S. stock market is declining. The data suggests that portfolios should overweigh commodities, Treasury bonds, international bonds, and cash equivalents during Fed tightening. The data also suggests that emerging markets, U.S. stocks, and developed markets should be underweighted. Table 13.9 is a statistical performance summary of seven

TABLE 13.9   Summary Statistics During a Declining U.S. Market

	S&P 500	T-Bonds	Corp. Bonds	Int'l Bonds	EAFE	Emg. Mkts.	GSCI
# of Months	103	57	98	60	102	22	103
# Years	8.6	4.8	8.2	5.0	8.5	1.8	8.6
Compounded Annual Return	−13.4%	8.3%	5.2%	7.1%	−7.9%	−37.3%	20.5%
Mean Monthly Return	−1.063	0.730	0.474	0.631	−0.535	−3.413	1.779
Median Monthly Return	−1.200	0.800	0.400	0.350	−0.200	−1.950	0.500
Standard Deviation	5.121	3.604	3.121	3.465	5.482	8.717	6.792
Kurtosis	3.348	−0.056	2.278	0.948	0.733	2.195	2.195
Skewness	−0.198	0.471	0.672	0.685	−0.091	−0.985	1.169
Range	38.3	16.3	20.4	16.7	30.0	39.4	37.3
Minimum	−21.5	−5.8	−7.7	−5.7	−14.4	−28.9	−11.5
Maximum	16.8	10.5	12.7	11.0	15.6	10.5	25.8

Source: Blythe Lane Investment Management

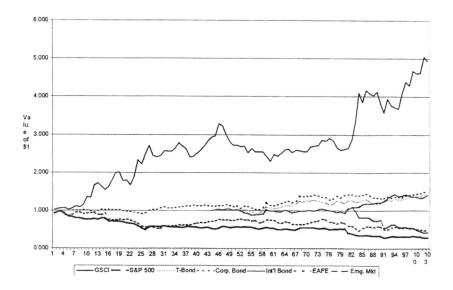

FIGURE 13.4   Performance comparison during bear markets.

different asset classes. During a declining market, the S&P 500 has compounded at a −13.4 percent rate of return. Figure 13.4 graphically illustrates the value of $1 compounded in sequential order during U.S. bear markets. The worse performing asset classes were emerging markets, which compounded at a −37.3 percent return, and developed markets, which realized a −7.9 percent return. The best performing assets classes were commodity-linked investments measured by the GSCI, which compounded at a +20.5 percent return. The asset classes that provided incremental returns for investors during a tough U.S. stock market were commodities (20.5 percent), Treasury bonds (8.3 percent), international bonds (7.1 percent), and corporate bonds (+5.2 percent).

Changes in monetary policy can clearly be a useful trigger to rebalance portfolios. When the Fed increases interest rates, the optimal portfolio has historically shifted considerably. Typically, the portfolio shifts away from U.S. stocks, foreign stocks, and corporate bonds, and buys investments in Treasury bills, managed futures, and natural resource stocks. Rebalancing at the industry level may also be effective. For example, avoid areas that typically perform poorly during restrictive monetary conditions including apparel, construction, and department stores. Traditional defensive industries, such as chemicals, petroleum, mining, and railroad, have historically performed better during restrictive periods and may be a better alternative.

CONCLUSION

The asset class risk of investing in equities is increasing. International equity and bond market correlations are unstable and increase during periods of higher volatility and U.S. stock market declines. Portfolio managers may have limited reduction in the risk of their portfolios when investing in foreign stock to diversify the risk of a declining U.S. stock market. The general risk of being in equities, whether or not they are domestic or foreign, is a significant concern when allocating capital. Estimates of an optimal portfolio can be distorted using long-term correlations. The risks may be understated due to the market shock phenomenon. This may lead to optimization results that allocate too much money in stocks and foreign securities when the stock market declines or volatility increases. Volatility tends to increase when the Fed is tightening monetary policy. This supports the use of tactical allocation strategies to reduce the risk of portfolios. Mean variance optimization methods may have less useful output if the time horizon is very long and may understate the short-term risk of the portfolio. Country selection may have limited value in diversification of a global portfolio in Europe. Industry-level security selection may become more prevalent in Europe. Rebalancing can be a useful tool to mitigate some of the risk of a global portfolio.

REFERENCES

Bookstaber, Richard M. "A Framework for Understanding Market Crisis." AIMR Conference Proceedings, 1989.

Chance, Don M. "Managed Futures and Their Role in Investment Portfolios." The Research Foundation of The Institute of Chartered Financial Analysts, 1994.

Evensky, Harold R. *Wealth Management* (New York: McGraw-Hill, 1997).

Ghayur, Khalid and Paula Dawson. "Are Global Market Returns Converging?" *Asset Allocation in a Changing World*, AIMR Publication, 1998.

Goodsall, William A.R. "Tactical Asset Allocation." *Asset Allocation in a Changing World*, AIMR Publication, 1998.

Jensen, Gerald, Robert Johnson, and Jeffrey Mercer. "The Role of Monetary Policy in Investment Management." The Research Foundation of AIMR and Blackwell Publishers, November 2000.

Kaufman, Perry. *Smarter Trading* (New York: McGraw-Hill, 1995).

Lowe, Stephen. "Rebalancing the Portfolio." *Asset Allocation in a Changing World*, AIMR Publication, 1998.

Markowitz, Harry. *Portfolio Choice: Efficient Diversification of Investments* (New York: John Wiley & Sons, 1959).

Michaud, Richard O., Gary L. Bergstrom, Ronald D. Frashure, and Brian K. Wolahan. "Twenty Years of International Equity Investing." *The Journal of Portfolio Management* 23, no. 1 (Fall 1996).

Roulet, Jacques, Kpate Adjaoute, Michael Sabbatini, and Delphine Barbaud. "Equity Investing in an Integrated Europe." Morgan Stanley Capital International, www.msci.com.

Solnik, Bruno. *International Investments*, 3rd edition, (New York: Addison-Wesley, June 1996).

The Federal Reserve Bank of St. Louis. "FRED Database." February 2001.

Wang, Charles. "Term Structure of International Market Correlations." Acadian Asset Management, October 1997.

———. "The Geocultural, Economic, and Financial Reasons for World Equity Market Correlations." Acadian Asset Management, November 1999.

Warwick, Ben. *Searching for Alpha* (New York: John Wiley & Sons, 2000).

CHAPTER 14

Investing on the Edge of Chaos

Mike Howell

This chapter argues that if the investment world is chaotic (that is, nonlinear) and dominated by paradigm shifts, then diversification across managers offering different investment styles will prove more efficient than investments offering different asset classes. In short, investors should consider style selection rather than asset allocation as a more efficient means of generating above-average returns.

Diversification across different asset classes is the accepted means of risk reduction. However, asset allocation is best suited to a deterministic world. If the investment world is chaotic and dominated by paradigm shifts, then diversification across managers offering different investment styles will prove more efficient. In short, plan sponsors and trustees must consider style selection as well as conventional asset allocation.

KEY POINTS

- Large, leveraged, and more mobile capital and information flows have radically heightened the short-term co-variation of returns between asset classes.
- Investment returns reveal complex and chaotic patterns. They have non-normal distributions with unstable co-variances between asset classes.
- Financial series have fractal dimensions of around 1.5—in other words, they are complex and trending. Pure random series have fractal dimensions near 2, whereas mean-reverting series show values above 2.

- Distributions of returns from investment styles should demonstrate more stability than asset classes. Style investing is better suited to a chaotic investment world.
- By choosing portfolios of investment styles, such as hedge funds, and altering these systematically over the investment cycle, tactical style selection (TSS) can displace tactical asset allocation (TAA).

STYLE SELECTION, NOT ASSET ALLOCATION

Chaos refers to a deterministic, nonlinear dynamic process that is of such complexity that it produces random-looking results. A chaotic system has a fractal dimension or scaling; it is highly dependent on its initial conditions; it will converge to more than one position of stability; and it will prove virtually impossible to forecast beyond the very short term.

Alternative investments, or so-called hedge funds, are increasingly being viewed by investors as a way to increase investment returns. This chapter takes a different line. We argue that hedge funds provide a more efficient way to reduce risk, and one that is particularly well suited to a complex and chaotic investment world.

Larger, more leveraged, and more mobile international capital has combined with greater computing power and information flow through cyberspace. Together they have made the financial world inherently unstable, complex, and characterized by persistent disequilibrium and frequent nonlinear shifts. This new paradigm has been labeled *cyber finance*. It renders traditional fund management less and less useful. Cyber finance favors the greater use of hedge funds and the wider adoption of tactical style selection.

In short, to lower risk, investors should diversify across investment styles rather than across asset classes. Consequently, picking baskets of hedge funds will become an important part of the investment management activities of large pension funds and other institutional investors.

The theoretical justification for traditional asset allocation derives from modern economics and finance and their assumptions of a smooth, linear, rational, and deterministic world. Unfortunately, this paradigm cannot justify the persistence of certain return patterns, nor can it explain the statistically high occurrence of market crashes.

Two dubious concepts lie behind this orthodox investment model: the existence of an equilibrium, that is, convergence to some stable fair value level, and absent-minded investors, that is, markets have no memory.

Both are wrong. First, nature abhors equilibrium. In nature, evolutionary change occurs at far from equilibrium positions. Economic evolution also often takes place out of equilibrium. Indeed, attempts to force an economic equilibrium, such as the Soviet Union, have resulted in economic stagnation and social collapse. Second, investors clearly do have memories and their actions are likely to be heavily influenced by past events, that is, feedback effects. In short, persistence or trends are likely characteristics of financial markets.

Each characteristic far from equilibrium conditions and dynamic feedback effects is usually associated with nonlinear dynamic systems, or chaos. Chaotic systems generate two features that are familiar to investors:

- **Crashes.** "The straw that breaks the camel's back." In other words, at some specific point, markets will suddenly jump or plunge to a new value, for example, the 1987 stock market crash.
- **Poor long-term forecasts.** The sensitivity to initial conditions and nonlinear dynamics mean that only short-term forecasting is practical. Long-term prediction is virtually impossible.

Unfortunately, neither feature can be explained by modern financial theory. In reality, financial markets are the very opposite of that assumed by the theory. They are nonlinear, messy, and complex. Consequently, investment risk is forced to take on several new dimensions.

Table 14.1 shows how risk characteristics change according to the pattern of investment returns. Investment returns can be constant, and they can also vary randomly, deterministically, and chaotically. Each state implies a different structure for the variance/co-variance matrix of returns.

In the fictitious world of constant returns, asset allocation becomes trivial. Portfolios comprise entirely the highest returning asset. Modern finance does not go this far, but it does assume that we lie somewhere in between a completely deterministic world and an entirely random one; in other words, investment markets contain elements of both.

At one extreme, carefully crafted computer models attempt to accurately predict future asset returns. At the other, the Efficient Market Hypothesis

TABLE 14.1 Returns and Risks Under Different Assumptions

Investment Returns	Variance	Co-variances
Constant	Zero	Zero
Random	Constant and normally distributed	Low
Deterministic	Varying and normally distributed	Moderate
Chaotic	Varying and non-normally distributed	High and varying

Source: CrossBorder Capital

(EMH) argues that only unexpected news affects prices because all other information has already been thoroughly analyzed and discounted by the vast assembly of investors that populate financial markets. In short, asset prices simply cannot be wrong because so many people influence them. Moreover, given that yesterday's news is no longer relevant, investment returns must be unrelated to time. In other words, they will be unpredictable, independent random variables.

According to the Law of Large Numbers, as the number of these random observations (such as investment returns) grows, in the limit (as the total approaches infinity), the probability distribution will become normal with an identifiable mean and constant variance. If investment returns follow a normal probability distribution, then a battery of statistical tests and decision-making rules can be devised to optimize asset allocation.

These rules make up much of Modern Portfolio Theory (MPT). MPT includes Markowitz's efficient frontier, Sharpe's Capital Asset Pricing Model (CAPM), and Ross' Arbitrage Pricing Theory (APT). MPT, with its assumption of normal returns and its association of variance with risk, rationalizes the case for diversification across securities and across asset classes.

However, the real world is not constant, random, or deterministic. Financial markets fall into the fourth category: highly chaotic. Experience shows that the co-movements between asset classes tend to vary significantly over time. Investment returns are non-normally distributed and variances are unstable. The constant variance and normality assumptions are necessary conditions for the EMH. A high and varying co-variance undermines MPT. Ironically, these co-movements tend to jump during times of crisis when low correlations and diversification benefits are most needed. In a chaotic world, variance is a poor and inadequate measure of risk because the return distribution is skewed, kurtosis, and non-normal. What's more, the efficient frontier becomes unstable. Consequently, mean-variance optimization and use of the Sharpe Ratio become increasingly useless analytical tools.

WHEN PARADIGMS SHIFT

The investment process can be thought of in terms of a pyramid. The apex represents the ideal portfolio allocation and the base denotes the mass of all publicly available information. Sandwiched in between are two layers consisting of the range of assets, differentiated by duration and, just below, the range of investment styles, also ordered by duration. There are fewer assets than investment styles. See Figure 14.1.

In theory, investors should diversify over as wide a base as possible, that is, across the base of the pyramid, in order to ensure against even the most

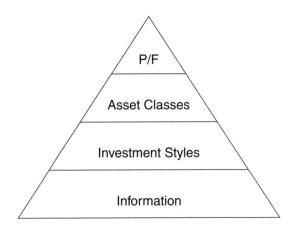

Source: CrossBorder Capital

FIGURE 14.1   The investment pyramid.

remote shock. This means diversification across the entire information set, but, by definition, this is impossible. The second best option is to move higher to the next tier in the pyramid. In other words, diversify across the range of investment styles (or managers) that synthesize the information set. It follows that diversification across asset classes, such as bonds and equities, which comprise the next level up, represents an inferior option.

Diversification across investment styles should reduce risk in a similar way to diversification across asset classes. In other words, each new management style can be thought of as a new asset. And combinations of investment styles should produce a return distribution that is closer to normal than the distribution of conventional asset returns.

Conventional investing may also fail to diversify efficiently because of consensus thinking. Financial information is neither evenly distributed nor smoothly acted upon. If consensus thinking dominates, there is likely to be a widely shared investment paradigm. This might, for example, center on forecasts of economic growth and inflation. Undoubtedly, managers will try to differentiate themselves by either having slightly better models and/or slightly better access to information. But, in practice, few differences exist either in the return generation process or in the forecast inputs themselves, which tend to be compressed together by the powerful forces of consensus.

However, if the investment world is complex and incompletely understood, there will more likely be a profusion of different investment paradigms and an array of different information sets, each associated with a different investment style. In a complex world, investors should diversify directly across these paradigms or investment styles rather than across traditional asset classes. Paradoxically, the theory behind diversification does not require that any of these investment paradigms be necessarily correct. Many may ultimately prove to be wrong-headed. But a basket of different styles does offer clear risk-reduction opportunities since it is unlikely that all will move together.

There is also another reason why conventional investing may prove less efficient. The traditional investment process assumes a constant or almost constant investment horizon, for example, 5 or 10 years. It is more likely that the length of the desired investment horizon changes frequently and that these changes are related to systemwide liquidity conditions. In other words, the investment horizon will likely be longer the more that liquidity is abundant. If the investment horizon is itself changing, then portfolio duration must also change with it.

The problem is that the effective duration of bond and stock portfolios within traditional asset allocation models are often similar and, anyway, average portfolio duration is rarely changed significantly over the liquidity cycle, in large part because of constraints, such as the inability to short sell. Essentially, conventional investment management limited by restrictions and hammered by consensus thinking has become too inflexible. See Figure 14.2.

Figure 14.2 shows that as well as offering the possibilities of greater leverage, alternative investment products give a wider range of duration possibilities. Hedge fund managers can be grouped according to their broad investment styles, such as arbitrage, market neutral, and directional. Not only do each of these three styles differ greatly in duration terms, but within each style duration can also vary significantly. For example, arbitrage funds tend to be duration neutral; market-neutral funds often run a small positive duration; and directional funds apply large positive and occasionally large negative duration positions.

We have argued that chaos theory may explain the changing co-movements between investment returns. Chaos theory contains elements of stochastic and deterministic processes. This complexity defies the rational analysis employed by most deterministic models to such an extent that the outcomes, such as investment returns, appear to be almost random.

Table 14.2 classifies four different investment regimes according to this complexity and the degree of disorder observed in the system. Complexity is judged from the number of rules required to describe behavior. Figure 14.3 depicts these four regimes quantitatively, measured in terms of risk and the degree of system complexity. We have joined states by a curve according to their disorder.

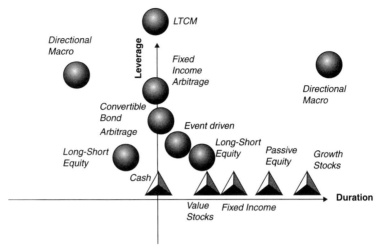

FIGURE 14.2   A taxonomy of investment styles.

TABLE 14.2   From Complexity to Chaos—Investment Returns
Under Different States

	Ordered World	Disordered World
Simple World	Constant	Random
Complex World	Deterministic	Chaos

Source: CrossBorder Capital

This taxonomy suggests that traditional asset allocation tries to invest during periods of disorder and order by successive shifts away from and toward a benchmark or passive index portfolio—in other words, from a random to a deterministic world. This is illustrated in Figure 14.3 by a shift between the top left and the bottom right of the diagram. It applies if the real world alternates between randomness and rationality.

But in a complex, messy world there is another method of controlling risk. Visually, this can be represented as a movement from the bottom left to the top right in the diagram—in other words, from a constant to a chaotic environment. This technique requires allocating a portfolio between cash and

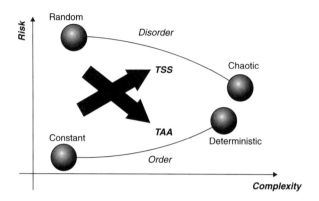

Source: *CrossBorder Capital*

FIGURE 14.3 From TAA to TSS.

alternative investments, such as hedge funds, and it applies when the real world alternates between occasional constancy and frequent chaos. It is a more likely description of today's investment environment.

Looked at another way, investors should hold baskets of management styles, not baskets of assets. Investment style is more likely to be invariant to chaotic change or paradigm shifts than traditional asset classes. Rising co-movements between these assets mean that in times of crisis they all move together in the same direction—for example, bond and equity prices collapse. Investment styles offer greater diversification benefits in a chaotic world.

CONCLUSION: CYBER FINANCE FAVORS TSS, NOT TAA

Traditional asset allocation would work well if we could ignore the unpredictable but periodic shocks, which heighten portfolio variance and tighten the cross-correlation between asset classes. Unfortunately, we cannot. The world is complex, nonlinear, and messy; consequently, investment returns are non-normal. This fact challenges orthodoxy and negates the conclusions of MPT. Specifically, three and four sigma events are fairly common and investment returns reveal persistent trends. This strongly suggests that they are generated by nonlinear dynamic processes. In short, they are chaotic.

If the world is complex and chaotic and therefore difficult to understand, then two heads will always beat one. Hedge fund managers are not necessarily better investors than conventional managers (some are and some are not), but the risk characteristics of a portfolio of hedge funds styles will likely reduce risk more efficiently than a portfolio of assets.

In a chaotic world characterized by paradigm shifts, methods of cyber finance should be adopted. For example, TAA between bonds, equities, and cash will likely be an inefficient method of reducing risk. More effective is TSS. This approach starts by selecting manager styles, such as different hedge funds, and holding a diversified but changing basket of these investments.

HOW CHAOTIC ARE FINANCIAL MARKETS?

History gives us good reason to doubt that the world is normal in a statistical sense. In fact, recent mathematical techniques are able to demonstrate that the world in general, and financial markets in particular, display chaotic behavior.

The pattern of investment returns can be best described as *leptokurtic*. In other words, they come from spiky, fat-tailed distributions, where three and four standard deviation events are common. Table 14.3 shows this bias in U.S. equity return data. The high degrees of (negative) skewness and (lepto-) kurtosis reported confirm that the distribution is non-normal. Skewness measures the presence of long -tails (normally distributed data has a skewness coefficient of zero). A significant negative number denotes a long

TABLE 14.3 Are Stock Market Returns Non-normal?
(U.S. annualized returns from 1920 to 1999)

Decade	Mean	Standard Deviation	Skewness	Kurtosis
1920s	8.1	26.1	−1.41	18.97
1930s	−5.8	30.4	0.18	3.77
1940s	2.5	14.1	−0.94	10.80
1950s	12.3	11.2	−0.84	7.86
1960s	4.3	9.9	−0.48	9.87
1970s	1.5	13.7	0.26	2.29
1980s	11.8	16.5	−0.83	7.32
1990s	14.8	13.8	−0.71	4.84
Overall	6.2	17.0	−0.60	8.22

Source: Peters (1991) and CrossBorder Capital

left-hand tail (higher odds of sub-par returns). A significant positive number measures a long right-hand tail (higher odds of above-par returns). Kurtosis measures the flatness or sharpness of the return distribution. The normal distribution has a kurtosis measure of 3. Readings below 3 indicate a relatively flat (or platykurtic) distribution. Readings above 3 suggest a leptokurtic or spiked return distribution.

These results severely challenge MPT. Non-normality means that the traditional mean-variance models will not be optimal. The CAPM will also be wrong since variance (the traditional proxy for risk) and return will not be linked in the way the theory says. Indeed, evidence shows that low-variance investments yield higher returns and high-variance investments yield lower returns than the CAPM predicts.

Fat tails in the return distribution either mean that information is released in clumps, or that investors react to it in clumps. In other words, the market has a memory. Investors likely react sometime after information is released, not as it is released. This may be because opinions are formed after several pieces of confirming information are gathered. It may also be because investors react as part of a crowd and crowds first need to build up size.

In nonlinear dynamic systems, the Hurst Exponent (H) tests for these memory or persistence effects. If H = 0.5, the underlying data series is random. In other words, if today's value is positive, there is a 50-50 chance of the next reading being positive. If the exponent lies between zero and 0.5, the data series is antipersistent or mean reverting. In practice, mean-reverting series tend to be very hard to find. Far more common are time series with Hurst Exponent values between 0.5 and 1. These show the data to be persistent or trend reinforcing. In short, H values near 0.5 identify randomness; values near 1 show well-defined trends.

The Hurst Exponent is related to a concept called the *fractal dimension*. The fractal dimension is a generalization of the more common Euclidean dimension familiar from basic geometry. It is defined as the inverse of the Hurst Exponent. Fractal dimensions measure persistence because a fractal is an object where the parts are in some way linked to the whole, but unlike the smooth Euclidean geometry, their dimensions are often rough, discontinuous, and noninteger; in other words, a fractal dimension of 1.4 is somewhere between a Euclidean line (= 1) and a Euclidean plane (= 2).

In Euclidean geometry, a line has dimension 1, a plane has a dimension of 2, and a solid has a dimension of 3. A purely random event would have a fractal dimension of 2, that is, 1/H where H = 0.5. A pure trend would have a fractal dimension of 1, that is, 1/H where H = 1. The fractal dimension of 1.39 often occurs in nature. Peters (1991) reports that Britain's coastline has a dimension of 1.30, whereas Norway's more jagged coastline has a dimension of 1.52. Sunspots have a dimension of 1.85.

TABLE 14.4 Are Financial Markets Chaotic? (Fractal dimensions of selected data series from 1959 to 1990)

	Hurst Exponent	Fractal Dimension	Cycle Length (months)
Currencies			
US$: Y	0.64	1.56	N/A
DM: US$	0.64	1.56	72
£: US$	0.61	1.64	72
Interest Rates			
US Long Bond	0.68	1.47	60
US Treasury Bills	0.65	1.54	N/A
Stock Markets			
S&P 500	0.78	1.28	48
MSCI Japan	0.68	1.47	48
MSCI UK	0.68	1.47	30
MSCI Germany	0.72	1.39	60

Sources: Peters (1991) and CrossBorder Capital

These statistics help us to characterize and describe data. Put another way, they confirm that economic and financial series derive from complex dynamic systems. In short, they are chaotic. A clear undeviating trend could be contained in a straight line. Hence, it would have a geometric dimension of 1. A pure random series would need to be contained within a plane. Therefore, it would have a dimension of 2. A chaotic series that sits somewhere in between it is neither completely random nor exactly linear. Consequently, its dimension lies between 1 and 2. Recall that the Hurst Exponent of a mean-reverting data series lies below 0.5. In other words, its fractal dimension exceeds 2. Table 14.4 shows the fractal dimensions of a number of financial series. The results show that all come from nonlinear dynamic systems—in other words, they are chaotic. None reveal mean-reverting characteristics.

REFERENCES

Lee, D.K.C. "Long Memory and the Asian Crisis," National University of Singapore, 1999.

Peters, E. *Chaos and Order in Capital Markets* (New York: John Wiley & Sons, 1991).

CHAPTER 15

Hedge Fund Risk

Brian Cornell

An excellent introduction to the many varied hedge fund styles and the risks associated with each. A more succinct overview of the strategies employed and their peculiar risks would be hard to find in current industry literature.

"Benign neglect is not an excuse for suffering a loss in a hedge fund"
—Brian Cornell

The evolution of the hedge fund industry has parallels to the development of the Internet. With the establishment of the first hedge fund in 1949 by A.W. Jones, the concept of alternative investment structures was born. Over the next 40 years, development in legal structures, technology, markets, and information flows facilitated the nascent growth of hedge fund offerings. The PC revolution then caused the rate of development to progress rapidly as models for exploiting inefficiencies were commoditized. With this technological expansion, new entrants and offerings under the guise "hedge fund" have exploded onto the investment landscape.

The backbone and principal of the Internet had existed for years as an efficient method of communication within the government, specifically the defense industry. The interconnectivity revolution spawned the rapid development of a wide variety of products and services designed to capture the new electronic economy. Although products and services shared rather quiet beginnings and were transformed by the Information Age, the paths taken reflect very different risks. Irrational valuations attached to concept businesses have proven to reflect bubble-like mania behavior. The rapid flow of funds into the hedge fund industry reflects prudent asset allocation at work. This is not to be mistaken for the overvaluation of hedge funds in general. However, this flow of funds requires a breadth of understanding of the risks peculiar to hedge funds.

Risk comes in many different forms. Structural risks include legal and regulatory issues. Market risks include liquidity, volatility, flow of funds, and investor psychology. Leverage risks include collateral, magnitude, duration, and volatility. Business risks include fraud, operations, administration, feedback loop, and management. Strategy risks include leverage, liquidity, scalability, and theory. Investment risks include lack of transparency, liquidity, relationships, fees, and conflicts of interest. None of these lists is exhaustive, yet collectively they underscore the complexity of understanding required to navigate the unregulated nature of hedge funds.

Before listing the particular styles of hedge funds and meeting the task of defining their respective risks, it helps to understand the basis for the lack of regulation of hedge funds. The Federal Reserve, through Regulation T, effectively reigned in the speculative fervor that persisted in the Roaring Twenties. To protect investors from the evils of excessive leverage, this decree set margin requirements for equity purchases at a maximum of 50 percent. In effect, leverage was limited to two to one under this mandate. For the unsophisticated investor, this regulation limited some of the irrational investment behavior people are prone to pursue. For the more knowledgeable market participant, however, this regulation was a tight leash on savvy investment innovation. As the legal profession is wont to do, a chorus of sophisticated investors developed, supported by a cadre of lawyers who pushed the agenda for regulatory exception. Through rules 3.c.1. and 3.c.7., the portal to the hedge fund industry was exploited. Therein lies the heart of many of the risks associated with hedge funds. The industry operates on regulatory exception. As with many human endeavors where rules and regulations are designed to benefit the masses, popularity of an exception to the point of the exception becoming the rule compromises the very nature of the purpose of the rules in the first place.

HEDGE FUND STYLES

Just as many styles, sizes, and strategies of mutual funds exist (active versus passive management, Fidelity Magellan versus Fidelity Select Pharmaceuticals, and equity versus fixed-income funds), hedge funds are equally, if not more, diverse in structure. The following examples are not an exhaustive list of strategies but do reflect the complex nature of the hedge fund industry.

Relative Value Strategies

Convertible Arbitrage   This strategy involves the purchase of a long convertible security (usually preferred shares or bonds) exchangeable for a fixed amount of other securities (usually common stock) at a fixed ratio or price while short selling the underlying equity. The convertible security is a hybrid instrument comprising fixed-income and equity features. The equity features reflect the convertibility of the bond into equity while exhibiting optionality. Convertible arbitrage requires an understanding of the conversion details, including timing and exchange value. These details provide the basis for the short position in the underlying equity. Value is extracted through perceived mispricing of the equity component of the convertible bond and the short equity position. This value may be driven by different judgments about volatility and/or the timing of convertibility.

Mortgage Trading   This is a long/short strategy that typically requires the purchase of a mortgage instrument while short selling credit and Treasury instruments to offset credit and interest rate risk. Mortgages are pooled and packaged in a variety of ways to isolate interest and/or principal components. The structure of the packaging may include leverage and/or inversions. These fixed-income instruments have the peculiar character of doubtable duration. As individuals pay down their mortgages early, the duration of the mortgage pool is shortened. Value is extracted through market inefficiencies in pricing the optionality of duration contraction as well as credit and interest rate risk.

Capital Structure Arbitrage   This strategy attempts to exploit mispricings within the capital structure of a company by maintaining long and short positions among various equity and fixed-income securities in a given publicly traded firm. Typically consisting of a long senior debt position offset by a short junior debt position in the same company, the arbitrage is designed to reconcile differences in valuation among different constituent holders of the debt. Measuring the debt covenants and interest coverage at each level of the capital structure enables valuation as to the probability of a company paying off its debt. As company fundamentals deteriorate, subordinated debt erodes in value first, followed by higher levels in the structure. Value is extracted through the identification of mispricings relative to similar debt in related companies or industries with similar financial positions. In addition, through ownership of a significant portion of one or more levels of debt, one can influence management and other bondholders to alter the structure of the company finances that can unlock significant profit.

Fixed-Income Arbitrage   This strategy typically involves holding an equal amount of debt long and short in order to neutralize market exposure while capturing a yield, duration, or other spread. Although this strategy may be applied in the corporate bond market, it is most commonly exercised in sovereign debt markets worldwide. The trade may be as simple as a long position in off-the-run Treasuries versus short on-the-run Treasuries. Or the trade may be a complex butterfly trade involving perhaps 2- and 10-year long positions versus a short 5-year position constructed to neutralize duration. Value is extracted through minute price differences among similar securities or through duration-engineered positions.

Options Arbitrage This entails holding long- and short-option positions against an index, a basket of stocks, or individual stocks in an attempt to extract volatility differentials. Individual equity volatility often differs from index volatility due to differences in diversification. Exploiting these differentials through carefully engineered baskets utilizing puts and/or calls can generate significant value.

Statistical Arbitrage This requires investors to hold long and short positions in equity securities in order to exploit a statistical relationship that exists between stocks. The statistical relationship may relate to one of over a hundred fundamental factors that explain stock price movement. In exploiting one or more of these factors, there may be a measured effort to neutralize many other factors. For example, in an attempt to isolate jet fuel contract price differences between major airlines, the trade may be constructed to neutralize dollar, beta, and capitalization exposures. Most statistical arbitrage is an attempt to take advantage of minute-factor-explained price differences over very short periods of time (perhaps a day or less).

Equity Market Neutral

Strategies involve maintaining an equal amount of equity long and short positions in order to neutralize market exposure while capturing a valuation spread. The objective is to capture the change in relative valuations. Like statistical arbitrage, market-neutral equity strategies attempt to extract value from mean-reversion price behavior. Unlike statistical arbitrage, however, the timeframe for mean reversion is typically longer, the value differential larger, and the valuation relationship looser. These programs tend to have more fundamental evaluation involved in the process. Consequently, these strategies have a greater tendency to be exercised within one or a few sectors rather than across a wide spectrum of sectors.

Event-Driven Strategies

These strategies invest in the outcome of specific corporate events with the objective of capturing the spread between the pricing of security before completion and following completion of the event.

Merger Arbitrageurs   These individuals invest in companies undergoing mergers, acquisitions, or other types of changes in control. They attempt to profit from the price spread that exits between the announcement and completion of the merger transaction. Pure merger arbitrage avoids speculation about rumored transactions. The trade is constructed through a long position in the acquired company and a short position in the acquiring company. The composition of the trade is engineered according to the unique character of the transaction structure. Once a deal has been announced, the relative prices of the stocks involved immediately price in the deal structure less a small discount. The discount represents time, regulatory risk in the acquisition, and other uncertainties. The value extracted in this strategy is properly setting up the arbitrage and experiencing a successful conclusion to the acquisition within a reasonable timeframe.

Distressed Investing   This strategy involves investing in the debt of companies undergoing debt restructuring. It is an attempt to profit from the increase in company and debt value as the company emerges from distress or bankruptcy. Distressed investing is most often a long-only strategy. It is typically quite labor intensive, as buyers of distressed debt often work closely with the company, bankers, or other interested parties in an effort to affect change in the direction, financing, or operation of the company. Many traditional debt holders become forced sellers when certain low price levels are hit or covenants are compromised. Value is extracted through the purchase of debt from these holders at prices that do not accurately reflect the intrinsic value of the underlying collateral or the potential of the company to fix their problems.

Loan Origination

In this strategy, strategists arrange privately structured senior debt to companies to satisfy the short-term need for capital. The strategy attempts to profit from the need for shorter-term financing with full collateral protection in case of default. When companies are faced with short-term financing needs, they may seek alternative sources of lending away from traditional lines. They may be at their credit limit with traditional lenders or find an advantage through alternative means. Value is extracted through fees, high interest rates, and potential warrants.

High Yield

In this strategy, managers invest in below-investment-grade debt in order to capture enhanced yield and price appreciation. This strategy is most often practiced on the long side only. After a thorough evaluation of a company's fundamentals, one attempts to profit from the payment stream and potential price increases if an anticipated rating increase occurs.

Multistrategy/Special Situations

This category includes class share arbitrage, one-off deal structures, and combinations of any or all of the previously mentioned strategies. The value in exercising a multiple strategy approach is the ability to shift capital to opportunistic situations as they arise. As the economy moves between boom and bust periods (notwithstanding the Greenspan-led Federal Reserve rate activism), different strategies enjoy relative periods of outperformance. A fund that can move with these cycles may provide greater value than a single strategy fund.

Long/Short Equity Strategists

These individuals hold unequal amounts of long and short positions in equities while maintaining a bias in one direction. The direction of the bias may be held constant or vary with market conditions. The objective is to capture equity market-like returns with lower volatility.

Long Biased

These funds typically maintain net market exposure between 30 and 80 percent long. Some funds operate within a narrow band of fixed net long exposure while others fluctuate dynamically. The theory behind fixed exposure strategies lies in the belief that market timing calls are not within the purview of the manager. Dynamic exposure managers often profess that exposure is driven by ideas generated while others proclaim a macroeconomic analysis capability. Gross exposure (long plus short exposure) generally runs from 80 to 200 percent or more. Value is most often extracted through stock-picking skill.

Classic Jones Model

This type of investing involves a capital structure that is long approximately 100 percent of account value and short approximately 50 percent of account value, with the objective of maintaining between 30 and 50 percent net long exposure. This is a classic version of the long biased strategy first expressed in A. W. Jones' 1949 portfolio. Gross exposure runs around 150 percent most of the time. Although alpha is generated on the long side, often short-side exposure is designed to provide a hedge rather than provide alpha.

Low Net Biased

These funds maintain a net market exposure between 0 and 30 percent long. This portion of the spectrum tends to operate more dynamically in terms of exposure. Gross exposures often run between 40 and 120 percent. Short exposure tends to be more of an alpha generator in this case.

Neutral Biased

These funds maintain a net market exposure between -10 and $+10$ percent. This area of long/short equity is focused largely on generating alpha from both sides of the portfolio equally. Gross exposure has a tendency to remain in the 40 to 200 percent range depending on market conditions.

Short Biased

These funds maintain a net market exposure between 0 to -60 percent. Sometimes long/short equity and sometimes just modestly short only, this group of funds offers alpha generation on the short side. Long exposures are often constructed to hedge-specific risks while lacking alpha. Gross exposure is usually lower than in many of the other long/short strategies, usually 10 to 80 percent.

Dedicated Short Selling

With this strategy, strategists maintain net market exposure approaching 100 percent short. This strategy is not for the faint of heart as the theory goes against the long-term upward bias of the market. The strategy is often sold as a market-hedge, contrarian-style portfolio diversifier. Fee structures are more creative in this space as positive return is not always the objective. Instead, a benchmark such as the inverse of a popular index may be the measure of success.

Other Strategies

Many funds offered in today's marketplace have utilized the label "hedge fund" to their advantage. Some of these offerings are truly hedge funds in the classic sense, while others stretch the boundary of definition for marketing purposes.

Macro   This is the all-weather strategy in more ways than one. This strategy employs any of the strategies listed previously and in the following sections to capture the opportunistic value. The most sophisticated of strategies and usually the most difficult to assess, macro trading exploits a wide variety of market opportunities globally. Value is derived in an infinite number of ways in creative trade engineering. The edge created through the synergies of operating a broad set of strategies is unparalleled. These funds can grow to enormous size and have a great deal of influence in the market.

Currency   Managers attempt to exploit value differences among currencies through long and short positions (currency pairs) worldwide. This strategy had more dynamics prior to the advent of the euro, but the principal remains the same. The economic engines of the world run at different speeds and central bankers operate with differing policies. These competing forces keep the relative values of currencies in a state of flux. Perceptions of economic trends and interest rate changes are the drivers of fundamental analysis in this strategy. Value is extracted through trend capture.

Commodities and Futures   In this strategy, portfolios are built with long and short positions across a wide spectrum of derivative markets. An increasing number of commodity funds is marketed as hedge funds. In most cases, no hedge is involved. A number of spread traders exist in the business, but the vast majority of these programs involves trend following in nature based on intramarket analysis. Value is generally captured through the capture of price trends.

Regulation D   This involves the purchase of restricted stock in publicly traded companies at a discount to the current market value. Capture spread in value between unrestricted and restricted stocks when restructured stock becomes registered. The market for this strategy has blossomed in recent years. Companies have found the rapid rise of capital through this regulatory window advantageous relative to traditional underwriting. Funds that exploit this area attempt to hedge their position through short sales of unrestricted stock. Value is captured through the discount offered on the restricted stock.

Mutual Fund Timing   This entails the purchase of mutual funds for short-duration holding periods. The strategy employs a timing model based on a variety of price-based factors. The most successful programs exploit *time zone arbitrage*, whereby purchases of foreign benchmarked funds are allowed up to the closing bell in the United States. To the extent that foreign markets exhibit follow-through correlation with our domestic markets, the arbitrage exploits the free look offered through purchases after the foreign markets close. In domestic mutual fund timing, models are more dependent upon serial correlation behavior.

STRATEGY RISKS

Very little pure arbitrage takes place in the world. To the extent that it exists (two instruments that at a defined point in the future become one and the same), the efficient market theory is defied. On the other hand, one could say that the efficient market theory requires arbitrage to bring similar instruments into equal value. Many of the strategies in the hedge fund industry incorporate the word *arbitrage* into their design, theory, or rationale, yet the convergence theory exploited in most instances carries a risk that arbitrage does not. For example, time, volatility, correlation, and regulation are but a few of the risks in the relationship between similar instruments that most hedge fund strategies are attempting to exploit. However, these risks, by definition, exclude the examples from the world of arbitrage. In fact, although many purport the idea that these strategies are arbitrage-like, some linkages are temporal at best while others are nonexistent at worst.

Nowhere in the hedge fund industry is the word *arbitrage* more misleading than in the relative value strategies. Take statistical arbitrage, for instance. Efficient market theory would essentially say that two companies that enjoy similar capital structures, market shares, and production costs in a competitive market should be priced fairly equally if they are producing similar earnings. However, the ivory tower world of analysis rarely exists in the real world. Subtle differences exist in the way the companies operate, in the strength of their market share, in their respective management teams, and in their strategic visions, among many other factors. Labeling statistical arbitrage as *arbitrage* connotes security and safety in the relationship between the two securities. A pair of companies is not destined to become one and the same at a specific point in time in the future. Accordingly, no true arbitrage takes place . When one thinks of all the relevant factors that can explain stock price and the tremendously diverse blocs of constituents that may buy or sell a stock, it is easy to see that an error factor in the mathematical relationship could easily consume the microscopic valuation differences statistical arbitrage strategies hope to exploit.

Many will argue that statistical arbitrage is just the removal of price differential along certain factor lines or vectors. The argument may continue that this is a pure example of the efficient market theory at work. This line of argument rests in the crucial assumptions of statistical arbitrage theory. These assumptions identify and isolate specific statistics about a balance sheet, income statement, or some other financial measure and through comparison with similar companies find different values attached to the item measured. Efficient market theory suggests market forces will erase these differences. This is not an exercise in arbitrage. The complexities of all the factors that may explain stock price make it difficult to isolate any one variable and its explanatory power in price movement or valuation with a great deal of accuracy. Statistical arbitrage is more arbitrage-like (in other words, relative-value-oriented) than pure arbitrage.

Market-neutral equity investing comes in many different forms, but it remains a close cousin of statistical arbitrage. This is a much simpler strategy by design and forgoes the arbitrage label. The theory is fairly similar, though, in that like companies should behave similarly in the market. When one takes into consideration structural differences, competitive advantages, and management, the relative value of similar companies may be better understood. Utilizing the theory of mean reversion, market-neutral practitioners build subset portfolios of long and short positions within a market segment trying to neutralize dollar exposure, beta, market capitalization, and so on. Let's picture a roller coaster. The track is the market behavior, while the string of cars that rides the track represents a group of companies, such as airlines. As the airline industry is affected by the economy, fuel prices, and labor, the companies ride the track together. As subtle differences emerge, such as targeted price wars, targeted labor problems, a plane crash, or weather problems in an area dominated by one carrier, the cars riding the roller coaster track reach tops and bottoms at different times. Buying the relatively undervalued airlines and shorting the relatively overvalued airlines, in this example, are designed to exploit the rotation of value within the industry while remaining neutral to market and economic factors. The risk is a car decoupling from the rest of the cars. Buying Braniff, Eastern, or Pan Am risks these companies going out of business rather than becoming mean-reverting value plays.

In both statistical arbitrage and market-neutral investing, the primary risk is the uncoupling of a previously measured tight statistical relationship. The most successful models operate on a theoretical basis with a substantial body of evidence that supports the theory. Weak models depend more upon perceived statistical relationships uncovered through data mining. Just like the Super Bowl investing theory and the presidential cycle theory, weak models rely on statistical anomalies that appear strong but are supported by small amounts of data. The risk for investors is determining the integrity of the research process, the breadth and depth of the models, and the volume of evidence supporting the conclusions the model will draw. With the most robust models, however, risk still exists that long-term theoretical relationships will break down. Without a method for examining models for deterioration and for testing new market information for consistency with historical data, the research process fails to maintain a robust character over time.

Fixed-income arbitrage investing entices high levels of leverage utilization in specific instances due to discreet differences among similar securities.

We will address the risk of leverage and financing in a later section, however. A central risk to fixed-income arbitrage is that duration plays along the yield curve. In a mature arena like the United States Treasury securities market, the breadth and depth of the constituent buyers and sellers maintains a fairly smooth yield curve whether steep, shallow, or inverted. Anomalous pricing among securities along the curve is routinely arbitraged away through basis trading. Other G-10 fixed-income markets are either less mature, provide less depth, have fewer competing constituents, or encompass a combination of these factors. The shape and continuity of the yield curve is less stable as a result. The risk in these strategies rests in the changing shape of the yield curve. If duration plays along the curve, one can mistake what turns out to be the beginning of a shift in the shape of the curve for an anomalous price occurrence. Just as in the example of the airline that breaks from the pack on its way to bankruptcy, an inflection point in the yield curve can develop in the early stages of a curve shift. Since so many of these trades can be placed in a large size with little or no margin requirement, an unexpected inflection in the curve can bring down the house in a hurry.

Mortgage arbitrage has the appearance of being the most consistent performer of all the fixed-income strategies. The market lacks a price discovery exchange impeding access to marginal utility information. This market is a dealer-run community where the product is inconsistent and structural leverage has run amok. The essential base of all products in this arena is a pool of mortgages packaged up and resold through Wall Street houses. Information is available on the character of the mortgages in order to facilitate knowledge of the credit worthiness, duration, and payment behavior of the mortgage holders. Wall Street buys pools of mortgages and carves up the package into products that are interest only (IO), principal only (PO), inverse IOs, and a variety of other levered structures. Mortgage arbitrageurs attempt to offset credit risk through swaps and high-yield index shorts. They attempt to mitigate or eliminate duration risk through short positions of similar maturity. Finally, they limit interest rate risk through short Treasury security holdings of similar interest rates. The single largest risk remaining in the arbitrage is the prepayment risk associated with the mortgage holders peculiar to a specific pool.

Economic theory provides a rational model for determining prepayment behavior, but mortgage holders, as a group, rarely act perfectly rational. Behavioral finance theorists have broadened the sophistication of the prepayment models to a marginal extent. Finally, market psychologists have added their two cents to model construction. Despite all the theorists and practitioners, prepayment risk remains the most unpredictable element of mortgage investing. This risk befuddles the duration component of the models destabilizing the arbitrage aspect of the trade. The risk is akin to matching fixed costs with variable financing. Without a model that can predict human behavior perfectly, no arbitrage exists. Rather, the trade becomes relative-value-oriented with odds dictated by actuarial tables of behavior that are constantly in need of updating.

Capital structure arbitrage is another misnomer among relative value strategies. The key to capital structure trades is identifying the inflection point in the capital structure where interest coverage ceases to exist with respect to cash flow and collateral. Given the disparate objectives of the buyers of equity and debt, it is no surprise that valuations attached to different parts of the capital structure seemingly have little or no connection. This strategy attempts to exploit these different points of view as to valuation. However, no arbitrage exists. Only a relative value opportunity is within one's assessment of the inflection point of protection among debt holders. The relative value opportunity exists if your valuation of the inflection point differs from that of the market.

A typical capital structure arbitrage trade consists of a long senior debt position and a short subordinated debt or equity position. The theory behind the trade is that a troubled company will suffer problems in their equity and junior debt while the senior portion of the debt is covered by cash flows, collateral, or both. The risk in this trade lies in the health of the company. If perceived troubles do not persist, equity can become a darling of the value-investing crowd and begin a significant appreciation. A short junior debt position is usually preferable to the extent that the value behaves more like capped equity, thus limiting risk on the short side. These trades are difficult to evaluate since the timing of the value realization is difficult to predict. If the timing of the desired value realization is postponed significantly, the return on capital is compressed to levels not reflective of the original risk taken. This is akin to winning the battle but losing the war. Finally, if the health of the company turns out to be poorer than originally diagnosed, even the long senior debt position may deteriorate, compressing the spread in the capital structure trade.

Convertible arbitrage is one of the most complex hedge fund strategies in existence. Convertible securities consist of a fixed-income instrument, an equity component, and an option on the equity. Since the convertible security is ultimately exchangeable into equity at a specified point in the future with a defined price, an arbitrage is truly in existence. Getting your arms around the moving pieces is the difficult part. Valuations on the fixed-income portion of the security require credit analysis, duration analysis, and yield curve analysis. Valuations on the equity portion of the security require analysis of the covenants of the security conversion, fundamental analysis of the company, and relative value analysis of the instrument to similar instruments issued by similar companies. To compound the issue further, the option component requires volatility analysis combined with duration analysis. With all these elements well understood, however, the cost of financing and the persistency of stock borrow must still be contended with. All these moving parts work in concert to make this trade difficult to engineer for the duration of the arbitrage process and are fraught with risk.

Any portion of convertible analysis that is incorrect can destroy the value of a seemingly well-engineered trade. The most common risks that are difficult to endure revolve around the option component of the trade. Volatility contraction and premium compression are the most common risks in a convertible arbitrage portfolio. The models used to measure and value these components have become generic and are now commoditized. Ten years ago, firms invested millions of dollars to develop their models. With the majority of firms using fairly standard and widely available models, less difference exists in competing valuations among convertible arbitrageurs. This scenario makes the strategy more risky, as a material change in one aspect of a trade will be identified by numerous holders virtually simultaneously. The potential risk from this perspective is the group behavior of heading for the exit all at once.

Regulation D provides companies with access to the capital markets quickly through a private market transaction that ultimately converts into public equity. Restricted stock is issued when a company is in trouble and needs to raise cash quickly. The price paid for this access to capital is often exorbitant and the equity holders are diluted in the process, yet this access to capital may be the event necessary for a company to stave off bankruptcy. Whatever the case may be, the risk in these transactions revolves around the illiquidity of the security held by the hedge fund offering the capital. The trade structure consists of a long restricted stock and a short unrestricted position. Here the stock borrow may come under pressure, the company may not survive, and the marketability of the security is sorely lacking.

Merger arbitrage is often referred to as risk arbitrage. Once a merger acquisition deal has been announced, the market reprices the company marked for acquisition just shy of the announced deal value. The difference between the new price for the stock and the announced purchase price reflects a variety of risks present in the proposed transaction that may prevent the deal from occurring at the announced price and suggested timetable. The most common risk is one of regulatory interference due to the prospective risk of unfair competition presented by the combined new entity. In the United States, the Department of Justice reviews corporate mergers and acquisitions for such traits and may require the divestiture of some business components by either the acquirer or acquiree. Or, the regulators may simply rule that the proposed deal will create an environment of unfair competition and consequently nix the deal.

Other risks in such transactions include financing, corporate governance, and shareholder approval. Many companies making strategic acquisitions lack sufficient cash to complete the transaction. In such cases, companies will look to bankers for capital. Lenders may determine that the acquisition lacks sufficient synergies to support the debt-servicing requirements of such a loan. The inability to locate efficient financing presents a risk to the completion of an acquisition. In cases where the leaders of the companies involved in a merger are both headstrong, it may not be possible to work out a governance structure satisfactory to both. Ego is an elusive trait to evaluate in these circumstances. Finally, shareholders may prevent a proposed transaction for a variety of reasons. These may include dilution, a lack of corporate synergy, inadequate valuation, and so on. These risks to deal completion play a significant role for investors in risk arbitrage. Although the upside potential in these deals may generally represent two to four times the risk-free rate, their breakage may cost a large multiple of this amount. Although the vast majority of mergers and acquisitions (M&A) deals announced do close successfully, the exceptions are very costly. The primary risk in this strategy is the clustering of several broken deals in a short period of time. A lesser risk is the flow of capital attempting to exploit this strategy and its impact on squeezing all the opportunity out of the market.

Distressed investing is typically a more proactive strategy than most other hedge fund strategies. Often, the hedge fund manager becomes involved with management and/or bankers to satisfy specific lending requirements, enforce loan covenants, or force changes upon the company. The reward for such activity can be great if the distressed investor's plan works efficiently. The risks usually entail the consequences of friction involved in pursuing a workout solution. For example, an agreement among lenders and management may be difficult to achieve, and an agreement among bondholders of one class may not be that easy either. Of course, forcing management to change course is the most difficult of all to accomplish. The result may be delays or failure to achieve the desired workout plan. In either case, the original rate of return on capital will likely be reduced. The risk in this strategy is that significant delays and/or failure to implement a workout plan may reduce the risk/reward ratio envisioned by the manager. In addition, since positions required to exercise influence in the process may become control positions, liquidity is compromised by the regulatory restrictions placed on large bondholders. The combination of these risks is the worst of all worlds—illiquid investments where the reward is diluted in favor of greater risk.

Equity strategy risk is ultimately akin to the risk in traditional equity investing. The real value in these strategies lies in good stock picking, regardless of the underlying approach. Without stock-picking skill, portfolio construction and risk management will do little to overcome the deficiency of poor investment decisions. Notwithstanding the obvious, many other risks are present in equity hedge fund investing.

A critical component of equity hedge fund investing is the objective of the long portfolio versus the short portfolio. Many hedge fund managers focus on one side for alpha generation, while the other is utilized primarily for hedging macro, sector, and/or specific stock risks. For example, many managers excel in constructing long portfolios while using short index positions to hedge out market or sector risks. This style of active management investing, relative to passive index investing, is designed to dampen volatility associated with the long portfolio. In extended bull market runs, like the one from 1995 through the first quarter of 2000, the risk in this approach is underperformance. In addition, index hedges may not insulate the long portfolio as intended, due to the differences in volatility between specific stocks and indexes in general. Worse yet, the use of a modest amount of index hedges may be utilized only to justify charging hedge fund fees.

Short sellers may employ long index positions in a similar fashion to dampen volatility. By nature, short sellers tend to have more aggressive personalities due to the contrarian nature of their business of always fighting the crowd. They also suffer from the inequity of the math of short selling; the most you can make is 100 percent on a position while the potential loss is infinite. In the course of identifying numerous shorts over a long period of time, cynicism becomes a natural by-product. Employing a long hedge in the form of index positions may provide little protection in the event of a short squeeze or error in judgment.

A purer form of equity hedge investing attempts to generate alpha on both sides of the portfolio. This takes a high level of skill to master both long-side and short-side investing. The risk in this form of equity hedge fund lies in the construction of the portfolio. Ideally, the relationship between the two portfolios provides for a natural hedge in either direction depending upon general market movement. This style of portfolio is usually labeled relative value and was addressed earlier in the discussion on statistical arbitrage and market-neutral investing. In a long/short construct that is not market-neutral by design, the risks are similar. Does the long portfolio and the short portfolio have some connection? A major risk in these strategies is a dislocation of relationship between long and short positions. In other words, the combination of longs and shorts in one portfolio may present a greater risk rather than a dampening of volatility.

Macro investing includes many of the risks mentioned already. In addition, a primary risk is the nature of macro investing essentially making market timing calls. With the flexibility to shift capital among a wide variety of opportunities on a global scale, the primary market call employed is the choice of opportunity. This expression of choice of opportunity is typically well protected in order to retain the value of such decisions. Accordingly, these funds tend to be the least transparent of hedge funds by class. The risk to investors is the lack of knowledge about the risks taken by the hedge fund manager. Even due diligence may be compromised by the lack of transparency afforded to potential investors. In many cases, the investment is made solely on past track records of performance, which the regulators frequently remind us is no guarantee of future success.

Currency trading is perhaps the most liquid of all trading strategies and the currency markets are the deepest and most liquid of all financial markets. Liquidity, however, has several layers. Primary currencies, such as the dollar, yen, and euro, are the most liquid; the currencies of other industrialized nations are the next liquid; and the emerging market currencies remain the least liquid. With the advent of the euro, many liquid currencies disappeared from trading, reducing the diversification available among the most liquid currency set. The risk now, in this strategy, is the dependence upon less liquid currencies for diversification purposes. Emerging market currencies are subject to political unrest, currency controls, and weak banking systems to support the free flow of capital. These risks present a clear and present danger for investors.

Derivative trading, futures trading, and commodity trading can all be rolled into one discussion. These instruments incorporate leverage into their very structure. Unlike equities that are subject to Regulation T margin requirements of 50 percent, these instruments routinely require a 5 percent margin or less to hold in your account. The greatest risk present in this strategy is the abuse of leverage in an otherwise diverse portfolio. The vast majority of funds operating in this strategy arena are model or price driven. The lack of fundamental work incorporated into the average commodity fund is alarming when compared to equity funds. The risk in these price action models is the research employed to discover trading opportunities. A seemingly endless supply of data must be researched, but most of these markets are less than 20 years old. In a statistical sense, the amount of data relative to the number of fundamental cycles experienced in these markets is very small. The risk in this sense becomes the lack of economic cycle experience upon which these models may rely.

Options arbitrage is designed to exploit the differences in volatility in similar instruments. Index arbitrage is the exploitation of single-stock volatility versus the dampened volatility of an index (due to diversification). Volatility relies, to a large extent, on expectations about a variety of factors. When attempting to measure and evaluate expectations, one is delving into market psychology, which can change rapidly and without good reason. This presents a significant risk to the timing- and price-level factors that are incorporated in option pricing models. Sudden shifts in volatility can wipe out a well-structured trade due to the leverage and duration components of the option changing with the change in volatility.

LIQUIDITY RISKS

Market liquidity is the most obvious form of liquidity risk. The volume of transactions is a primary component, but the breadth and depth of market participants are critical, too. Discussions with hedge fund managers will reveal that not all equity liquidity is the same. For example, measuring the total volume traded on an average day may suggest adequate liquidity for trading purposes. However, the nature of the volume may have institutional participation (which facilitates large block transactions) or it may be more retail oriented (potentially weaker liquidity as depth may become a problem). In the momentum-driven daytrading frenzy of 1999, many stocks traded only 100 shares for each eighth-point move. For a manager to be nimble in such an environment, these stocks were basically off limits. In most cases, however, mid- to large-capitalization stocks have sufficient liquidity for most managers. The issue to focus on is the size of position a manager wants to own. As managers attract larger pools of capital to employ, their normal allocation (percentage of capital) may exceed the average daily trading volume in stocks in which they would ordinarily invest. This forces the manager to choose to migrate to larger capitalization stocks, further diversify his or her portfolio through smaller position sizes, or take on the additional risk of illiquid positions in a portion of the portfolio.

Another form of market liquidity risk comes in the form of restricted positions. Whether due to the size of the stake in a company, a Regulation D investment, or another form of restriction on a stock, hedge funds sometimes hold illiquid positions. If an investor elects to exit a hedge fund while it holds a restricted position, the investor may not receive his or her entire value until the position is ultimately liquidated.

Hedge fund liquidity is another form of liquidity risk. This risk may come in the form of infrequent opportunities to exit a hedge fund. Typical liquidity rights may only be offered at month end, quarter end, or year end to investors. In addition, the exercise of this right may require a notice period of 30 to 200 days or more. Today, with investors pushing for greater transparency, the discovery of a problem that leads to a liquidation request still faces the stumbling block of waiting until the next window of liquidity opens. In many cases with limited or no transparency, the investor may not discover a problem until the damage has already occurred.

Until recently, the practice of prophylactic liquidation notices used to occasionally occur. Investors who were contemplating portfolio changes near a liquidation window would often send in a liquidation notice to a manager in order to have the option of liquidation. If they chose not to proceed with the exit from the fund, they would simply call the manager right before the liquidation window closed and withdraw the liquidation notice. This practice was the exception rather than the rule and was frequently accommodated with minimal grumbling from the manager.

In the fourth quarter of 1998, that all changed. So many investors issued contingent or prophylactic liquidation notices due to the uncertainty during the volatile aftermath of the Russian crisis and the collapse of Long-Term Capital Management (LTCM) that many managers were forced to liquidate large portions of their portfolios only to realize that many of the potential liquidations were not confirmed. As the news spread within the hedge fund community that this practice was not isolated but rather widespread, the reaction was swift. Many managers issued notices that future redemption requests could not be withdrawn, penalties for cancellations were instituted, and liquidity gates were written into contracts. All these actions effectively killed off the exception that, for a short time, became the rule.

Liquidity may not arrive in the form in which you want to receive it. The legal agreements governing limited partnerships, limited liability companies, and offshore funds invariably include clauses for distribution in kind liquidations if it is in the best interest of the remaining partners. What this entails is the distribution of your pro-rata share of the investment portfolio via equity or debt positions, as the case may be. Investors are required to open an account in which to receive the stock or debt, and then they must liquidate the positions themselves. The problem with this scenario is the likelihood that the positions probably have little or no market available for them (part of the problem for the manager in the first place). Compound this situation with the probability that other investors are in the same situation holding the same positions wishing they had liquidity too. Sounds like an opportunity for a macro manager.

The most problematic experience in hedge fund investing is the suspension of liquidation rights. In the case of severe market disruptions, such as those existent in the liquidity crisis of 1998, many funds opted to suspend liquidations altogether in order to protect their own capital and the remaining investors' capital. In these cases, the limited partners have few rights to exercise. Letters, phone calls, and lawsuits may not do anything to change the situation. The manager may choose to work out a plan of liquidation that suffers the least market impact (in his or her estimation) and extends over a period of months, or even years.

LEVERAGE RISKS

Regulation T was a desirable curb to the speculative fervor of the Roaring Twenties and brought about a greater respectability to equity investing. Since human nature is such that greed is difficult to contain, regulators determined that the health of the markets is better served through this type of rule. Hedge funds may enjoy certain regulatory relief, but this is not one they are exempt from. However, many managers get around this rule by trading through the London desk of their prime broker. Offshore trading is not subjected to Regulation T. Consequently, hedge fund managers can lever their portfolio beyond the limits of this rule with the assistance of Wall Street. Investment banks used to run larger proprietary trading operations than they do today. By facilitating this type of trading for hedge funds, the investment banks have increased the stable earnings derived from commissions, financing, and stock lending while becoming less dependent upon the instability of trading profits from the proprietary desks.

Fixed-income investing is not subject to the same restrictions as equity investing. Margin requirements are established by prime brokers depending on the perceived risk in a trade. In sovereign debt long/short trades, the risk may be relatively small, as in the case of basis trades. In these cases, the similarity of the instruments may be so great that they are true arbitrage trades. The nature of the riskless transaction of pure arbitrage does not adequately describe the entire situation. A transaction may be riskless to the extent that at a defined point in the future the positions are equal or interchangeable. However, during the life of the trade, the price difference may widen between the two similar securities. This matters to the extent that little or no margin is required in many instances. Many managers will lever these trades 10, 20, or 30 times the capital in their fund. In this example, a spread widening may have a severe mark to market impact on the fund.

Many fixed-income trades are not so arbitrage-like. Trades exploiting mispricing along the yield curve may be mistaken for arbitrage trades. Yet, in most cases, no arbitrage exists but a very close relationship exists between securities. Many of these trades can be placed with a minimal margin requirement, which leads to high levels of leverage. A far greater risk exists that these spreads will widen a great deal more than basis trades. To the extent that too much leverage is employed, the risk of ruin is very high.

As one moves further out the risk spectrum in fixed-income investing, many opportunities are available for exploiting leverage and raising the stakes of risk. Spreads between sovereign debt instruments of different countries is a dangerous move since it is dependent upon a relationship that may appear consistent in the data but has no theoretical foundation. In these cases, a breakdown in the connection between the securities can result in a significant loss. It is easy to see how investment managers may view these trades as low risk. A great deal of data that supports such a conclusion can be a powerful persuasive tool. Yet politicians and bankers are prone to acting unpredictably, which undermines the experience demonstrated in the data. Prime brokers may fail to see these risks as well, as they may be competing for business and make mistakes in judgment about the margin required for such a trade. These risks are ever present in fixed-income trading due to the high levels of leverage that are available to hedge fund managers.

Investors leveraging their capital through intermediaries willing to finance increased investment in hedge funds are compounding the risk profile of the industry. Many managers are unaware of the leverage employed in the investments in their funds. Insurance companies and banks are willing to lend against the collateral of hedge fund assets when they review the low-volatility profile that many funds exhibit. However, the risks outlined previously do not reflect normal distributions of returns. In statistical parlance, this means we experience the occasional fat left tail result. With so much structured product in the marketplace dependent upon low-volatility profitable returns, market crises that arise can precipitate a domino effect of liquidation demands.

To the extent that liquidation may not be accommodated in funds experiencing problems (see earlier), liquidation requests may be pursued in more liquid funds. This is known as *collateral damage*. Many hedge fund managers were surprised to receive liquidation notices in the fourth quarter of 1998 after performing well all year. Investors in these funds were negatively impacted when managers were forced to sell portions of their portfolios to meet liquidation requests during a volatile and less liquid timeframe. With more and more levered and structured products in the marketplace, the risk of leverage impacts not only highly levered funds, but investors in unrelated funds may also be adversely impacted through the collateral damage liquidation effect.

BUSINESS RISKS

One mistake commonly made by investors in hedge funds is overlooking the business aspect of the investment. Hedge fund investing is investing in a business. In most cases, it is an investment in a small business. Consequently, the experience will differ widely from one manager to another. Thus, it is important to investigate the manager's business acumen and resources.

Many emerging managers (a term used to describe a startup hedge fund) grossly underestimate the management skill necessary to operate a business.

A common presumption is that all that is involved is trading and marketing. The operational aspect of running a small business can be very time consuming. With the amount of focus required to make excellent investment decisions, the distraction of paying bills, replacing equipment, and meeting with lawyers can dilute the effectiveness of good analysis. Investors must undertake the time to evaluate the past business experience of the principals of a hedge fund and the allocation of responsibilities among them. The risk of failure is greatest among inexperienced businesspeople operating these funds.

An increasing opportunity exists for skilled analysts to join forces and open up a hedge fund today. Finding complementary skill sets in an investment approach is difficult enough. Compound this with allocating management responsibility and real problems may develop. It is important for each partner in a new venture to understand what he or she is expected to do and what he or she is expected not to do for the business. Without a written plan of responsibility, assumptions are easily made, expectations easily concocted, and disappointment readily experienced in the development of a new relationship. Investors eager to support cache investment experience may be disappointed by the poor results generated by partners without a plan.

Investing in human capital is another important aspect of starting a new hedge fund or operating a growing hedge fund. The duties of trading, accounting, administration, marketing, and legal and regulatory compliance are all areas of specialty that can be outsourced to third parties or employed in house. Small shops often attempt to execute these duties with only one or two people who are not experienced in all of these areas. This may work when the fund is small since adequate time is available to work through a long list of responsibility. The risk in these operations is the failure to invest in more skilled people to handle the rapid growth these businesses can experience. Failure to plan far enough in advance and train personnel in specific skill sets necessary for the operation of the business can create a significant distraction for the management team.

Early in the life of a fund, the need for working capital can be acute. In order to build systems, hire personnel, and finance travel for research, a poorly funded operation will make compromises that can lead to poor performance. In addition, the fear of running out of capital prior to building critical mass in the fund can become a distraction to the focus of investing. Working capital borrowed from others may carry a high rate of interest or require a piece of equity as an enticement. Borrowed money also requires frequent progress reports that can hamper the pure execution of the trading strategy in favor of behavior that is intended to exhibit more consistent returns. Why would one argue with that? Because the altered behavior rarely accomplishes the goal of lower volatility without significantly impairing returns. Investors should look into the working capital requirements of a new hedge fund prior to investing to determine the staying power of the management team.

Fraud and deception are easily perpetrated on unsuspecting investors through hedge fund vehicles. The lack of regulatory oversight, transparency, and liquidity associated with the average hedge fund enables the criminal element to operate undetected for a great length of time. Investors generally want to believe their investment is working and do little to check out the background of the principals, verify the results of the fund's performance, or seek independent references. These are the most obvious steps in detecting fraudulent activity. Experienced hedge fund investors have an edge in this regard because they can draw upon so many resources to check out a hedge fund. At the same time, they are the most vulnerable since they are competitive in identifying the newest manager or the hottest manager in a strategy and may take shortcuts in their due diligence process. It takes a very skilled person to perpetrate a fraud in this business, but it takes an even greater skill to detect one.

Communication is an underrated service in the operation of a hedge fund. Investors want more information and hedge fund operators want to communicate less in favor of doing more research. A good flow of useful information between parties can facilitate a greater understanding between investor and manager as well as solidify expectations. A lack of communication may foster false expectations and do irreparable damage to a relationship. The risk that investors run is the request for information for which they have no process to evaluate. This creates work for the manager and yields no better comfort for the investor. More information may provide a cloak of security for the investor, but just like the emperor's new clothes, the information may provide little substance. It is important for investors to understand the risk in the investment strategy and work with the prime broker to provide a platform for risk diagnostics that is understandable.

Client service is another aspect of business that has its risks. First, the client service personnel may not have the expertise necessary to communicate the strategy, the performance attribution, or the new risks discovered in the portfolio effectively. Investors dependent upon client service that turns out to be inadequate run the risk of not understanding fully the risks they have employed with their capital.

Conflicts of interest come in many forms for hedge funds. When a shop runs multiple products, conflicts may arise in the allocation of resources, trades, and risk management. If two products have moderately different mandates, how does one choose which fund to allocate to, how much to allocate, and how to manage the risk? In mutual fund operations that are sponsoring hedge funds, how does the manager short a stock in the hedge fund that is a long position in one of the mutual funds? Chinese walls are supposed to exist in some cases, but how effective are they?

Some funds enable trading by the principals outside the fund. How much time is spent researching these ideas and how much capital is at risk by the principal can become a large conflict of interest in the eyes of the investors. It is common, therefore, for managers to "eat their own cooking" by having most of their liquid net worth invested in the fund. If a manager does not invest heavily in his or her own fund, the investor should think twice about why he or she doesn't.

Incentives should align the interests of the hedge fund manager, employees, and investor alike. To justify the compensation derived from a profit-sharing arrangement with the investor, the hedge fund should bear some risk in compensation if it fails to achieve specific goals. High watermark levels need to be surpassed after a losing period before the fund manager should be in a position to capture an incentive payout again. Key analysts should have a similar arrangement that encourages teamwork reward and risk. However, the incentive structure should not penalize analysts for the poor performance of a fund to the extent that they don't earn anything. This situation builds resentment toward analysts that contribute the losses and creates an environment where individuals must work for free for some period of time before reaping the benefits of an incentive fee again. A blend of fixed compensation, incentive bonus, and a modest vesting schedule keeps many analysts happy and employed for the benefit of the investors.

Other investors in a fund can disrupt an otherwise successful investment. In late 1998, as noted, many profitable hedge funds were hit with substantial liquidation requests because they were liquid, had not lost money, and would be open to reinvestment at a later date. The investors enduring such a shift in capital are harmed on the exodus through poor marks due to heavy selling. They are also harmed on the return of capital through the dilution of the portfolio at that time and the effort required to put the capital to work. Investors must endeavor to understand the kind of capital invested in a fund they want to own, the amount of leverage behind that capital, and the concentration of investors that can disrupt the normal operation of the fund.

STRUCTURAL RISKS

A common practice in the hedge fund industry today is the facilitation of tax avoidance through insurance vehicles. Owing to an insurance industry loophole in the tax code, offshore investments through insurance products like annuities or life insurance policies enjoy the benefits of tax deferral until the end of the life of the investment. Since a portion of the capital in such a structure is available for investment purposes, many attempts are being made to engineer hedge fund investments (with and without leverage) as the underlying investment vehicle. The risk in these structures is the nature of the insurance risk. There has been little testing of the viability of this structure in the eyes of the IRS, but it is clear that a bona fide risk of insurance loss should accompany the investment if it is to pass muster in tax court.

Not all partnerships are created equal, nor are all hedge fund vehicles. Many managers operate onshore and offshore versions of their hedge fund. More often than not, a difference exists in the liquidity provisions of the funds in favor of offshore investors. When these funds charge the same fee for the same portfolio but provide monthly liquidity to offshore investors while offering only quarterly liquidity to onshore investors, the onshore investors run the risk of having a run on the bank take place outside their liquidity window. This can be an enormous risk, especially in fixed-income funds where leverage tends to be higher. Some funds charge different fees to reflect the liquidity premium that some investors receive versus others. The level of that fee and whether it is adequate compensation is subject to debate.

Liquidation gates are gaining popularity in the hedge fund industry. A gate is designed to limit the outflow of capital in any given period by charging a fee on flows exceeding a specified level. The objective of this structure is to protect the remaining investors by passing the fee into the fund. The typical gate includes an escalation feature to make larger liquidations more onerous. Lockup periods act similarly to gates in that new capital must stay in a fund for a specified length of time before liquidity windows are offered to those investors. The purpose behind these features is to create a more stable capital environment for the investors. It also creates a more stable capital flow for the hedge fund manager. The risk is whether the fund manager must abide by the gate as well.

SCALABILITY LIMITS

Hedge fund strategies that employ true arbitrage are designed to die. This may be an overstatement, but it contains an element of truth. Any free lunch that has a low barrier to entry will attract sufficient capital to effectively close the market inefficiency. Many of the strategies widely employed in the 1980s have gone by the wayside in the last 10 years thanks to the increased horsepower of the PC and the commoditization of many arbitrage modeling techniques. A similar phenomenon is taking place in some of the relative value strategies today. The low barrier to entry, the ease of access to models, and the low-volatility, high-reward character of these strategies are attracting large pools of capital. The result is spread compression at the margin in some of these strategies. This is a great example of the efficient market theory at work.

Strategy dependence may limit the size a fund can reach. For example, effective option arbitrage is limited in scale due to the lack of continuous liquidity and pricing in a large number of options. A portfolio may generate attractive returns at $100 million in capital. At a billion dollars, though, the effectiveness may be challenged through a limited opportunity set. Equity hedge funds seem to have the greatest scalability due to the depth of the equity markets. However, alpha generation becomes more difficult the larger the fund becomes for two reasons: liquidity and short selling. Liquidity is challenged, as mentioned, by forcing migration to higher capitalization levels or through a diminished ability to trade in and out of a position in a timely manner. Short selling alpha becomes more difficult to achieve in a large fund due to lack of short selling opportunities or the need to generate more ideas. These changes required for a manager to accommodate growth may push the fund into areas beyond the manager's ability to generate alpha or manage his or her business along the original principles for the fund.

Many hedge fund firms close to new investments in order to avoid the complications of scaling the business. The risk with this approach is the potential loss of key analytical talent to competitor funds that can offer a greater reward or equity for their effort. The risk to investors is understanding the value added that key analysts bring to the fund and what impact their loss may have on the performance of the fund. If the hedge fund chooses to pursue another investment strategy to accommodate the aspirations of their analysts, the move may be distracting or diluting to current investors.

Very few funds actually return capital to investors when they get too large. This is the ideal behavior from an investment point of view since the hedge fund manager is in the best position to determine the proper scale of the business. At the same time, this approach is the worst behavior for an investor to endure since the relative size of his investment is continually shrinking relative to the rest of his portfolio (assuming success in the other investments).

A common dilemma facing growing hedge funds is whether to increase positions' sizes or the number of positions. Increasing size limits the nimbleness or liquidity. Increasing the number of positions brings on a host of other problems. A limit exists to the number of positions each analyst can follow effectively. More positions require more analysts. Integrating more analysts into a fund brings the risk of culture change, management change, internal communication expansion, a potential lack of compatibility in the portfolio construction process, and a need for greater risk management controls. This alters the nature of the business materially. In fact, several managers of large organizations have returned a significant portion of their capital in recent years to get out of the business of managing people and get back into the business of managing assets.

In addition to the integration problems of growth, the problem with more positions in the portfolio is the dilution of individual positions and their impact on performance. Statistically speaking, the ability to generate above-average returns consistently diminishes in accordance with the law of large numbers. That is, the probability of each additional position added to a portfolio yielding the same marginal utility is remote. Many studies have analyzed the performance of new versus older funds and find that performance diminishes over time. This is a statistical expectation that only few managers are able to overcome for extended periods of time.

Putting capital to work is another problem with scaling a business. In an era where larger amounts of capital flow into funds more readily, a real problem is being encountered by existing investors in that their investment is diluted until capital can be deployed. In equity strategies, this is less of a problem than with narrower strategies like convertibles and merger arbitrage that have limited means from which to draw upon for ideas. Short sellers are particularly sensitive to large chunks of new capital since their activity generally requires less visibility to maintain effectiveness. Investors must undertake the effort to understand growth and marketing plans of the funds they intend to invest in to guard against diluting activity brought about by other investors.

Stretching for return is a common problem among relative value strategists that continue to accept capital. As the number of ideas generated fails to keep pace with an increased pool of capital, managers sometimes begin the incremental stretch for additional return. They begin accepting lower thresholds for making investments in order to get capital invested. In spread-related activity, this may also result in an increase in leverage. Investors may be unaware of the creep in the character of the portfolio risk until their investment is no longer productive or the risk is exposed.

ANALYTICAL RISKS

Model-building techniques are difficult to assess even for experienced model builders. Without actually performing the process of theorizing, testing, and tweaking a model, it is difficult to discern good research from rationalized data mining. The amount of data, the context in which data is generated, the theory that is derived and tested, and a host of other aspects of building a model require a vigilant focus on objectivity. Deviations from that objectivity along the research path can imbed structural flaws in the model's output. These structural flaws manifest themselves in portfolio bets the manager may not realize until it is too late. Real-time testing of a model is often done with real money. The researcher embraces mistakes with further research and a tightening of the process. The investor embraces mistakes with a liquidation notice and an expensive lesson learned.

Regulation fair disclosure (FD) is changing some of the fundamental work that hedge funds have traditionally practiced. The concept behind full disclosure is the elimination of unfair advantages in the dissemination of information about public companies by their management teams. Analysts who relied on management interviews for accessing information that others may not have are limited in their efforts as corporate executives adjust to the new regulation. This places a greater emphasis on different kinds of fundamental work like analyzing the quarterly and annual reports issued by companies. Investors in funds that relied heavily on management interviews for an investing advantage may find their investment losing its alpha engine.

Forensic accounting is a skill set emphasized by many short sellers in the quest for fraud identification or for the early detection of cash flow problems in a company. Given the flexibility that corporate management has in reporting their financial condition, it takes a skilled practitioner to detect the subtle practices that usually foretell a company on the brink of disaster. Of course, the mental fortitude it takes to persist in fighting Wall Street and the vast majority of investors by emphasizing short selling is taxing. In this line of work, though, it is easy to fall into the trap of looking only for confirming information for your investment thesis. At risk for the investor is the willingness on the part of the hedge fund manager to turn a blind eye to the information that negates his thesis. This is not a common occurrence, but it presents an analytical risk to this strategy.

CONCLUSION

Hedge funds are considered risky by most investors due to a lack of familiarity and understanding. This chapter merely scratches the surface in facilitating a better understanding by demystifying many aspects of hedge fund investing. Much of the investing done in this arena is really a logical extension of traditional investing in traditional markets through modestly more sophisticated approaches. The risks are real to the extent that regulators have encouraged the development of this industry through regulatory exception. Awareness of the risks spelled out in this chapter should provoke a more thorough investigation of all aspects of investing in this unregulated marketplace. Benign neglect is not an excuse for suffering a loss in a hedge fund.

CHAPTER 16

The Risk of Informationless Investing: Hedge Fund Performance Measurement Bias

Andrew B. Weisman

Weisman evaluates three strategies common to the hedge fund industry that tend to generate significant alpha over relatively long periods, though they demonstrate no theoretical basis for doing so. The dangerous implication of their enhancement is the statistical bias they attract that ultimately impairs quantitative optimization of portfolio components.

DANGEROUS ATTRACTIONS

Hedge funds have emerged as an important investment category for institutional investors. They are attractive because they promise superior, noncorrelated rates of return compared to traditional industry benchmarks. This popular perception of hedge funds, in conjunction with the institutional desire to improve risk-adjusted performance, typically characterized by some form of mean-variance efficiency, has led to dramatic capital flows into this investment class.

Institutional investors have not, however, always had pleasant experiences with their hedge fund investments. For example, Brown, Goetzmann, and Ibbotson (1999) observe in their examination of offshore hedge funds that the hedge fund industry is characterized by very high rates of attrition, estimated to be about 20 percent per year, as compared to the approximate 5 percent rate for mutual funds.[1]

The failure to meet investor expectations is typically the result of two related factors. First, many institutional investors, investment consultants, and academicians lack a basic understanding of the return-generating processes of many hedge funds. Second, because of this basic lack of understanding, there tends to be an over-reliance on conceptual frameworks and technologies that are appropriate to the traditional investment world, but highly inappropriate for hedge funds.

To avoid such pitfalls, it is useful to consider some of the basic investment techniques that are widely employed in the hedge fund industry—in particular, a widely used class of investment techniques referred to as *informationless investment strategies*. Informationless strategies tend to produce return enhancements over relatively long periods even though they frequently provide no theoretical long-term benefit.

The most important consequence of such strategies is that they tend to systematically bias statistically derived performance measures, such as mean, variance, and measures of association. Subsequently, quantitative optimization will tend to systematically worsen overall portfolio performance in the context of hedge fund investing.[1] Indeed, as demonstrated in this chapter, when they select managers to maximize an ex post measure of risk-adjusted return, portfolio managers may be virtually guaranteeing a bad outcome.

My purpose, therefore, is to present three specific informationless investment strategies peculiar to the asset management industry in general, and the hedge fund industry in particular, and their consequences with respect to performance measurement and asset allocation.

SHORT-VOLATILITY INVESTING

The first informationless strategy relates to the reasonably common practice of structuring investments that are essentially equivalent to writing insurance policies against low-probability events, that is, *short-volatility investing*. Short-volatility investing is typically operationalized by using derivative securities that possess optionality. Options (or certain active management strategies that mimic them) permit a trader to collect a premium for assuming the risks associated with low-probability events.

A wide variety of hedge fund investment strategies derive their returns from short-volatility investing. These investment strategies typically involve the purchase of one or more securities and simultaneous short sale of one or more securities, where the long security is viewed to be undervalued relative to some perceived equilibrium relationship with respect to the short security. Positive payouts accrue to the investor as the relative valuations of the securities converge to the perceived equilibrium, while losses accrue as the relationship becomes increasingly strained—thus the term *short-volatility investing*.

Strategies such as merger arbitrage, various forms of fixed-income arbitrage, and statistical arbitrage (pairs trading) can all be classified as short-volatility investing programs.

Short-volatility investments are typically initiated when the relationship between the long and short securities is estimated to be at an extreme valuation, so a continuation or further straining of the relative valuation is determined to be a low-probability outcome. In fact, the tendency to structure individual investments with a high probability of a successful outcome is a hallmark of such strategies.[2]

Such investment strategies are usefully thought of as a process of selling insurance policies written against perceived low-probability events. Viewed in such terms, the general performance characteristics of short-volatility investing become analytically tractable, and, most important, it can be demonstrated that short-volatility investment strategies can be easily constructed that appear to provide performance enhancement for reasonably long periods without in fact doing so. In so doing, such strategies can systematically bias statistically derived estimates of risk, return, and association.

Sample Short-Volatility Investment Program

To clarify this point, consider an investment strategy I discuss in Weisman (1998). Assume the current risk-free rate is 5 percent. A hypothetical manager invests all of his or her capital at the risk-free rate. At the beginning of every month, the manager writes (sells) a series of fairly valued calls and puts that expire at the end of the month. The strike prices are, respectively, 2.5 standard deviations (with respect to the prevailing market volatility) above and below the current market price of some unspecified financial instrument. The manager writes (sells) a sufficient number of these strangles so that in the event the market remains within the 2.5 standard deviation collar, the manager will take in enough premium to double the risk-free rate.

Using Monte Carlo simulation, we can define the probabilities associated with various related outcomes. Figures 16.1 and 16.2 depict two randomly generated 5-year outcomes for this investment strategy.

The performance of this investment strategy can be summarized as follows. The manager has (approximately) an 88 percent chance of outperforming the risk-free rate in any year and almost an 86 percent chance of doubling it. The manager has an almost 50 percent chance of doubling the risk-free rate over any 5-year period. The expected time to a volatility event

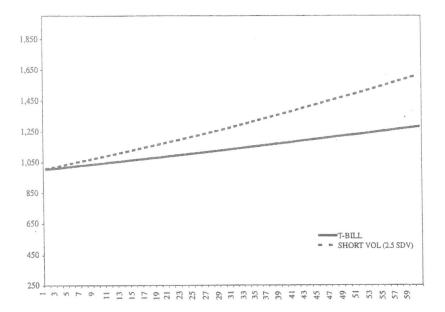

FIGURE 16.1 Randomly generated 5-year performance—T-Bill versus short-volatility strategy.

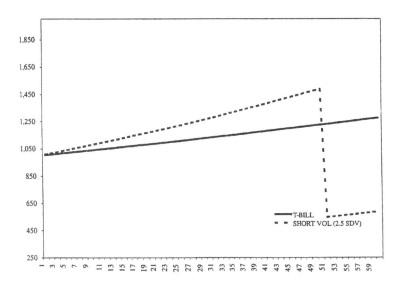

FIGURE 16.2 Randomly generated 5-year performance—T-Bill versus short-volatility strategy.

(when the underlying security trades outside the collar by any month-end, resulting in a loss of capital) is almost 7 years.

As we note, the options are assumed to be fairly valued, so the informationless process of selling options is assumed to have a zero expected value, and an equalizing event is therefore necessitated. The equalizing event is that when a volatility event occurs, the expected loss of capital is approximately 32 percent.

This example can be extended by including additional options with different strikes in order to clarify the relationship between the probability of outperforming the risk-free rate in any year and the extent of the expected loss of capital. Tables 16.1 through 16.4 present the results of the analysis, whereas Figure 16.3 summarizes the relationship between the probability of outperforming the risk-free rate in any year and the magnitude of expected future periodic loss of capital.

Figure 16.3 illustrates that as the probability of outperforming the risk-free rate increases, the extent of the anticipated loss of capital grows at an increasing rate. This graph illustrates one of the most serious issues associated with the interpretation of hedge fund performance data. For managers who use short-volatility strategies, a stellar performance history, characterized by (for example) a high Sharpe ratio, may be an indication of a very high degree of assumed risk. Most important, statistically derived estimates

TABLE 16.1 Probability of Outperforming Risk-Free Rate of Return

Distance to Strike	1 Year	Time Period 3 Year	5 Year
Standard Deviations			
1.50	0.57	0.50	0.47
2.00	0.70	0.58	0.52
2.50	0.88	0.73	0.65

TABLE 16.2 Probability of Doubling Risk-Free Rate of Return

Distance to Strike	1 Year	Time Period 3 Year	5 Year
Standard Deviations			
1.50	0.18	0.01	0.00
2.00	0.57	0.19	0.06
2.50	0.86	0.63	0.46

TABLE 16.3 Expected Time to Draw-Down (Capital Loss)

Distance to Strike	Length of Time
Standard Deviations	Years
1.50	0.80
2.00	1.97
2.50	6.83

TABLE 16.4 Expected Draw-Down (Capital Loss)

Distance to Strike	Percent Loss of Capital
Standard Deviations	
1.50	−2.96
2.00	−9.00
2.50	−31.92

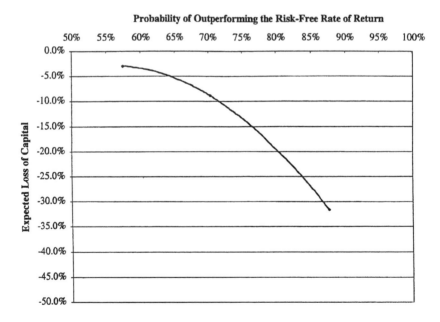

FIGURE 16.3 Probabilities of outperforming risk-free rate of return versus expected draw-down.

of the manager's risk-return characteristics will be diametrically incorrect; in other words, high in-sample risk-adjusted returns may imply poor out-of-sample performance.

As per Figure 16.3, in the context of short-volatility investments, it is rational to argue that the strategy of selecting managers by maximizing an ex post measure of risk-adjusted return is, in fact, a *negative selection* process. Such a conclusion is especially likely when the track records are brief enough to exclude a major volatility event.

This reality is clearly demonstrated in the example, where it is shown that an investment strategy could be devised that is simultaneously constrained to provide no long-term performance enhancement and a high likelihood of generating high risk-adjusted rates of return for a fairly significant period of time.

Perhaps the most startling conclusion with respect to short-volatility investments is that very high, statistically derived estimates of risk-adjusted return can be directly linked with an increasing probability of an unacceptably large loss of capital.

Short-Volatility Regression Bias

Short-volatility investing also severely complicates the process of determining a measure of association between a manager's returns and likely return-generating factors. I show in the following section that regression analysis is unlikely to reveal the importance of the association between a short-volatility manager's performance and movements in the price and volatility of the underlying asset class traded. As long as the analyzed period includes no major volatility events, that is, as long as the market remains within the collar, the manager's outcomes will be positive regardless of market direction.

Figure 16.4 should serve to clarify this issue. The first half of the randomly generated market performance presented in Figure 16.4 depicts a positive-trending market without any major volatility events, whereas the second half depicts a negative-trending market without any major volatility events.

With no major volatility events, the manager's returns will be statistically positively associated with the market for the first half, negatively associated for the second half, and unrelated for the entire period.

Most important, however, a statistically derived measure of association is unlikely to adequately describe the highly elastic response the manager's returns will exhibit during a sharply down-trending market; that is, derived regression coefficients will underestimate the tendency for the manager to become highly correlated during such turbulent conditions.

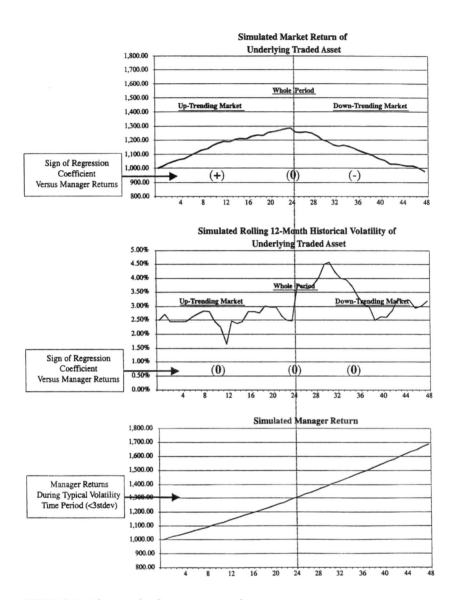

FIGURE 16.4 Short-volatility regression bias.

This point has very serious implications for both hedge fund investors and academicians who are attempting to analyze hedge fund performance, and probably necessitates a reexamination of much of the research.[3]

Short-Volatility Summary

The net result is that portfolio managers who naively make use of certain standard optimization strategies, in conjunction with statistically derived inputs, will tend to systematically overallocate to managers who have a short-volatility profile and systematically maximize a future period loss. The tendency for portfolio managers to overallocate to such investment strategies is referred to as *short-volatility bias*.

Short-volatility bias is a direct result of an overestimate of the manager's risk-adjusted returns and an underestimate of the manager's correlation during volatile market conditions.

ILLIQUID SECURITY INVESTING

The second informationless investment technique simply involves expressing basic market exposures using illiquid securities. To better understand the consequences of this simple informationless strategy, consider a simple two-manager world. Managers 1 and 2 operate investment programs that have precisely the same performance characteristics, except that Manager 2, due to the illiquidity of the securities in her portfolio, is unable or unwilling to accurately value the portfolio on a periodic basis. Manager 2 therefore employs the simple informationless strategy of systematically understating both the periodic increases and decreases in value of the portfolio and subsequently generates the appearance of performance enhancement.

Assume the following notation:

$\bar{x}_i$ = trend (average) return for Manager i;
σ_i = reported standard deviation of returns for Manager i;
$\bar{x}_i = X$;
$\sigma_i = \sigma$; and
δ = proportion of the standard deviation of return that is reported by the manager, referred to as proportional valuation lag, where $0 \leq \delta \leq 1$

Therefore,

$$[(\sigma - \delta\sigma/\sigma)]100 = (1-\delta)100$$
$$= \text{percent reduction in reported volatility}$$

Similarly, where r_f = the risk-free rate,

$$[((\bar{X} - r_f)/\sigma) - ((\bar{X} - r_f)/\delta\sigma)]/((\bar{X} - r_f)/\sigma)100 = [(1/\delta) - 1]100$$

$$= \text{percent improvement in reported Sharpe Ratio}$$

It is worth noting that the performance of Manager 2 is in no way superior to Manager 1; Manager 2 merely represents herself as being superior due to the stability of her returns—which is in fact merely a consequence of the inability or unwillingness to accurately value the portfolio.

Figure 16.5 illustrates the relationship between the proportional valuation lag and the improvement in reported risk-adjusted returns as represented by the Sharpe Ratio. Note that Sharpe Ratios can be highly sensitive to proportional valuation lags. For example, a lag factor of 0.5 will result in a 100 percent overstatement of risk-adjusted returns, whereas a lag factor of 0.15 will result in a 567 percent overstatement.

Therefore, when managers face difficulties in performing accurate periodic valuations of their portfolios, there is substantial opportunity for overstating risk-adjusted performance. When performance is systematically overrated by individual managers, or systematically overstated for certain classes of managers, statistically derived performance measures will by definition mischaracterize performance. Subsequently, there will be a tendency to overweight such individuals or investment classes.

Once again, one could rationally argue that ex post Sharpe Ratio optimization is a negative selection process when applied to unadjusted man-

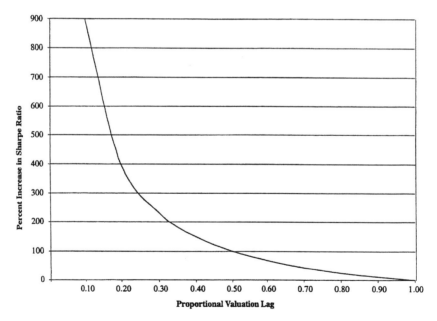

FIGURE 16.5 Illiquidity bias.

ager or index performance data. If manager data are not appropriately normalized, quantitative optimization strategies will systematically bias a portfolio toward illiquidity and de facto reduce risk-adjusted returns.[4] This tendency is referred to as *illiquidity bias.*

Illiquid securities create problems for an investor beyond suboptimal allocation. Most important, the tendency to under-report volatility implies the occurrence of predictable financial calamities. To better understand this issue, consider the anatomy of a typical illiquidity-based financial crisis.

At the commencement of trading, a manager invests in a selection of illiquid securities. The securities are valued at the purchase price. Therefore, initially the reported net asset value (NAV) of the portfolio is approximately equal to the true or liquidation value of the portfolio. At the end of a period, the securities will have changed in value. Given the illiquidity of the securities, the manager cannot determine their precise values, nor can any objective third party. Consequently, the manager will tend to systematically understate the periodic change in the NAV of the portfolio.

The manager produces a periodic NAV by augmenting the prior period's NAV by some proportion of the difference between where the portfolio was previously valued and its current true value. This strategy results in periodic over- and undervaluations of the reported NAV compared to the true NAV. The extent of these misstatements is a function of three key variables: the true mean ($\bar{x}$) and standard deviation (σ) of the underlying portfolio, and the extent to which the manager captures the periodic difference in value between the prior period's reported NAV, and the current true NAV, that is, the proportional valuation lag (δ).

A crisis typically results when a manager's prime broker or investment partners become concerned about the possible difference between the reported and actual NAVs and force a liquidation of all or a portion of the investment portfolio. A difference that exceeds some crisis threshold value (L) typically evokes such concern.

Figure 16.6 presents a randomly generated example of just such a manager. It graphs actual and reported NAVs as well as a histogram of the periodic valuation differences. In this example, σ is assumed to be 30 percent, $\bar{x}$ is assumed to be 15 percent, δ is assumed to be .15%, and L is assumed to be 20 percent. Using these assumed parameter values in conjunction with a simple Monte Carlo simulation, we can determine an estimated time to financial crisis (T). Simply put, $T = f(\bar{x}, \sigma, \delta, L)$. In this example, the expected time to crisis is 49 months.[5]

Figure 16.7 is a graphical representation of the relationship between the extent to which a manager understates volatility and the expected time to crisis expressed in months. Table 16.5 presents the discrete data points that are used to generate Figure 16.7.

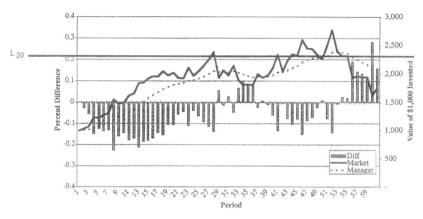

Mean = 0.15, sigma = 0.30, lag valuation = 0.15.

FIGURE 16.6   Reported NAV versus actual NAV.

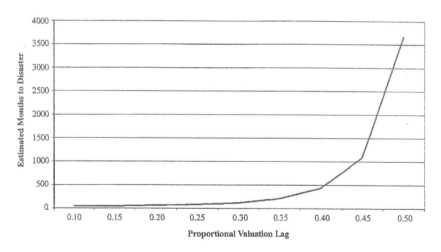

FIGURE 16.7   Proportional valuation lag versus estimated months to disaster.

Finally, it is worth noting that the use of illiquid or over-the-counter securities is particularly endemic to the hedge fund industry and is rarely satisfactorily addressed in academic studies of hedge fund performance. When you are researching the return-generating factors of hedge funds or evaluating

TABLE 16.5 Values for Generating Figure 16.7

Lag Valuation Parameter (δ)	Expected Time to Crisis (Percentile$_{10}$)	Expected Time to Crisis (Percentile$_{50}$)	Expected Time to Crisis (Percentile$_{90}$)
0.10	5	44	161
0.15	7	49	167
0.20	9	59	192
0.25	12	77	253
0.30	18	113	390
0.35	32	204	691
0.40	67	437	111
0.45	165	1088	3702
0.50	560	3668	6000+

$\bar{x} = 0.15; \sigma = 0.30; L = 0.20.$

such research, it is a good idea to give serious consideration to the impact of illiquidity.[6]

ST. PETERSBURG INVESTING

To understand this informationless investment technique, it is first necessary to consider a concept known as the St. Petersburg Paradox. This concept refers to the seemingly paradoxical expectations associated with a simple betting strategy.

This informationless strategy involves making a single unit bet on the outcome of a binomial process such as a coin toss. If you win, you bet again with the same unit size. If you're wrong, you double up by betting two units on the subsequent trial. If you're wrong again, you double up once more by betting four units. You continue doubling up until you eventually win, at which point you return to betting the starting unit amount.

This better strategy has some unique properties. First, even though the coin is assumed to be fair, this strategy has an infinite expected value. Second (and here's the paradox), you will, with a probability of one, eventually become bankrupt. With absolute certainty, you will eventually encounter a long enough series of losing bets so that, for any finite amount of capital, you will lose everything. Clearly, if a manager increases leverage as he goes into a draw-down (as he loses capital as result of investment losses), he is subjecting his investors to a substantial amount of risk.

The solution to this problem is to avoid managers who engage in this sort of behavior. Yet, due to the return patterns generated by managers who employ some form of informationless, double-up, betting strategy, it is frequently the case that inexperienced asset allocators actively select for such managers.

Sample St. Petersburg Investment Strategy

To better understand such a money management strategy, it is worth considering the returns associated with a simple St. Petersburg-like investment strategy. At the start of the first week of trading, a hypothetical manager makes an investment (bet) risking 50 basis points (0.5 percent) of capital. If the bet fails, the manager makes a second bet at the beginning of week 2, risking 100 basis points. The manager continues to double up, as a percentage of the remaining equity, at the beginning of every week until successful, at which point the manager reverts to making the initial unit bet of 50 basis points of capital. Finally, to introduce an opportunity component, the manager reports returns only at month-end.[7]

With this limited amount of information, we can use Monte Carlo simulation to characterize the manager's likely future performance. For the purpose of this simulation, we assume that the manager has no systematic skill or lack of skill—in other words, there is a 50 percent chance of being right in any given week.[8]

Figure 16.8 presents a randomly generated sample monthly performance history for our fictitious manager. It depicts precisely what we would expect from a firm employing inappropriate (St. Petersburg-style) money management. There is a fairly prolonged period of consistent profitability. The manager appears to recover brilliantly and rapidly from any loss of capital. Finally, the manager goes out of business in spectacular fashion. It is worth noting that this is a very common life cycle for hedge funds.

Given our precise specification of this strategy, we can once again use Monte Carlo simulation to accurately describe the associated expectations. These expectations are summarized in Figure 16.9.[9]

Figure 16.9 describes the relationship between a specific percentage loss of capital and its expected time to occurrence. You can see from the graph that the expected time until a month-end loss of 50 percent of capital is approximately 400 weeks, or 7 3/4 years.

It is worth considering the significance of a 7 3/4-year expected time to a 50 percent loss of capital. First, the sales cycle for a hedge fund is far shorter than 7 3/4 years. Typically, hedge funds come up for serious consideration after 3 to 5 years. Additionally, as our sample performance history in Figure 16.8

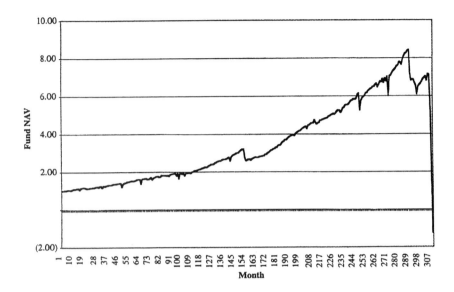

FIGURE 16.8 ACME hedge fund performance.

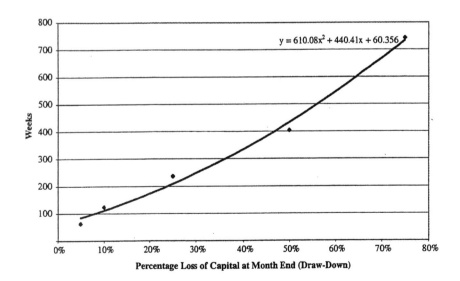

$$y = 610.08x^2 + 440.41x + 60.356$$

FIGURE 16.9 Comparison of percentage draw-down versus mean time to occurrence (derived via Monte Carlo simulation).

indicates, prior to experiencing a large loss of capital, the manager's performance is quite compelling.

Monthly reporting tends to obscure much of the fund's volatility; the draw-downs (loss of capital) have a very limited duration, and the returns are consistently positive. In fact, right up until its fiery death, such a fund would generate approximately a 15 percent annualized rate of return with about a 12 percent annualized standard deviation and would be profitable approximately 78 percent of all months.

One further interesting trait associated with this strategy is, given that the manager is simply making a series of unrelated weekly wagers, it is unlikely that the overall return series will have any long-term systematic correlation with any particular index. In short, we have defined a seemingly high risk-adjusted return product with a low correlation with other managers and indexes.

Bear in mind that all of this wonderful performance is consistent with the a priori structure of this experiment—the manager is employing an informationless strategy and is assumed to have no systematic skill. As a consequence, statistically derived in-sample performance measures will by definition significantly mischaracterize potential out-of-sample results.

St. Petersburg Summary

The most frightening result of this experiment is just how easy it is to create a St. Petersburg-type investment program that will probably generate a long period of superior performance and very low correlation relative to many traditional benchmarks. Subsequently, when structuring a portfolio by naively maximizing an ex post measure of risk-adjusted return, one may actually be selecting for managers who employ money management strategies that imply a catastrophic loss of capital.[10]

I call the tendency to allocate to such managers *St. Petersburg bias*. Anecdotal evidence indicates that the St. Petersburg bias, allocating to managers who increase leverage as they go into a draw-down, is quite prevalent in the alternative investment industry.

CONCLUSION

Short-volatility bias, illiquidity bias, and the St. Petersburg bias are important considerations to bear in mind when attempting to apply established investment concepts and technology to the world of hedge funds. As I demonstrate, hedge fund managers have the ability to engage in essentially informationless strategies that can produce the appearance of return enhancement without necessarily providing any value to an investor. Consequently, statistically derived estimates concerning risk, return, and association frequently mischaracterize hedge fund returns. These mischaracterizations have significant negative implications for both the asset allocation process and the validity of considerable academic research.

Note: The author thanks Jerome Abernathy, Mark Anson, and Masao Matsuda for their thoughtful comments; Richard Michaud for his guidance and wisdom; Tim Birney for excellent quantitative research assistance; Adam Albin for editorial assistance; and finally the Institute for Quantitative Research in Finance and its April 2001 conference participants for their thoughtful questions and comments. The views expressed in this article are the opinion of the author and should not be taken to represent those of his employer.

NOTES

[1] As Michaud (1998) notes, mean-variance optimization is highly prone to error maximization because such procedures tend to overuse statistically estimated information and thereby magnify the impact of estimation errors.

[2] Such strategies tend to produce very compelling stick-like performance histories (that is, rates of return, when graphed, that appear smooth and upward sloping over fairly long periods). A high probability of success on a given trial, however, should not be confused with the notion of a positive expected value that takes into account the payoffs associated with various outcomes.

[3] See, for example, Fung and Hsieh (1997), McCarthy and Spurgin (1998), Schneeweis and Spurgin (1998), and Liang (1999).

[4] Normalized to compensate for the impact of estimated lagged valuation.

[5] In my opinion, these parameter values represent an eminently realistic example. Furthermore, this framework for analyzing illiquidity goes a long way toward explaining the highly deterministic and cyclical nature of such events.

[6] The pervasive tendency for certain managers, or classes of managers, to include illiquid securities in their portfolios calls for a reexamination of much of the published research in this area.

[7] Providing an opportunity to engage in unreported, intramonth, overly aggressive trading.

[8]In my experience, the example is not an extraordinarily unrealistic example of the money management practices employed by certain hedge fund managers, especially with respect to the directional investment strategies typically employed by commodity trading advisors.

[9]We use Monte Carlo simulation for solving this problem primarily because we are interested in incorporating the effect of periodic month-end reporting. If this were not the case, this problem could be solved deterministically.

[10]Interestingly, Edwards and Ma (1988) note that there is actually a significant empirical negative relationship between in-sample pro forma track records provided in commodity fund offering memoranda and subsequent out-of-sample performance.

REFERENCES

Brown, S., W. Goetzmann, and R. Ibbotson. "Offshore Hedge Funds: Survival and Performance 1989–95." *Journal of Business* (January 1999): 91–117.

Edwards, F. and C. Ma. "Commodity Fund Performance: Is the Information Contained in Fund Prospectuses Useful?" *Journal of Futures Markets* 8, no. 5 (1988).

Fung, W. and D. Hsieh. "Empirical Characteristics of Dynamic Trading Strategies: The Case of Hedge Funds." *The Review of Financial Studies* 10, no. 2 (Summer 1997).

Liang, B. "On the Performance of Hedge Funds." Ass263ociation for Investment Management and Research, July/August 1999.

McCarthy, D. and R. Spurgin. "A Review of Hedge Fund Performance Benchmarks." *The Journal of Alternative Investments* (Summer 1998).

Michaud, Richard O. *Efficient Asset Management* (Boston: Harvard Business School Press, 1998).

Schneeweis, T. and R. Spurgin. "Multifactor Analysis of Hedge Fund, Management Futures, and Mutual Fund Return and Risk Characteristics." *The Journal of Alternative Investments* (Fall 1998).

Weisman, A. "Conservation of Volatility and the Interpretation of Hedge Fund Data." Alternative Investment Management Association, June/July 1998.

Accounting, forensic, 245
Aggregation formulas, 161
Alpha, 149, 151–153
    classic Jones model, 224
    hedge fund strategies, 233
Ambiguity aversion, 12, 13
Analytical risks and hedge funds,
    244, 245
Appraisal Ratio, 116
Arbitrage, 227
Arbitrage Pricing Theory (APT),
    210
Asset allocation, 87, 88, 98, 126,
    149, 150. *See also*
    Rebalancing portfolios
    diversification, 82, 207
    and downside risk measures, 85,
        87, 88
    global equities
        country versus industry
            allocation, 199, 200
        markets, 189, 190
        risk measures, 106–109, 125,
            126
    style selection. *See* Style
        selection
Asset mix, 28, 32
Average performance, 4, 5

Bank of International Settlements,
    149
Banks, 147–149
Barings Bank, 147, 148
Behavioral portfolio theory, 175
Below-target probability (BTP),
    102, 109, 122

Below-target risk (BTR), 103, 108,
    109, 122, 125
Below-target variance (BTV), 102,
    103
Benchmarks, 149, 150, 152
    benchmark-relative VaR, 121,
        122
    choosing, 179, 180
    and goals, 175
    options on time and
        benchmarks, 181–183
    regret, pride, and options on
        time, 183, 184
    time and choices, 180, 181
    time and losses, 179, 180
Beta, 85, 104
Bias
    illiquidity bias, 257
    short-volatility regression bias,
        253–255
    St. Petersburg bias, 262
Black-Scholes model, 130, 132
Bonds, 179, 180, 192, 194, 195
    and risk, 177
    and time diversification, 176
Business experience, 238, 239
Business risks and hedge funds,
    238–241

Capital Asset Pricing Model
    (CAPM), 79, 80, 103–106,
    115, 116, 210, 216
    downside risk measures, 79–81,
        83
    problems with, 81–83
    single-factor models, 104

Capital structure arbitrage, 221, 230
Cash conversion value, 31
Cash cows, 88, 92
  and downside risk measures, 89, 90
Cash needs and portfolio risk, 30–32
Chaos, 208
  and analytical tools, 210
  complexity, 212, 213
  crashes, 209
  financial markets, 215–217
  long-term forecasting, 209
  nonlinear dynamic systems, 209
Chicago Board Options Exchange (CBOE), 58, 67
Chicago Mercantile Exchange, 67
Choices and risk, 175
Cognitive difficulties, 5
Collateral damage, 238
Commodities and futures, 226, 234
Common sense, 20, 21
Communication and hedge funds, 240
Compartmentalization, 84, 85, 88
  and downside risk measures, 85
Compounding, 37
Conflicts of interest and hedge funds, 240, 241
Continuous returns, 38
Convertible arbitrage, 220, 221, 230, 231
Correct coverage, 162
Correlation
  and asset allocation, 190
  global equity correlation, determinants of, 196, 197
  and integration of Europe, 197

Corroboration, 153
Crash option contract, 70–74
Critical value, 39, 40
Currency trading, 226, 234
Cyber finance, 208, 214, 215

Daily absolute return contract, 67–70
Decision making, 3, 4, 15
  Prospect Theory. *See* Prospect Theory
Decision models, 3, 4
Degrees of belief, 5
Derivatives, 129
  short-volatility investing. *See* Short-volatility investing
  trading, 234
Discounting, 22–26
Distressed investing, 223, 232
Distribution. *See also* Standard deviation
  asymmetric, 49, 51, 101
  independent identical distribution (iid), 36, 157
  lognormal, 37, 38
  normal, 36, 100, 101, 119
  probability, 46–51, 99
  symmetric, 101
  VaR distribution, 118
Diversification, 82
  and investment process, 210, 211
  time diversification, 87
Dollar-averaging, 185
Downside protection, 175, 176
Downside-risk framework, 175
Downside risk measures, 102, 108, 109, 122
  asset allocation, 85, 87–88
  CAPM. *See* Capital Asset Pricing Model (CAPM)

cash cows, 89, 90
compartmentalization of
    investment goals, 84, 85
diversification issues, 82
generally, 79, 80
high-growth companies, 92
investor behavior, 80, 82, 83, 92
lower partial moment (LPM),
    79, 85, 89, 90, 92
modern portfolio theory, 80, 93
product life cycle, 88, 89
risk aversion, 86
semivariance, 79
startup companies, 91
time diversification, 87
utility
    function, 85, 86, 91, 92
    theory, 79, 81–84
Downside semivariance, 102

Economic equilibrium, 208, 209
Efficient frontier, 86, 90, 107–109,
    210
Efficient Market Hypothesis
    (EMH), 147, 209, 210
Efficient market theory, 227, 228
Efficient portfolios, 107
EGARCH model, 58, 62–63
    absolute return contract results,
        69, 70
    crash option contract, 74
    principal components analysis,
        65
    regression analysis, 66, 67
    value at risk (VaR), 75, 76
Eigenvalues, 163, 165
Emerging markets, 194
Emotion and self-control, 5
Equity strategy hedge fund risk,
    232, 233
Error risk, 152

Ex ante risk. *See* Risk
    measurement
Ex post risk. *See* Risk management
Exception report, 123
Exponential GARCH. *See*
    EGARCH model
Externality, 153
Extreme events, forecasting,
    165–167
Extreme value theory (EVT),
    165–167

Factor analysis, 150
Factor-mimicking portfolios, 106
Failure of invariance, 8–10
Fat tails, 71, 120, 215, 216
Financial advisors, 85, 86, 93
    and CAPM, 80, 81
First passage time problems, 40
Fixed-income arbitrage, 221, 222,
    228, 229, 237, 238, 249
Fractal dimension, 216
Framing, 176–178
Fraud and hedge funds, 240

Game theory, 4
GARCH model, 58, 60–63, 158,
    159, 161
    absolute return contract results,
        69, 70
    crash option contract, 74
    principal components analysis,
        65
    regression analysis, 66, 67
    value at risk (VaR), 75, 76
Generalized autoregressive
    conditional heteroscedasticity
    models, 58
GJR model, 58, 63, 64
    absolute return contract results,
        70

GJR model (*continued*)
crash option contract, 74
principal components analysis, 65
regression analysis, 66, 67
value at risk (VaR), 75, 76
Global equity markets
determinants of correlation, 196, 197
generally, 189, 190
increasing correlation of, 190–196
and integration of Europe, 197
market shocks, 197–199
portfolio management techniques, 199–204
Goals, 175

Hedge funds, 208, 212, 214, 215, 245
classic Jones model, 224
commodities and futures positions, 226
currency positions, 226
dedicated short selling strategy, 225
development of, 210
equity market neutral strategy, 222
event-driven strategies, 222, 223
high yield strategy, 223, 224
informationless investment strategies. *See* Informationless investment strategies
institutional investors, 247, 248
lack of regulation, 220
leverage risks, 237, 238
liquidity risks, 235, 236
loan origination strategy, 223
long biased strategy, 224
long/short equity strategy, 224

low net biased, 225
macro trading, 225, 226
multistrategy, 224
mutual fund timing, 226
neutral biased, 225
Regulation D, 226, 231, 235
relative value strategies, 220–222
risks, 220
analytical, 244, 245
business, 238–241
leverage, 237, 238
liquidity, 235, 236
scalability limits, 242–244
strategy, 227–235
structural, 241, 242
short biased, 225
strategy risks, 227–235
High-growth companies, 88
and downside risk measures, 92
High yield hedge fund strategy, 223, 224
Hit sequence, 162, 163
House money effect, 8
Hurst Exponent (H), 216

Idiosyncratic risk, 98, 99, 104, 105
measures of performance, 114–116
Illiquid security investing, 255–259
Incompleteness theorem, 83
Independent identical distribution (iid), 36, 157
Indexes, 81, 93, 152
Information Ratio, 128
Informationless investment strategies, 248
illiquid security investing, 255–259
short-volatility investing generally, 248, 249, 262
sample investment program, 249–253

short-volatility regression
   bias, 253–255
St. Petersburg investing
   example, 260–262
   generally, 259, 260, 262
Insiders, 23
Insurance products and hedge
   funds, 241, 242
Interval forecasting, 161–163
Inverted reasoning, 18–21
   double inversion, 19
Investment horizon and portfolio
   risk, 28
Investment managers, 149
Investment style. *See* Style selection
Investor behavior, 80, 82, 83
   downside risk measures, 92
   rational investors, 82, 83
   and VIX index, 59

Jensen's alpha, 115, 116
Jones model, hedge fund strategy,
   224

Kurtosis, 71, 102, 215, 216

Law of Large Numbers, 210
Leptokurtic distribution, 102, 215
Leverage risks and hedge funds,
   237, 238
LGK estimator. *See* Logarithmic
   Garman Klass (LGK)
   estimator
Liquidation gates, 242
Liquidation notices and hedge
   funds, 236, 238, 241
Liquidation rights, 236
Liquidity risk, 235, 236
   hedge funds, 235, 236
Loan origination, 223
Logarithmic Garman Klass (LGK)
   estimator, 58–61

absolute return contract results,
   70
crash option contract, 74
principal components analysis,
   65
regression analysis, 66, 67
value at risk (VaR), 75, 76
Lognormal distribution, 37, 38
Long biased hedge fund strategy,
   224, 233
Long-horizon volatility, 155, 156
   formal aggregation, 161
   scaling, 156–161
Long/short equity strategy, 224
Loss aversion, 7, 9
   myopic, 178
Loss avoidance, 148, 149
Loss likelihood
   critical value, 39, 40
   multiperiod annualized loss, 38,
   39
   single-period loss, 35–38
   table, 41
Losses, 175
   framing, 176–178
   paper losses, 176, 177
   realized, 176, 177, 181–183
Low net biased hedge funds, 225
Lower partial moments (LPMs),
   54, 55, 79, 85, 88
   downside risk measures, 85, 89,
   90, 92–94

Macro trading, 225, 226, 233, 234
Market-neutral equity strategy,
   222, 228
Market risk, 98, 99, 117
Market shock, 190, 197–199
Mean-downside risk portfolio
   optimization, 108, 109
Mean-variance-efficient frontier,
   108

Mean-variance-efficient portfolios, 108
Mean-variance optimization, 107–109
Measurement, subjectiveness of, 5
Measurement of risk. *See* Risk measurement
Mental accounting, 9, 10
Merger arbitrage, 223, 231, 232, 249
Models. *See also* Risk models
  analytical risks, 244, 245
  assumptions, 131
  Black-Scholes, 130, 132
  CAPM. *See* Capital Asset Pricing Model (CAPM)
  constructing, 133, 134
  domain knowledge, 132
  factor models, 150
  financial modeling as imperfect science, 139–142
  limitations, 132, 133
  opinions and values, 131, 132
  rational model, 4, 27, 28
  single-factor, 104
  software, 132
  types of, 130
  uncertainty, 132
  variables, 131
Modern portfolio theory, 80, 93, 210
  and chaos, 214, 215
  efficient portfolio, 107
  and non-normality, 216
Modified Sharpe Ratio, 112–114
Monetary policy and rebalancing portfolios, 201–204
Money illusion, 180
Monte Carlo simulation, 120, 139, 249, 260
Moral hazards, 148
Mortgage trading, 221, 229, 230

Multistrategy hedge funds, 224
Mutual funds, 93
  bond funds and risk, 177, 178
  timing and hedge funds, 226

Neutral biased hedge funds, 225
Nonlinear dynamic systems. *See* Chaos

Options
  arbitrage, 222, 234, 235, 243
  short-volatility investing, 248
Over-the-counter securities, 258
Overestimating risk, 149
Owner's risk, 31

Pairs trading, 146
Performance evaluation, 98
  risk-adjusted returns. *See* Risk-adjusted performance
Portfolio optimization, 108
  mean-downside risk, 108, 109
Portfolio risk, 108
  asset mix, 28
  and cash convertibility, 30, 31
  cash obligations, 31, 32
  investment horizons, 28
  new risk paradigm, 28, 29
  owner's risk, 31
  performance measurement, 28
  rational model, 27, 28
  volatility, 28–30, 32
Potential, 175, 176
Predictability, 31
Pride, 183–185
Principal components analysis and volatility forecasting, 64–66
Probabilities
  below-target, 102
  loss likelihood, 36–40
  shortfall, 52–54
Probability judgments, 11, 12, 25

Product life cycle, 88
  and downside risk measures, 88, 89
Prospect Theory, 4–15, 48
Protected Equity Notes (PENs), 178, 179
Psychological factors. *See* Investor behavior
Public opinion, 17, 18, 23

Quadratic programming, 108

Random Walk Hypothesis, 146, 147
Rational model, 4, 27–28
Rationality, 13, 14
RATS-5, 60, 77
Real consumption growth, 106
Rebalancing portfolios. *See also* Asset allocation
  monetary policy, 201–204
  and risk-adjusted returns, 200
  trigger-based, 200, 201
Regression
  analysis, 66, 67
  and average performance, 4, 5, 14
  to the mean, 14
Regret, 183–185
Regulation D, 231, 235
  hedge funds, purchase of restricted stock, 226
Regulation Fair Disclosure, 245
Regulation T, 237
Relative semideviation, 55
Relative semivariance, 55
Restricted stock, 235
  purchase of and hedge funds, 226, 231
Return to Risk Ratio, 110, 111
Risk-adjusted performance, 110, 150

measures of, 109–116
risk-adjusted returns, 98, 99
Risk aversion, 6–9, 48–50, 85, 86, 180, 181
  and downside risk measures, 86
Risk budget, 124
Risk horizon, 118
Risk management, 45, 46, 98, 116, 117, 147–149, 156, 166–168
  and changing world economy, 189, 190
  market risk measurement
    and asset allocation, 125, 126
    downside risk measures, 122
    ex ante measurement, reasons for, 122–124
    generally, 116, 117
    Value at Risk (VaR), 117–122
  time horizons, 155, 156
  volatility forecasting considerations, 74–76
Risk measurement, 126
  error variance, tracking, 51, 52
  ex ante risk and ex post risk compared, 97, 98, 126
  lower partial moments (LPMs), 54, 55
  market risk, 98, 99
  probability distribution, 46
  relative semivariance, 55
  semivariance, 55
  shortfall
    expected, 53, 54
    probability, 52, 53
  standard deviation, 46–51
  total risk, 99–103
Risk models. *See also* Models
  correct model but inappropriate use, 135, 136
  correct models and incorrect solutions, 135
  developers of, 138

Risk models (*continued*)
　discrepancies, 138
　dissemination of, 138
　generally, 129–131
　inapplicability of, 134
　incorrect models, 134, 135
　interdisciplinary nature of, 137
　testing complex models,
　　137–138
　user interface, 138
Risk seeking, 6, 7
RiskMetrics model, 61–62
Runs test, 163, 165

Safety-first framework, 175
Sample period, 109, 110
Sample statistics, 100
Sampling, 5
Scalability limits and hedge funds,
　242–244
Scaling, 156, 157, 161
　example, 159–161
　independent, identically
　　distributed (iid)
　　environments, 157
　non-iid environments, 157–159
Scientific method, 153
Security, 175
Semivariance, 55, 79
　downside, 102
Sharpe Ratio, 111, 112, 114, 115,
　121, 251, 256, 257
　Modified Sharpe Ratio, 112–114
Short biased hedge funds, 225, 233
Short-selling, dedicated, 225
Short-volatility investing
　bias, 253–255
　derivatives, 248
　example, 249–253
　generally, 248, 249, 262
Shortfall
　expected, 53, 54

probability of, 52, 53
Shortfall-risk framework, 175
Simulation, Monte Carlo. *See*
　Monte Carlo simulation
Single-factor models
　CAPM. *See* Capital Asset
　　Pricing Model (CAPM)
Skepticism, 18–20
Skewness, 102, 120, 215
Sortino Ratio, 114
Speculation, 21, 22, 24, 25
St. Petersburg investment
　technique
　example, 260–262
　generally, 259, 260, 262
St. Petersburg Paradox, 50, 259
Standard deviation, 36–38, 55,
　84–85, 99, 100, 119, 190. *See*
　also Distribution
　and risk measurement, 46–51
　variance, 50, 51
Startup companies, 88
　and downside risk measures, 91
Statistical arbitrage, 146, 147, 222,
　227, 228, 249
Strategy risks and hedge funds,
　227–235
Structural risks and hedge funds,
　241, 242
Style selection, 207
　and asset allocation, 208–210
　and shifting paradigms,
　　210–214
Systematic risk, 98, 99, 105
　factors, 103–106
　measures of performance,
　　114–116

Tails, 166, 167, 215, 216
Taylor series expansion, 50, 51
Technology
　anchoring, 145, 146

curvefitting, 145, 146
importance of, 144, 145
over-reliance on, 146
overconfidence, 145
Time diversification, 87, 173–175, 184
benchmarks, 179–184
and bonds, 176
Time series, 100
Time zone arbitrage, 226
Total risk
measurement of, 99–103
measures of performance, 110–114
systematic risk factors, 103–106
Tracking error, 51–53, 112, 152
Treynor Ratio, 115, 116
Tripwire, 123, 124

Uncertainty, 4, 7, 24
and risk measurement, 45
Unconditional coverage, 162
Upside potential, 175, 176
Utility functions
compartmentalization, 84, 85
and downside risk measures, 79, 81–86, 91, 92
expected utility, 50
investor's utility function, 50
mean-variance utility function, 68, 69
quadratic, 56, 86
Utility satisficing, 83
Utility theory, 79, 81

Value at risk (VaR), 57, 58, 67, 117, 147–150, 161
alternatives to, 122
and asset allocation, 125, 126
benchmark-relative VaR, 121, 122
crash option contract, 71

distribution, 118
ex ante measures of market risk, 122–124
measures of risk for performance compared, 117–119
and measures of risk for performance evaluation, 121
methods of calculating, 119–121
volatility forecasting considerations, 75, 76
Variance, 55, 87, 99–101, 106, 117, 119. *See also* Standard deviation
below-target, 102
error variance, tracking, 51, 52
lower partial variance, 54, 55
semivariance, 55
and utility functions, 50, 51
weighting, 69
VIX index, 58–59, 67, 77
absolute return contract results, 69, 70
crash option contract, 71–74
principal components analysis, 65
regression analysis, 66, 67
value at risk (VaR), 75, 76
Volatility, 28, 31, 32, 48
forecastability at different horizons, 161–164
forecasting models. *See* Volatility forecasting models
long-horizon, 156–161
as measure for risk, 101
measurement of, 99, 100
model-free assessment of volatility forecastability, 161–165

Volatility (*continued*)
   persistence, 164, 165
   as proxy for risk, 29, 30
   and risk measurement, 45
   short-horizon asset return, 155,
      156
   testing forecastability,
      163–165
Volatility forecasting models
   analysis, 66, 67
   analysis of components, 64–66
   considerations, 74–76
   crash option contract, 70–74
   daily absolute return contract,
      67–70

   EGARCH model. *See* EGARCH
      model
   GARCH model. *See* GARCH
      model
   generally, 57–64
   GJR model. *See* GJR model
   Logarithmic Garman Klass
      (LGK) estimator. *See*
      Logarithmic Garman Klass
      (LGK) estimator
   regression analysis, 66, 67
   RiskMetrics model, 61, 62
   Value at Risk (VaR). *See* Value
      at Risk (VaR)
   VIX index. *See* VIX index